Pedagogical Tact

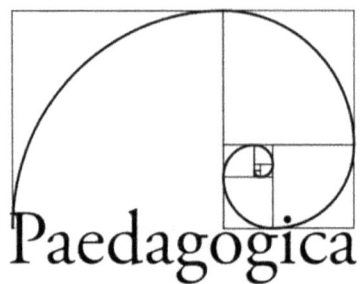

Paedagogica

Sebastian Engelmann, Norm Friesen, and Karsten Kenklies
General Editors

VOL. 4

Norm Friesen and Thomas Senkbeil (eds.)

Pedagogical Tact

Reconnecting Theory and Practice in Education

PETER LANG

New York · Berlin · Bruxelles · Chennai · Lausanne · Oxford

Bibliographic information published by the Deutsche Nationalbibliothek
The Deutsche Nationalbibliothek lists this publication in the Deutsche Nationalbibliografie; detailed bibliographic data is available online at http://dnb.d-nb.de.

Library of Congress Cataloging-in-Publication Data
Names: Friesen, Norm, editor. | Senkbeil, Thomas, 1985- editor.
Title: Pedagogical tact: reconnecting theory and practice in education /
   edited by Norm Friesen, Thomas Senkbeil.
Description: New York: Peter Lang, [2026] | Series: Paedagogica, 2769-5158; vol. 4 |
   Includes bibliographical references.
Identifiers: LCCN 2025015845 (print) | LCCN 2025015846 (ebook) |
   ISBN 9783034357401 (hardback) | ISBN 9783034358651 (paperback) |
   ISBN 9783034358668 (pdf) | ISBN 9783034358675 (epub)
Subjects: LCSH: Teacher-student relationships. | Tact.
Classification: LCC LB1033 .P515 2025 (print) | LCC LB1033 (ebook) |
   DDC 371.102/3--dc23/eng/20250528
LC record available at https://lccn.loc.gov/2025015845
LC ebook record available at https://lccn.loc.gov/2025015846

Cover Image Credits: Photograph by Drazen Zigic; Licensed from Shutterstock
Cover Design: Norm Friesen

ISSN 2769-5158
ISBN 978-3-0343-5740-1 (Hardback)
ISBN 978-3-0343-5865-1 (Paperback)
ISBN 978-3-0343-5866-8 (E-PDF)
ISBN 978-3-0343-5867-5 (E-PUB)
DOI 10.3726/b22911

© 2026 Peter Lang Group AG, Lausanne (Switzerland)
Peter Lang Publishing Inc., New York (USA)

info@peterlang.com

All rights reserved.
All parts of this publication are protected by copyright.
Any utilization outside the strict limits of the copyright law, without the permission of the publisher, is forbidden and liable to prosecution. This applies in particular to reproductions, translations, microfilming, and storage and processing in electronic retrieval systems.
This publication has been peer reviewed.

www.peterlang.com

Table of Contents

PART I
Introduction

Pedagogical Tact: A Historical Overview — 3
Norm Friesen

Chapter Synopses — 33
Norm Friesen

PART II
Theorizing Tact

Reconsidering Tact — 43
Eirick Prairat

A Matter of "Character, Mind, and Heart"? On the Role of Ethos in Preparing the Tactful Teacher — 59
Severin Sales Rödel

Tact as Pedagogical *Daimon*? Arendt on Tact, Exemplarity, and Judgment — 79
Morten Korsgaard

PART III
Tact in Context

Pedagogical Tact and the Limits of Community — 97
Hans-Rüdiger Müller

Pedagogical Tact and Education in the Family — 113
Dominik Krinninger and Kaja Kesselhut

TABLE OF CONTENTS

PART IV
Embodiment and Tact

Antinomies and Aporias: The Reciprocal Ambivalence
of Tact and the Body 135
Norm Friesen

Tactful Views: On Forms of Educational Measure and Precaution 153
Jörg Zirfas and Daniel Burghardt

Creating Contact, Making Things Sound: Resonance and
the Expression of Tact in the Classroom—Respect and Timing as
Mediators of Self-World Relations 169
Jens Beljan

Postscript

Pedagogical Tact and Teacher Professionalization: A Conceptualization 195
Thomas Senkbeil and Norm Friesen

Notes on Contributors 213

PART I

Introduction

Pedagogical Tact: A Historical Overview

Norm Friesen

At a time when education is becoming ever more standardized and technocratic, there is renewed interest in the interpersonal, even intimate phenomenon of pedagogical tact. Some speak of a "renaissance" (e.g., Fageth, 2021, p. 14).[1] But what exactly is pedagogical tact? Like tact in general, it is "a ready and delicate sense of what is fitting and proper in dealing with others" (Oxford English Dictionary). In pedagogy, these "others" are typically children, youth, or students. More broadly, and in keeping with its origin in the Latin *tangere*, meaning touch, tact refers to "a keen faculty of perception or discrimination likened to the sense of touch" (Oxford English Dictionary). Pedagogy, meanwhile, is understood here not as various techniques of teaching, but as a way of *being* with children and the young, a way of being oriented to their maturation and eventual autonomy. In this context, pedagogical tact refers to attuned ways of being, acting, and speaking that are most appropriate for the child or student. In social relations generally, tact often serves the interests of the one exercising it. To be pedagogical, however, tact must be attuned above all to the needs of the Other. Pedagogical tact thus begins to reconnect theory and practice not by imposing prescriptions on everyday activity, but by putting the relationship of theory and practice into question. Indeed, it sometimes inverts this relationship, seeing *practice* as defining aspects of *theory*.

This introduction begins by revisiting the origin of the notion of pedagogical tact and the beginnings of the pedagogical tradition with which it originated. Then, it traces some of the ways that pedagogical tact has been interpreted and conceptualized more recently. Significantly, concern with tact and pedagogical tact is closely tied with social and political change and upheaval. The concepts of tact and pedagogical tact emerge around the time of the French and American revolutions, and they are subsequently preserved—without being significantly changed or developed—for over 100 years. Only by the twentieth century, partially as a response to the two World Wars, were tact and pedagogical tact substantially renewed and revised[2]—a renewal necessitated by still further changes in the social order. The final phase in the story of pedagogical tact is its contemporary renaissance, marked by the publication of books in German, English, and French. Indeed, three of these volumes are by authors or editors whose contributions are included in this collection. The historical overview provided here forms the background for short summaries of the content and themes of the various chapters of this book. (Relevant aspects of these chapters are also highlighted parenthetically when they arise in this overview.)

Pedagogy, Theory, and Practice

Ways of understanding pedagogy that are integral to pedagogical tact emerged about 200 years ago.[3] They were developed by the founders of pedagogy as a "science"—as a rigorous way of reflecting and theorizing. However, these figures have since been forgotten or simply ignored. The first is Johann Friedrich Herbart, who was translated and widely read in English in the late nineteenth century (Beiser, 2022), but who was forgotten and even suppressed in the decades that followed. Herbart's discussion of pedagogical tact is found in a lecture he gave to student-teachers in 1802, a lecture that focuses on pedagogical theory and practice as well as on their interrelationship.

Herbart begins by emphasizing how, on the one hand, "theory claims to be universal, and in this sense stretches over a vast expanse" (2022, p. 31). Theory "passes over all details, over all circumstances that surround the practical teacher at any given moment" (p. 31). Surrounded by these innumerable circumstances, the teacher must be able to translate theory (for example, principles of justice or equality) into practice. According to Herbart, this cannot happen quickly or directly; only a "supernatural being," he says, could undertake an immediate and "complete application of scientific propositions" in this way. This means that "a link intermediate between theory and practice" (p. 32) is required (or "involuntarily inserts itself" as Herbart also puts it): "By this [link,] I mean a certain tact, a quick judgment and decision that is not habitual and eternally uniform… [but that] answer[s] the true requirements of the individual case" (p. 32). For Herbart, then, tact can help the educator be responsive to the child or student by enabling a type of action that is speedy or quick. It does this by overcoming habit (*Schlendrian*), by being improvisational (or not "eternally uniform"). Tact is related to theory or "science" but at the same time, it is involuntary and intuitive (suited to what Herbart calls "art"). Finally, tact informs action addressed to the individual student and their uniqueness. In this way, the innumerable concrete circumstances of pedagogical practice can be reconciled with the generality and abstraction of theory.

The second founding figure of the modern "science" of pedagogy is Friedrich Schleiermacher (1768–1834). In the decade or two that followed Herbart's remarks, Schleiermacher lectured both on tact and pedagogy as well as on theory and practice in education. Schleiermacher defined education in the most general terms: as a kind of influence[4] exercised by those already established in the world on those entering it. Accordingly, pedagogy is not simply what takes place in educational institutions; it is instead what unfolds between generations more broadly, in terms of the "relationship between the older and the younger, and the obligations of the one to the other" (1826/2023, p. 24). Schleiermacher believed that the more self-aware and informed the older, the educating, generation could become, the more "complete and perfect" its educational influence would be. As a result, he worked to develop a theory, that at least in part, is intended to help the older generation in this task.

Like Herbart, though, Schleiermacher knew that the help that theory could provide is limited. But while Herbart (1802/2022) took the "fundamental correctness" of theory "on faith" (p. 32), Schleiermacher actually regarded practice as more important than theory. Schleiermacher emphasized that *practice* necessarily takes on a certain primacy and *dignity* in relation to theory: "it would be incorrect to say that practice gains its character and specificity only through theory. The dignity of practice exists independently from theory. Theory only makes practice more conscious" (1826/2023, p. 26). Schleiermacher briefly mentions tact several times in his lectures in the 1813–1814 and 1820–1821 academic years on education. He defines it specifically as a "general mediator of order and measure"—a capability that "must operate unconsciously" (1814/2000, p. 255) and that "stand[s] in the safest balance between the two extremes" (p. 214). In keeping with Schleiermacher's insistence on the primacy of practice, these two balanced extremes or opposites are different from Herbart's. Tact does not appear as the singular interconnection of theory and practice, but as the dialectical unification or equalization of multiple opposites, extremes, or antinomies in educational practice—such as the general and particular, protection and exposure, or proximity and distance. For example: A teacher must reconcile the special treatment of any one student (e.g., who is struggling) with the need to treat all students alike; they must also support the child's good behavior while counteracting what is not so good; educators, finally, must be ready to help (i.e., be proximate), but without being intrusive. In each of these cases, tactful or sensitive pedagogy is a matter of balance between the individual versus collectivity, support versus counteraction, distance versus proximity.

Schleiermacher's general perspective on education can be updated for the present through Hannah Arendt, who studied Schleiermacher's work. In a 1958 lecture on education, Arendt appears to effectively put Schleiermacher's definition into her own words: "what concerns us all," she says, "is the relation between grown-ups and children in general." "In even more general and exact terms" she continues, this is a question of "our attitude toward the fact of natality: the fact that we have all come into the world by being born and that this world is constantly renewed through birth" (p. 196). At the heart of our being with children, in other words, is an orientation that sees the future as *open*—as being realized precisely through the unique and precious novelty that the child, youth or younger generation bring with them into the world.[5] And although

Arendt did not speak explicitly about tact and pedagogical tact (see Chapter 5 in this volume), she *did* see education as being both an intergenerational matter and a question above all of adult *concern* or *attitude*: an issue of care, regard, and consideration. As already suggested, pedagogy is a matter of what one could call a way of being or an orientation in relation to another.

Pedagogical tact, then, is not a type of pedagogical flair, an inexpressible *je ne sais quoi*. It is instead inseparable from ways of understanding pedagogical theory and practice. It is also embedded in the intrinsically ethical, relational, intergenerational enterprise that *is* pedagogy. This approach to pedagogy has been labeled "the European pedagogical tradition" or simply "continental pedagogy" (e.g., Friesen & Kenklies, 2023). Tact is an ongoing concern in this tradition, introduced as a constitutive element of this way of thinking and acting near the beginning of the nineteenth century, and then undergoing substantial development and revision only later in the twentieth and early in the twenty-first centuries. Some of these changes and developments are reflected in the individual chapters in this volume. Again, before introducing these chapters and the volume as a whole, this introduction provides a historical overview of the concept of tact. This overview begins in prerevolutionary France and extends to its "renaissance" today.[6] This discussion then concludes by suggesting some reasons why pedagogical tact (and tact more broadly) is now of renewed relevance. It also outlines what this collection offers in the context of the current renaissance of pedagogical tact.

The History and Politics of Pedagogical Tact

The First 50 Years: Voltaire to Schleiermacher

As a name for a social sensitivity or virtue, tact first appeared at the end of the age of absolutism, well into the European Enlightenment. Based on a dinner-time suggestion from Prince Frederick II of Prussia, Enlightenment thinker Voltaire began work on his famous *Dictionnaire philosophique* in the 1750s. Under the entry for taste (*goût*), Voltaire declared that "the man of taste," the connoisseur of arts, "has other eyes, other ears, and another *tact* from the uncultivated man" (1776/1879, p. 172; emphasis added). This is the first known use of the term. Not long after, the word appeared in a volume on moral philosophy by Dugald Stewart, a representative of the Scottish Enlightenment. Stewart refers in passing to "the use made in the French tongue" of the word "tact" to describe how one "feels" one's "way in the difficult intercourse of polished society" (Stewart, 1793/1864, p. 25). Retaining its philosophical pedigree, tact was also adopted by Enlightenment philosopher Immanuel Kant to designate what he called "logical tact," a notion introduced in his 1789 *Anthropology from a Pragmatic Point of View* (2007). Like

Herbart, Kant also defines tact not as a matter of taste or feeling, but as a capacity or power of judgment. It is one that is exercised, Kant explains, without reference to "academic and artificially drawn-up principles," but instead relies on "general and innate rules of understanding" which remain "in the obscurity of the mind" (p. 250). However, it is only later, in a popular press article from 1793, where Kant produces a formulation that is echoed in later accounts, above all by Herbart:

> A set of rules, even practical rules, is called a theory if the rules are conceived as principles of a certain generality and are abstracted from a multitude of conditions which necessarily influence their application… However complete… [a] theory may be, it is obvious that between theory and practice there must be a link [*Mittelglied*], a connection and transition from one to the other. To the intellectual concept that contains the rule, an act of judgment must be added whereby the practitioner distinguishes whether or not something is an instance of the rule. (Kant, 1793/1974, p. 39)

Although Kant does not explicitly say anything about tact in this text, the similarity of this description to the words of Herbart (quoted above) is likely *not* coincidental: For not only did Herbart inherit Kant's chair in philosophy in Prussian Königsberg (today Russian Kaliningrad), Herbart also sided with Kantianism in critiquing the excesses of contemporary Romanticism (Beiser, 2022). The similarities linking the two accounts are remarkable: Both Herbart and Kant begin by defining theory. For Kant it is "a set of rules, even practical rules… conceived as principles of a certain generality"; for Herbart, it is "an orderly combination of propositions …claim[ing] to be universal."[7] Practice, on the other hand, is described as a context in which "a multitude of conditions … necessarily influence [the] application" of this theory (Kant), or—pedagogically speaking—as "all [of the] circumstances that surround the practical teacher at any given moment" (Herbart). For both theorists, what is essential in this context is a "link" (both use the term *Mittelglied*) that connects theory and practice: "It is obvious that between theory and practice there must be a link," as Kant says, or that "a link intermediate between theory and practice involuntarily inserts itself," as Herbart puts it. While for Kant, this link is characterized as "an act of judgment… a connection and transition from" theory to practice, for Herbart, it is tact itself: "a certain tact, a quick judgment and decision that is not habitual and eternally uniform." And in the end, both descriptions conclude by saying that this linkage animates practice in its relationship to theory: For Kant, it allows "the practitioner [to] distinguish whether or not something is an instance of the rule"; for Herbart, it allows to the teacher "to be faithful …to the laws articulated by pedagogic science in its universality."

Through their remarkably similar articulations of tact or of judgment-in-action as the singular "link" between theory and practice, Kant's and Herbart's descriptions take a decisive step beyond Voltaire and Stewart. Whereas earlier definitions of tact associated it with qualities like cultivation, taste, and polish, Kant's logical tact and Herbart's pedagogical tact see it as much more analytical and abstract. The norms of convention and taste referenced by both Voltaire and Stewart become, with Kant and Herbart, rules of understanding or principles of *theory*. As a result, tact itself becomes something relatively independent from subjectivity and social change. Both Kant and Herbart are also of one mind that tact is not just a form of social finesse or aesthetic sophistication; instead, it is something separate from both theory and practice—while it simultaneously takes on their mediation.

At the same time, early references to tact or judgment—whether of Voltaire or Stewart, Kant or Herbart—should be viewed in the context of cultural and historical developments that came to a head near the end of the eighteenth century. The rapid proliferation of the term "tact" across Europe coincides with the violent rejection of monarchical absolutism in the American and French Revolutions (1776 and 1789, respectively), and with the rise of a relatively new political class in Europe and America, the bourgeoisie. Writing in *Minima Moralia: Reflections from a Damaged Life*, critical theorist Theodore Adorno describes the role that tact came to have in the social relations of this period:

> Tact, we now know, has its precise historical hour. It was the hour when the bourgeois individual rid himself of absolutist compulsion. Free and solitary, he answers for himself, while the forms of hierarchical respect and consideration developed by absolutism, divested of their economic basis and their menacing power, are still just sufficiently present. (p. 36)

Adorno concludes: "The precondition of tact is convention no longer intact yet still present" (p. 36; *Voraussetzung des Takts ist die in sich gebrochene und doch noch gegenwärtige Konvention*). The historical hour of tact coincides with a reshuffling of what once appeared as an objective, even universal social order. It was also a time when "social convention [still] remain[ed]" in place, but when it was "no longer felt to be total and totalizing"—as British literary historian David Russell puts it (p. 6). These declining social conventions still allow for individual freedom and decision. At the same time, though, they provide ways of orienting this newfound independence so that it is responsive to that of others. "There are gaps" in these social conventions, Russell explains; and it is precisely these spaces that provide "room for the maneuver by which one might make [these] social forms one's own" (p. 6).

Meanwhile, the social class in whose interest tact is said to operate—the bourgeoisie—is defined *not* by inherited rank or conventions of social hierarchy, but rather, as Adorno makes clear, by *individuality*. This is illustrated, for example, in the genre of the *Bildungsroman*, the novel of formation or of coming-of-age. Many examples of this literary genre, such as *Jane Eyre* and *Wilhelm Meister's Apprenticeship*, appeared around the same time as the term "tact" was spreading through Europe. They describe their young protagonists as undergoing a process of finding and defining their own place in society. This happens through their own efforts in a kind of self-directed development or *Bildung*. This process, in turn, requires improvisation, negotiation, and creativity in a world that no longer has a strictly predetermined place for them. Whether it is a question of "gaps" in the social order or of the inadequacy and bland universality of theory, tact can be said to appear historically as an individualized, compensatory, and improvisatory accommodation or "stopgap" measure. The need for tact arises in the face of the inadequacy of something that is common, given, or inherited—whether it be of a specifically theoretical or broadly social in nature. And in response, tact is indeed able to provide a means of feeling one's "way in the… intercourse of… society" (Stewart) or alternatively, to provide "a quick judgment and decision [that] answer the true requirements of the individual case" (Herbart).

The Nineteenth Century: Herbartianism

In the historical hour identified by Adorno, educational thinkers Herbart and Schleiermacher both turned the already conceptually laden notion of "tact" to pedagogical purposes. Each of them did this in their own way, and the two ways of approaching pedagogical tact they developed remain important to this day: As H.-R. Müller (2015) explains, for Herbart, pedagogical tact appears as the *"transformation… of pedagogical or moral knowledge into practical action."* It represents, in other words, the *"mediation of the theoretical and general into the particularity of pedagogical practice"* (p. 15; emphasis in original). For Schleiermacher, as Müller also explains, tact is configured in more broadly dialectical terms—as an *"orientation of action in the field of tension of contradictory demands* of pedagogical practice" (Müller, 2015, p. 17; emphasis in original).[8] Just as Herbart's conception of tact has its roots in Kantian critical philosophy, Schleiermacher's dialectical approach references Aristotle and his notion of the golden mean. This is based on the ideal of *mesotes*, an ideal that posits that "every ethical virtue is a condition intermediate… between two states, one [of] excess, and the other, deficiency" (Aristotle, as quoted in Kraut, 2022, para. 23). Schleiermacher combined this approach to ethics with an "awareness of pedagogical antinomies" that were becoming popular "in his time," Müller (2015, p. 17) explains. This was the age of the dialectic, of change driven by historical contradictions—an idea developed by Hegel and others before being inherited by Marx. Schleiermacher's dialectical understanding of pedagogical capacity as the negotiation of extremes, Müller continues, "determine[s] theoretical, pedagogical discourse to the present day" (p. 17).

In German contexts today, Schleiermacher's dialectical understanding of the teacher's "artful action" provides the basis for defining the "professionalization" of the teacher—the acquisition of pedagogical capacities and sensibilities through specialized work and self-development (e.g., Hainschink & Zahra-Ecker 2018; Helsper, 2021; Schlömerkemper, 2018). So, if Herbart defines tact as a link between theory and practice, then Schleiermacher can be said to expand this idea of the linking of oppositions to the mediation, combination, even abrogation of any and all of the tensions that might arise in education as a field. Schleiermacher sees tact, in other words, as the way that oppositions and extremes are dialectically resolved, specifically by dint of the primacy and superiority of *practice* over theory (Friesen, 2023).

Over the course of the nineteenth century, it is largely Herbart's many followers, the Herbartians, who continue the tradition of pedagogical tact. Tuiskon Ziller (1817–1882), among the most famous of these, identifies two forms of tact as relevant: "naturalistic tact" and "rational tact." The first, Ziller says, is acquired and developed only through routinized practice and cannot rise above the execution of this practice. It is a reflexive or instinctual tact, neither teachable nor open to theorization. Rational tact, on the other hand, is "formed by theory" and "keeps itself in agreement with its [i.e., theory's] reasonable results" (p. 38). Reflecting Herbart's definition of pedagogical tact more broadly, Ziller adds that rational tact affords "ease, speed and certainty in judging and acting" (1876, p. 33). It appears as a way of enabling theory to support and inform effective practice.

Other Herbartians, including ones working in English, often did not expand Herbart's original notion of pedagogical tact, but rather simplified it into a one-dimensional phenomenon. Seeing Herbart's psychology as presenting positive "laws" by which both instruction and the mind of the child operates, Charles McMurry, in *The Method of the Recitation* (1897),[9] refers to pedagogical tact exclusively as "instinctive tact":

> The whole question of freedom and originality in the teacher is a question either of obeying the laws of nature in the child life [sic], or of constantly blundering in the effort to be free and original. The teacher must have either an instinctive tact or a conscious insight into the simple laws of mental life and action. (1897, p. 308)

Theory, the laws governing the child's mind, are no longer so complex that they need to first be mediated by tact in order to be put into practice. Instead, the action these theoretical laws require can be executed immediately, without the translation or transformation that tact makes possible. Tact consequently becomes simply a kind of in-born capacity to operate on the basis of natural laws and a way of avoiding excessive "blundering."

The Twentieth Century: Nohl, Blochmann, Muth, van Manen

In the first few decades of the twentieth century, German-language pedagogy passed through a progressive phase that went by the name of *Reformpädagogik*. This movement—like progressive education more broadly—envisioned learning and education as natural process: Education, as Dewey famously said, is not a "preparation for future living" but the "process of living" itself (Dewey, 1897, p. 7). As a result, questions of balancing theory with practice, or of moderating distance with proximity lose their urgency. What is paramount is to be able to engage with learning productively simply as it is, as a natural process—while discarding artificial school exercises and instruction.[10] In Germany, however, progressive pedagogy gave way to a somewhat less reformist "human science pedagogy" (*geisteswissenschaftliche Pädagogik*), which remained the dominant paradigm in education until the introduction of empirical and positivistic approaches in the last three decades of the twentieth century. Regardless, human science pedagogy—and *Reformpädagogik* before it—represented a firm rejection of the laws and instructional prescriptions of the Herbartians. Human science pedagogues instead saw themselves as developing a kind of "theory *of* practice *for* practice" (Biesta, 2011, p. 186), effectively positioning Schleiermacher's notion of "the primacy of practice" in the center of their pedagogy. They consequently had little need for a particularly strong conception of theory or science. Consequently, they also did not require a definition of tact that would bridge the gap between this theory and pedagogical practice.

In human science pedagogy, tact was relegated to a position of a second order concept. For example, in his pre-WWII writings, Herman Nohl, arguably the most prominent of the human science pedagogues, was concerned above all with the idea of the pedagogical relation. This he defined as an emotionally laden "relation between a mature person and one who is becoming"—specifically for the sake of the one becoming (1933/2022, p. 78). Characterizing this pedagogical dyad as nothing less than "the basis" of all "education," Nohl effectively locates pedagogical tact as only a moment within it; as the "most refined expression… [of] the singular *distance* … that the educator takes to his subject as well as to his student" (1933/2022, pp. 80–81; emphasis in original). Here, Nohl can be seen to be working with pedagogical antinomies—in this case, student and teacher (and student and curriculum) and the proximity and distance manifest between them. He sees this opposition as essential to understanding the pedagogical relationships that can arise between the educator and those being educated.

After Nohl's brief reference to tact as distance, it is nearly two decades later, well after World War II, that Nohl returns to this subject and to the Aristotelian ideal of balance or measure. In a short 1958 essay titled "Figures of Education" (*Erziehergestalten*), Nohl characterizes "the first secret of any formation of the educator" as the attainment of "the sovereign knowledge of the polarity of all of our tasks or duties" (p. 82). The acquisition of such knowledge is especially challenging in the context of Postwar Germany, Nohl emphasizes. This is due to the ongoing neglect of all tactful balance, of any sense of measure or Aristotelian *mesotes*:

> The *ideal of moderation* ... which was known in antiquity and humanism ... has been lost to us ... Because of the forgetting of this ideal, our people and their leadership declined ever more rapidly, and were finally cruelly overthrown [*sic*]. The ancient world saw hubris—losing measure in relation to the gods—as the real sin. (1958, p. 82; emphasis in original).

Nohl here is framing engagement with polarities or extremes as an ability or sensibility that is not only indispensable for the pedagogue, but vital also for society and culture more broadly. Not only should it guide the instructional and interpersonal engagement of the educator according to Nohl, but it has a world-historical, even cosmological role in the rise and fall, the sinning and redemption of whole empires, peoples, and civilizations. Such grandiose (and ultimately tasteless) theoretical gestures—combined with Nohl's own historical entanglements with National Socialism[11]—have significantly limited his impact since WW II.

Fortunately, after the horrors and atrocities of the 30s and 40s in Germany and the rest of Europe, there were some who saw the question of measure and tact in education rather differently than Nohl. For them, balance was not a question of the fate of whole peoples and epochs, but a matter of everyday sociability. Elisabeth Blochmann, a favored disciple of Nohl's and a student of English-language and literature, offers an important example. A Jew, Blochmann was forced to emigrate to Oxford in the 1930s, and—unlike Nohl—would likely *not* have seen the overthrow of the Nazi regime as "cruel." Instead, on her return to Germany, Blochmann wrote about the importance of tact both in pedagogy and in social convention (*Sittlichkeit*) more broadly. In two quasi-autobiographical articles published in 1950 and 1951 in the human science pedagogy journal *Die Sammlung: Zeitung für Kultur und Pädagogik* (*The Collection: Journal for Culture and Pedagogy*), Blochmann describes tact neither in terms of grand civilizational ideals nor of Aristotelian *mesotes*. Blochmann instead points to experiences of tact in the form in a "style of favorable social engagement" that she observed during her exile in England (1951, p. 592). From this very different starting point emerges a distinctive approach to pedagogical tact:

> Not only I, but other German educators who, like me, found a new field of work as emigrants in England, have had to learn one thing above all, regardless of where they were employed—whether in kindergarten, school or university. And that one thing is a much greater composure and restraint toward young people. (1950, p. 719)

The question of tact is here again rising to importance at a moment when, to borrow Adorno's words, "convention" is "no longer intact yet still present." Like German cities and industries in general, German culture and ways of life lay largely in ruins in 1950, following a moment of defeat sometimes referred to as the *Stunde null*, the zero hour. It is in the context of the overall *absence* of social conventions, then, that Blochmann seems to have found a kind of convention that, at least for her, remained viable. This is convention that was in evidence across the English Channel, in a culture and society quite different from the one to which Blochmann had returned. According to Blochmann, emigree German intellectuals—which would have also included Ludwig Wittgenstein and Norbert Elias—had to learn in Britain how to relate to young people in what for them was a different way. She admits that in place of the composure and restraint shown by British educators, the relationship between children, students, and pedagogues in the German context could be marked by violence and brutality:

> Out of high motives, for the sake of order or moral value, one is all too easily inclined as an educator to be too aggressive and to intervene violently in a young life. This became clear to me only in England. We need much more *Gelassenheit*[12] in education. After all, everything that is right and good can only be achieved in the long run if young people grow up unbroken, unoppressed, and secure in themselves. (1951, p. 591)

In asking for more *Gelassenheit*, serenity, letting be, or letting go, Blochmann can be seen to bring attention to a radically new dimension in the discussion of pedagogical tact. Up to this point, with perhaps only the exception of Nohl's prewar reference to its "singular distance," pedagogical tact had been defined as a mode of artful *influence, action*, and *engagement*. This tactful activity, moreover, was expected to be responsive, decisive, and rapid. In addition, educationists through to Nohl ignored the possibility of significant teacher failure or even outright teacher error in the context of their relationships with students.[13] However, in defining tact more overtly as matter of *Gelassenheit*, Blochmann frames both teaching and tact itself above all as an exercise in restraint, of *not* acting, *not* intervening, but rather of respecting and encouraging the free development of those being educated. Significantly, in discussing the dialectic of tact, Adorno references Wolfgang von Goethe to make a similar point: In a broader social sense, tact represents "the saving accommodation between alienated individuals… [the] renunciation, the relinquishment of total contact" (pp. 35–36). However, in keeping with the dialectical nature of tact, both Adorno's tact-as-renunciation and Blochmann's own tact-as-*Gelassenheit* can only exist in tension with its opposite. The opposition here is not one between theory and practice or proximity and distance, but between *Gelassenheit* on the one hand and the action or contact implied in pedagogical influencing on the other. Blochmann asks:

> Is it not one of the features of the essence of that which is pedagogical that it leads, guides, influences, and also punishes, so that [it is] in any case the intervention of the older, the more experienced, the stronger on the younger person, for whose development the older is responsible? And is not the actual essence of tact a holding of oneself in reserve, a wanting not to intervene? How can these things be united? (1951, p. 589)

Blochmann here asks how tact as reserve can coexist with what today we might call adult guidance, reinforcement, and correction. Schleiermacher would answer Blochmann's question by saying that these opposites could be united through practice and its intrinsic dignity. Blochmann, however, calls for a new type of practice. In this sense, her words echo Herbart's original characterization of tact as leaving behind mere habit or *Schlendrian*—a term that also means sloppiness or neglect, and against which Blochmann also explicitly warns (1951, p. 591). This new practice, Blochmann makes clear, is one in which the freedom and protection of the one being educated is seen as necessitating the limitation, curtailment or renunciation of pedagogical interventions and demands. Indeed, this can be regarded as a new, third way that pedagogical tact can be understood: In addition to serving as the mediation of the theoretical and practical, and as a negotiation of the many other contradictory demands of pedagogical practice, it can also be seen to take the form of "the self-limitation of pedagogical logic (*Rationalität*) and expectations," as Müller (2015, p. 21) puts it. What Blochmann's contemporaries and immediate successors show is how this self-limitation of pedagogy is necessitated by recognition of both the *freedom* and the *otherness* of the child or the student.

Two years after Blochmann's and Adorno's remarks were published, the question of pedagogical tact arose as an urgent matter in a rather different setting—a 1953 UNESCO report on "The Teaching of Philosophy." Authored by an international committee that included Georges Canguilhem (also a philosopher of science) and Eugen Fink (educationalist and student of Husserl and Heidegger),[14] the report appears to share Blochmann's postwar political concerns. The report frames tact, specifically what it calls "philosophical tact," not in terms of the activity of the educator, but in terms of freedom, above all the freedom of the student. The definition of tact it provides is captured in the phrase the "contact of two freedoms" (Canguilhem et al., 1953, p. 14)—the freedom of both the educator and the one being educated. In this context, one

> extremely important object is to preserve the virtue of philosophical tact or, in other words, the necessary conditions for the encounter of two freedoms—that of the teacher, which is essential if his teaching is to be individual and genuine, and that of the pupil, which is essential if his acceptance is to have any real intellectual virtue... This freedom, of course, is limited by the restrictions which tact and prudence impose upon the teacher or, in other words, by the consideration due to the pupil's freedom and developing personality. (Canguilhem et al., 1953, pp. 57, 61)

Although both are free, it is the teacher who must exercise self-restraint and make space, via distance and discretion, for the unfolding of students' freedom.

Chronologically, Jakob Muth's 1962 monograph on *Pedagogical Tact* is the next notable publication—and it is considered one of the more influential German works on the subject. It treats pedagogical tact by distinguishing its broadly pedagogical manifestations from ones that are more specifically didactic or instructional in nature. Muth opens his study with the observation that "pedagogical tact is a concept that one encounters frequently in today's literature on pedagogy and instruction" (1962/2022, p. 88). He takes as an example Elisabeth Blochmann's own biography and her article on "Morality and Pedagogical Tact":

> It is certainly not by chance that it is a woman, returning to Germany after the war, who has addressed this issue. To her, the heinous uniformity and conformity of the Nazi era—which extended well beyond orthodoxy of thought to include elements like clothing—was the diametric opposite of tact. (p. 88)

Going further, Muth can be seen as taking Blochmann's idea of pedagogical tact-as-*Gelassenheit* and describing it in terms of "reserve," a quality that is "manifest... through its non-influence, its non-interference" (1962/2022, p. 92). This, Muth says, constitutes one of "two essential moments" that are closely interrelated in pedagogical tact. The other is "sensitivity," defined as "a feeling for the 'you' (or *Thou*), for one's fellow human being, for the singularity and singular rights of the Other; it is a respect for the ultimate inaccessibility of the Other" (p. 92; emphasis added). Reserve and sensitivity converge in Muth's text in the form of the self-limitation of pedagogy as a kind of influencing. This self-limitation is one that is above all individualized and responsive to the singularity of the situation and the Other. It can be said to be a *tactful* form of self-limitation insofar as it respects the Other as ultimately inaccessible to our will, knowledge, and perception, and insofar as we must consequently rely only on "a *feeling* for the 'you'" or Thou of the Other (p. 92; emphasis added). In this version of tact, the incalculability of circumstances identified by Herbart (and Kant before him) are radically increased, extending well beyond theory and knowledge. This is the case not just because of the manifold complexity of what is at stake, but also because there is something explicitly unknowable involved.

Here, Muth makes it clear that he is taking up the notion of the ethical relation between I and Thou (*Ich und Du*), between oneself and another as his frame of reference. In this relation, the other that is directly involved is addressed not as *Sie* or you, but in the more intimate familiar form—as one would address God in a prayer. *I and Thou* is the translated title of a work published by Martin Buber in German during the interwar period (1923/1970). The I-Thou relationship, cast as the special pedagogical relation between the educator and the educated, is understood in opposition to what Buber labels the "I-It" relation. This is a type of relation we have with the world in general—one often marked by objectification and instrumentalization:

> When I confront a human being as my Thou and speak the basic word I-Thou to him, then he is no thing among things, nor does he consist of things. He is no longer He or She, a dot in the world grid of space and time ... Neighborless and seamless, he is Thou and fills the firmament. Not as if there were nothing but he; but everything else lives in his light. (p. 59)

Today we might paraphrase Buber by saying that in these and other ways, alterity or (in Muth's terms) "the Other," can be all too readily assimilated to the order of "the self": That which is other is so often categorized, labeled, and placed in service to interests other than its own. To prevent this, in the event of the encounter with the "Thou," this Other is to be recognized as located in an order that is *not* one's own, but is singular, filling the firmament. Accordingly, this Other is to be engaged both reciprocally and dialogically. Pedagogically speaking, the Thou, the Other, is not only recognized as impenetrable, but generally also as being vulnerable and in need of care. Although it is formulated in different ways, this sentiment remains prominent in all of the subsequent work on pedagogical tact discussed below.

For Muth (1962/2022), the connection with the Other constitutes an event, an existential encounter "in the concrete, unforeseeable situation in which one finds oneself"—an unplannable moment in which one is "suddenly confronted, needing to protect others, to help others—insofar as another is in need of help" (p. 92). The event of the encounter with another is beyond planning and calculation. For Muth, the most important of unplannable acts are *reserve*, inaction, and nonintervention that by definition are *not* part of an educator's instructional advanced planning: The *"reserve of the educator toward the child"* Muth says, *"points to the unintentional nature of original educational action, which sees the involuntary as pedagogically meaningful"* (p. 89; emphasis in original). As already suggested, for this reserve to be pedagogical, the educator or adult must engage in it not "for their own sake," but only for the sake of the Other. The openness and singularity that are a part of this pedagogical response cannot be reliably guided by the "ideal of measure"; nor is it addressed through the linkage of theory and practice. Filling the firmament—with everything else living in its light—the Other asks for something rather different from either "quickness and dexterity" or measured "balance." Instead, what is needed is realized through restraint.

Nonetheless, the exercise of tact—a word that in German also refers to rhythm and tempo—does not imply that pedagogy is paralyzed in the face of alterity or otherness. Muth sees the planned action of the teacher and their moments of improvisation and self-limitation as forming a kind of rhythm, a sort of movement back and forth between spontaneous variability and planned invariability: "One must have a feeling for tact as irregularity in that which is regular" Muth (1962/2022) emphasizes: "*It is distinguished as dynamic irregularity in static regularity*" (p. 91; emphasis in original). These observations regarding rhythm, tempo, and variation open a number of possibilities for tact and its role in cultivating what has been called the "pedagogical *atmosphere*."[15] This refers to a shared mood or disposition that can assist growth and learning—by encouraging those being educated to extend their trust and be open to risk and uncertainty. Such an atmosphere has experiential affinities with other collective phenomena like rhythm and flow that are also all the more powerful because they similarly remain below the level of explicit control and awareness.

The next book-length study that is focused solely on pedagogical tact owes much to Muth's 1962 monograph. This is Max van Manen's 1991 *The Tact of Teaching: The Meaning of Pedagogical Thoughtfulness*.[16] Comparing this publication to Muth's 1962 *Pedagogical Tact*, Barbara Fageth (2021) observes that the two texts "define forms of expression of pedagogical tact" in ways that mirror each other "almost word-for-word"—covering aspects of tact "that are of pedagogical as well as of instructional significance" (pp. 24–25). Speaking of instruction, van Manen, like Muth, sees tact as manifest in "situational confidence" and as involving an "improvisational gift" (van Manen, 1991, pp. 157–160; Muth, 1962, pp. 74–81, 88–94). On the topic of pedagogical tact more broadly, van Manen follows Muth in characterizing it as "unplannable" (van Manen, 1991, p. 144–145; Muth, 1962/2022, pp. 88–90), as a kind of "holding back" (van Manen, pp. 149–152; Muth, p. 89), and as working to "prevent injury" (van Manen, pp. 144–148; Muth, p. 102–103). Tact for both, finally, is also closely allied with Nohl's notion of the "pedagogical relation" (van Manen, pp. 72–78; Muth, pp. 107–108).

Aspects of *The Tact of Teaching* are revisited and developed further in van Manen's 2015 monograph, *Pedagogical Tact: What to do when you don't know what to do*. In both volumes, however, tact is defined quite differently from the way that Muth—or anyone else—defines it: "Tact," van Manen says, "is the sensitive application of thoughtfulness in action" (2015, p. 102); it is "the most personal embodiment of a pedagogical thoughtfulness" (1991, p. 9). Or: Tact "is based on" or consists of "a certain kind of reflection or, better, on an active intentionality of thoughtfulness" (2015, p. 102; 1991, p. 209). This thoughtfulness, however, is *not* one that mediates or reconciles opposed terms: "Tact," van Manen emphasizes, "is not simply some kind of mediator between theory and practice" (2015, p. 102). Van Manen describes the thoughtfulness constitutive of pedagogical tact as "formed by careful reflection on past experiences" (2015, p. 100). Tact is the "process and product of self-reflective reflection on the life of human experience" (2015, p. 102; 1991, p. 127). Tact, in other words, gains its power from individual reflection and self-reflection on previous experience. Tact and thoughtfulness, meanwhile, together appear as an indivisible fusion, a single, inseparable unity of two elements: Pedagogical tact for van Manen is thoughtfulness *in* action, reflection *in* embodiment, an active intentionality *of* thoughtfulness. With tact, action has the quality of reflection, and thoughtfulness is itself active and engaged.

Tact for van Manen thus appears to exist independently of what Adorno regards as its indispensable "precondition"—the compromised but nonetheless residual objectivity and universality of "convention no longer intact yet still present" (1951/1974, p. 36). In the case of pedagogy, this weakened or broken convention can take the form, for example, of a standardized, instrumentalized practice or of one that is unresponsively habitualized (*Schlendrian*). Regardless, convention as a precondition still provides a point of reference outside of individual subjectivity and experience for judging a word or action as more or less tactless or tactful. But since tact as active thoughtfulness, as embodied reflection, is derived only from "reflective self-reflection" or "reflection on past experience," it does not possess any obvious external or conventional point of reference. To use Adorno's words, what seems to be missing from van Manen's account is the "universal which made up the very substance of the individual claim"—the universality implied in individuality that justifies tact in the first place (1951, p. 26). This challenge in conceptualizing tact is discussed further in the conclusion to this introduction.

Significantly, in both of his volumes on pedagogical tact (1991 and 2015), van Manen introduces a way of approaching alterity or otherness that is different from Muth's adoption of Martin Buber's "I-Thou relation"—and that also is significant for subsequent discussions of pedagogical tact. Van Manen does this by adapting the ethics of "the Other" as articulated by Emmanuel Levinas. For Levinas (1987), the Other is not a thing that is known or understood, but an event of encounter which is determined by one's responsibility for the Other: "If one could possess, grasp, and know the Other, it would not be Other," Levinas says (p. 90). Van Manen, on the other hand, sees "the essential being" of this Other as its "vulnerability": It represents for him "the weak spot in the armor of the self-centered world" (1991, p. 240; 2015, p. 202). However, the relation that Levinas outlines between self and other does not allow for the relative symmetry, mutuality, and reciprocity of the horizontal relationship of I and Thou. The encounter of the self with the Other is for Levinas asymmetrical and vertical. It unfolds as a kind of limit experience, with its ultimate incarnation being the experience of death, as van Manen (2015) himself recognizes. It is hard to imagine how pedagogical tact—for example, conceived as a refined and singular distance from one's student and subject—would be relevant to such an existential limit experience. As a result, the danger of the pedagogue being literally at a loss for words or for some other apt response arguably becomes more than just a theoretical problem. Despite its extreme character, references to Levinas' notion of "the Other" are common in recent literature on pedagogical tact (e.g., Burghardt & Zirfas, 2019, p. 84).

The Twenty-first Century: Prairat; Burghardt & Zirfas

The "renaissance" or rediscovery of pedagogical tact begins about a decade and a half into the twenty-first century. This renewal of interest is indicated not only by van Manen's 2015 text that revives his 1991 discussion. The publication of two ambitious monographs in the 2010s establishes the consequential and international character of this renewal: One of these is in French and the other in German: Eirick Prairat's 2017 *Educate with Tact; The virtue and competence of the teacher, (Éduquer avec Tact: Vertu et compétence de l'enseignant)*; and Daniel Burghardt and Jörg Zirfas' 2019 *Pedagogical tact: An educational problem formula (Der pädagogische Takt. Eine erziehungswissenschaftliche Problemformel)*.[17]

Prairat's *Educate with Tact* is an eloquent essayistic text, laid out in three chapters with each having three sub-sections—an organization that has been described as "classical, if not scholastic" (Go, 2017, para. 2). Early on in his book, Prairat notes that Herbart's work on tact has been translated in French no less than four separate times.[18] Despite this fact, Herbart's lecture, as Prairat notes, represents "a forgotten work, erased, like Herbart's name itself" (p. 5). For Prairat, this is less a predicament than an opportunity. He not only develops his own understanding of pedagogy more broadly, but he also reinterprets Herbart's idea of tact, for example, in social, legal, practical, and ethical terms. And as discussed below, one of the nine sub-sections in his text is entirely devoted to an analysis of the "disappearance" of tact.

Prairat follows the 1953 UNESCO document—as well as philosopher David Heyd (1995)—in defining tact as a special kind of virtue: Namely, one that is interstitial and marginal—not having "a political facet like justice or tolerance" and unable to "compete with courage, nor [with] the greatness of humility" (2017, p. 12). Tact for Prairat largely corresponds to Aristotle's definition of virtues of character, to an ethos (*aretê*), involving judgment and practical wisdom (*phronesis*) that is improved upon through practice. (This is an understanding of tact discussed further by Severin Sales Rödel, Chapter 2.) Referring specifically to the UNESCO report, Prairat goes on to describe tact by saying that it is an "interstitial" and almost "invisible virtue"—particularly "insofar as it reveals itself and excels in the interplay of exchanges and interactions" (p. 12). Its locus is the teacher-student relationship understood as an "interpersonal relationship within the impersonality of an institutional one" (Marcel Gauchet, 2003, p. 47; as quoted in Prairat, p. 62). Teaching itself for Prairat "is a profession of relationships," one that "open[s] up to a common world" in a way "that allows for an authentic encounter of subjectivities" (pp. 51, 60). Following Herbart and other scholars, Prairat defines pedagogical tact in terms of a "link," but not one that mediates primarily between theory and practice. Instead, in keeping with his definition of pedagogy as predominantly relational, Prairat sees tact as above all taking the form of a "concern for the *relationship*" between teacher and student "itself" (p. 77; emphasis added). It is also concerned with other more abstract relationships as well, such as that between expression and responsibility, or between the capacity for empathy and an ability to judge.

The final third of *Educate with Tact* is devoted to the question of learning or acquiring tact—specifically through examples that take the form "exemplars" and "dilemmas." Prairat invokes the idea of a "pedagogy" of such examples. Although the example appears elsewhere in works discussed here (e.g., van Manen, 1991, pp. 185–186; see also Chapter 5 by Morten Korsgaard in this volume), Prairat treats it with singular emphasis and depth. "The virtue of tact," he says, "feeds on and is impregnated with exemplary forms, because improvisation is never a creation *ex nihilo*; it always draws on the source of successful forms and acts" (2017, p. 111). Prairat continues:

> The example… is a suggestion, a proposal; it is also an opportunity: that of a return to oneself. The formative dimension of the example lies in the work of appreciation and critical appropriation that accompanies its discovery. The professional personality is constructed through a series of almost unconscious identifications of certain traits and ways of being of our elders, and by a set of fully assumed borrowings of that which we consider to be the most accomplished and respected in a professional tradition. (p. 111)

Examples—whether of exemplary acts or of pedagogical dilemmas—are instances of concrete particularity that can never be entirely subsumed to theoretical generality. At the same time, an example is also always an example *of* something in particular: It is a concrete instance which points to something more general. In thus connecting the particular and the universal, examples not only mirror the fundamental operation of tact, but like it, they also encourage reflection and deliberation. As Prairat says, examples initiate a return to oneself—a return that can occur by raising questions. For example: "What went wrong or right in the given example?" "On what basis is this 'wrong' or 'right' to be judged?" or "How could I do better—or worse?" Examples can make conscious what was earlier unconscious, and they offer opportunity for the embodied "in-corporation" of ways of acting and being. They do not designate an answer or solution, but instead provoke the recollection of past experience and the imagination of future or alternative possibilities.[19] Speaking specifically of a "pedagogy of dilemmas"—a response to situations marked by uncertainty, potential harm, or conflicting values—Prairat briefly describes an exercise called "le speed dating *éthique*": "It consists in asking the trainees to respond quickly, very quickly, to briefly described situations involving moral problems" (2017, p. 129). The value of this method, Prairat suggests, lies in its potential to cultivate "the ability to rapidly identify an issue and to propose a response" (p. 129)—a goal really not that different from the "quick judgment and decision" called for by Herbart 215 years prior.

As befits the first German-language monograph devoted exclusively to tact in over 50 years, Burghardt and Zirfas' (2019) *Pedagogical Tact: An Educational Problem Formula* provides an extensive overview of the ways that pedagogical tact has been and can be understood: "This book," the authors explain, "attempt[s] nothing more than to develop and compile [*erarbeiten*] knowledge of pedagogical tact that is as conceptually clear as possible" (p. 10). This is structured through a range of "perspectives" on pedagogical tact—for example, as historical, ethical, anthropological, embodied, and aisthetic.[20] (E.g., see Zirfas and Burghardt's discussion of aisthesis, tact, and the power of the look in Chapter 9.) Burghardt and Zirfas' characterization of their book, however, as "just" a compilation ultimately sells it short. Continuing the strand of scholarship that understands tact primarily as the mediation of opposites or antipodes, the authors define pedagogical tact specifically as "a 'response' to the pedagogical tension between determinacy and indeterminacy—between certainty and uncertainty, [or] necessity and contingency" (p. 9). However, it is its definition of tact specifically as a "problem formula" (*Problemformel*) that represents the principal contribution of this monograph. This particular perspective provides not only a way in which the recurring interest in and resilience of questions of tact in pedagogy can be understood; it also explicitly casts the role of pedagogical tact in a way perhaps most suitable to contemporary understanding:

> pedagogical tact is here decidedly not understood as a formula [for the] solution of pedagogical problems, but as a formula [for the] problematization of pedagogical issues. We understand this term in the sense of the Latin *problema* [i.e., a task, that which is proposed, a question (Online Etymology, 2023)] and regard pedagogical tact

as something offered, put forward, as an inescapable pedagogical question... that does not primarily aim at solutions, but at the generation and discussion of pedagogical questions; it defines the problematic nature of certain kinds of pedagogical action and initiatives, and it identifies and differentiates the dimensions of associated problems. (2018, pp. 10–11)

Pedagogical tact, in other words, serves as a kind of heuristic for the consideration, analysis, and interpretation of aspects of pedagogy and pedagogical action. In this sense, as a problem formula, tact can be seen as broadly resonant with Prairat's notion of a "pedagogy of dilemmas." It is also adopted as a way of understanding tact in the chapters in this volume by Müller, and Krinninger and Kesselhut. To see tact as a way of "identif[ying] problems," of addressing "pedagogical issues," and for "the generation and discussion of pedagogical questions" (Burkhardt & Zirfas, 2018, pp. 10–11) means that its relation to theory and practice is reconfigured. In fact, this relation is in a sense reversed: Tact is no longer primarily a way of attuning or sensitizing practice based (however indirectly) on theory. Instead, it is justified as a way of problematizing action and asking questions about it. It becomes, in other words, a way of theorizing—but one that remains close to concrete concerns and examples. In this sense, theories of these kinds would resemble the "theory of practice for practice" that human science pedagogues like Nohl sought to articulate. At the same time, though, this theory is notably different in that it is developed from the *problems* of practice rather than from any supposed solutions.

Quoting Adorno's *Catchwords*, Burghardt and Zirfas assert that as the mediator of practice and theory, tact itself can be neither predominantly theoretical nor practical. It must always exceed what can be specified in thought and what can be performed in action: "If theory and praxis are neither immediately one nor absolutely different, then their relation is one of discontinuity. No continuous path leads from praxis to theory" (Adorno, 1969/2005, p. 276; Burghardt & Zirfas, 2019, p. 44). Tact can consequently no longer be seen as "the immediate director of practice" (Herbart, 2022, p. 32); nor can it be envisioned as "artful action" to which "one must always return... in one's practice" (Schleiermacher, 2000, p. 352). Tact is no longer about leading *positively* and *pro*spectively to "knowing what to do when you don't know what to do" as van Manen (2015) put it. Zirfas and Burghardt instead emphasize the dialectical inverse, tact's *negative* potential. This refers to its capacity to work *retro*spectively to discursively *problematize* what has or might have already occurred. For Kant, Herbart, and Schleiermacher, tact appears as an ability or faculty, something whose capacity is expressed through active engagement. Later, starting perhaps with Nohl and more emphatically with Blochmann and Muth, tact takes on the quality of the appropriate negation or absence of such activity and intervention. However, even through this negation, pedagogical tact remains a quality or capacity evidenced through timing, rapidity, and being singularly opportune. Only later does tact cease to be a guide for practice and becomes a means of problematizing that practice.

Burghardt and Zirfas also point out that beginning with Herbart, the opposite of pedagogical tact was represented by the term *Schlendrian*—a term referring to habitual sloppiness or neglect. Such an interpretation of tact in terms of its opposite or antipode can be traced from Herbart all the way to Blochmann, who again mentions *Schlendrian* in 1951. However, Burghardt and Zirfas emphasize that today, the negation of tact is not so much habitual negligence as it is planning and action that is dictated by means-ends rationality, by the instrumentalization and automation or "technification" of educational processes. This instrumentalization includes not only technology itself, but also ways of thinking that have as their goal the maximization of efficiency and outputs. The result of this "technification" of education, Burghardt and Zirfas (2019) emphasize, is that "tact simply becomes tactics" (p. 44). This sentiment is echoed elsewhere in the texts reviewed here: For Muth, the enemy of pedagogical tact is ultimately "the means-ends thinking of our time"—one that he says constricts the "domain… of the unintentional and the involuntary" in everyday pedagogical engagement (1962/2022, p. 102). For Pairat (2017) meanwhile, technology leads to nothing less than destruction of sociality itself as the foundation for tact: "Technology was originally conceived with the sole ambition of increasing our independence," Pairat emphasizes. "Its only ideal has been the conquest of self-sufficiency" (p. 35).

Conclusion: "Convention No Longer Intact yet Still Present"

Tact, which began as a general social and then (also) a specifically pedagogical concept, has changed a great deal in both its substance and implications over the past 250 years. It first arose through revolutionary social change and upheaval, specifically as a form of discernment and discretion in contexts that could no longer be governed through habit and custom, but which required flexibility and improvisation. *Pedagogical* tact, meanwhile, was co-emergent in the early nineteenth century with pedagogy itself as a "science"—as a system of interrelated propositions requiring practical adaptation and simplification. Meanwhile, in the remainder of the nineteenth century, pedagogical tact was captive to a prevailing Herbartianism. It was later abandoned altogether by *Reformpädagogik*—and seems to have remained unknown in progressive education. The rise of fascism and the Second World War, however, gave the question of pedagogical tact a new urgency.

By mid-century, pedagogical tact was reinterpreted as the protection of an "other's" freedom precisely through appropriate distance, inaction, and passivity. It was also configured as the necessary "self-limitation" of a "pedagogical logic" of influence and intervention in the face of alterity (Müller, 2015, p. 21).[21] Today, we live in a time when education is seen as unavoidably "audacious" (Mollenhauer, 1983/2014, p. 129) and as inevitably marked by educators' "incompetence and dilettantism" (Reichenbach, 2001, p. 368).[22] In this context, pedagogical tact is once again relevant. Combining the insights of both Prairat *and* Burghardt and Zirfas, tact is effectively redefined as a heuristic for the analysis of pedagogical practice that works through examples, dilemmas, and reflection. But why now? What might be some of the broader social or political grounds for this development? Why is pedagogical tact undergoing a renaissance?

A possible answer to the question of the return of tact—a response with which this overview concludes—can be found by returning once again to Theodore Adorno's 1951 *Minima Moralia: Reflections from a Damaged Life*. In combining observations of twentieth-century life with discussion of world-historical events, Adorno effectively subjects his topic to a kind of negative dialectic. As signaled in the discussion of van Manen above, this movement of negation begins with the interrelationship of the general and in particular, between the universality of social convention and the singularity of the individual. Adorno (1951/1974) warns that tact has lost its capacity to mediate between these extremes:

> Convention represented, in however etiolated a form, the universal which made up the very substance of the individual claim.... Yet when emancipated, [tact] confronts the individual as an absolute, without anything universal from which to be differentiated, it fails to engage the individual and finally wrongs him. [It] helps what is most universal, naked external power, to triumph even in the most intimate constellations. (pp. 36–37)

The enfeebled and "unauthorized claims of convention" Adorno implies, are the universal on which the moment of tact and the singularity of the individual have depended. But because tact can no longer achieve the delicate equilibrium of these opposites, it falls "into irreparable ruin" (p. 37). As with his negative dialectic in general, the relationship between these opposed terms for Adorno can only be one of discontinuity. "Silence on sensitive subjects," as one example, consequently appears only as "empty indifference." And this is the case specifically because there "is no rule to indicate what is and what is not to be discussed" (p. 37).

Significantly, Prairat can be seen to expand on Adorno's reasoning in discussing the contemporary "eclipse" of tact. Prairat identifies three reasons for tact's decline: The first is the elevation of the individual—and of the individual's self-fulfillment—to the status of an absolute, above the claims of any larger order, including that of social convention. The second is the corresponding depersonalization of mass society, the dominance of legal frameworks and limitations—and the tactics to which they give rise—in even intimate relations. The third has already been covered: It is the impact of technology, of the general rationalization and optimization "on our ways of being" (p. 28) that the increasing technification of the lifeworld implies. Prairat quotes from Adorno's *Minima Moralia* in describing this process further: "Technology is making gestures precise and brutal, and with them men. It expels from movements all hesitation, deliberation, civility" (Adorno, 1951/1974, p. 19; Prairat, 2017, p. 33). In the case of tact, gestures and bodily dispositions can communicate a great deal—silently, but often with greater force and indubitability than mere words. However, in becoming ever more like the machines and devices that surround us, our bodies can be said to be gradually deprived of their capacity to express, for example, activity that is also receptive or passivity that is also attentive—or, as Prairat puts it, to express "the charm of a presence that is posed without imposing itself" (2017, p. 23).[23]

In describing the potential of tact to flip from relinquishment and renunciation to nothing less than naked external power, Adorno highlights something all too readily overlooked. This is the way that a supposedly tactful word or action is almost unavoidably haunted by its dialectical opposite, both in empirical analyses and discussions seeking to identify moments exemplifying pedagogical tact (e.g., Friesen & Osguthorpe, 2018; Friesen, 2021): Instead of being adroit, appropriate, and discreet, an otherwise tactful word or gesture might just as well be interpreted as maladroit, inappropriate, or indiscreet. This is particularly true in the case of pedagogical tact: Here, the significance of a tactful word or gesture is to be judged not by the actor, the educator, but ultimately by the receiver, the child or student—who may be in no position to render or communicate a decisive judgment. As Prairat (quoting Philippe Meirieu) explains, "nothing in the history of the Other is erased": In pedagogy, "a destiny can be changed by very little, by a clumsy sentence that is instantly forgotten by the person who pronounces it" (Meirieu, 1991, p. 67; Prairat, p. 22). Specifically in its pretention to address the unknown and unknowable Other—the one being educated ostensibly *for their own sake*, as Nohl emphasized—pedagogical tact can appear as little more than a "cynical ruse." This is how David Russell describes tact more broadly in his 2018 book on *Tact and Aesthetic Liberalism* in nineteenth-century Britain. Tact, Russell says, has recently and deservedly

> had some bad press. It may seem rather an old-fashioned term, even one best left in the nineteenth century. The word suggests a certain stuffiness, a retrograde attachment to social hierarchies, and a pedantic knowingness about the right thing to do, now all but useless in a modern and diverse world… Or, what's worse, tact might seem to survive,

even to thrive, from the nineteenth century to our own time as a cynical ruse—as a cover for dissimulation, and a technique of manipulation—in relationships, in politics, in business, in the media. (p. 2)

Perhaps tact, particularly pedagogical tact, is of interest today precisely because of proliferating dissimulation and manipulation which appear undisguised by any pretention to tactfulness.

Summarizing Prairat and Russell, and borrowing from contemporary sociology, one can say that the convention upon which tact depends has been significantly affected by a range of macro-level social processes. These include the specialization or functional differentiation of society and social roles (Luhmann, 1977), the widespread diffusion of digital technologies (e.g., Castells & Cardoso, 2005), and the pluralization of society (e.g., Rabushka & Shepsle, 2008). Pluralization—for example, in terms of race, culture, gender, and class—has been associated with the rise of new vocabularies and new ways of engaging socially. New terms such as "othering," "triggering," "decolonization," "implicit bias," "stereotype threat," and "microaggression"—can all be seen as responses to this macro-social process. Correspondingly, terms such as "doxing," "clickbait," "ghosting," or "shadow banning" are just a few of the words describing social practices now possible in digital social media. Both of these vocabularies, whose normative character is self-evident, represent relatively new ways of categorizing and arbitrating interaction and sociality. They are also expressive of new forms and types of awareness of social and cultural difference. These terms and forms of reference can be said to delimit nothing less than a new domain of civility and of novel forms of engagement with "the Other." In this sense, they can be compared to social conventions of the bourgeoise that Adorno saw in his own time as being in "irreparable ruin." However, these new forms appear not to be undergoing decline as much as development, change, and contestation. Nonetheless, they serve as examples of "preconditions of tact" that may now be "just sufficiently present," as Adorno put it, making a return to tact—in pedagogy and beyond—compelling and urgent.

Notes

[1] Fageth (2021) writes: "In the past five years in particular, a number of noteworthy monographs and anthologies have been published… whose contributions make pedagogical tact appear more topical than ever in the discourse of educational studies in the 21st century" (p. 15).

[2] One important contribution to German-language discourse from the interwar period not directly addressed in this chapter is Helmuth Plessner's *The Limits of Community: A Critique of Social Radicalism* (1924/1999), particularly the chapter "The Logic of Diplomacy. The Hygiene of Tact." As both the book and chapter titles suggest, Plessner brings the question of tact into connection with politics—all during the politically volatile Weimar era. He

defines tact as "a bindingness which does not bind," as a "sphere" in which "there should be neither good nor evil, neither truth nor error, but only the value of beneficence—the hygiene of the greatest possible nurturance [*Schonung*, or protection]" (pp. 163–164).

3   This understanding of pedagogy refers to a way of thinking that coalesced in Europe early in the nineteenth century and that continues to be elaborated today—particularly in German-speaking Europe. It is marked by a concern for the quality of the relation of educators to those educated. The words "pedagogy" and "pedagogical" in this book overall are meant to designate this Continental understanding and tradition (see: Friesen & Kenklies, 2023).

4   Schleiermacher uses the term *Einwirkung*, which can be translated not only as "influence," but also as "intervention" or "result."

5   While Arendt asks that the child and their natality be protected "so that nothing destructive may happen to him from the world," Arendt also makes it clear that the opposite is also true: "But the world, too, needs protection to keep it from being overrun and destroyed by the onslaught of the new that bursts upon it with each new generation" (p. 186). The two types of protection can be said to exist in dialectical tension.

6   I provide this account with the acknowledgment that it mixes a historical overview with a systematic one (i.e., a chronological account with changes in theory or conceptualizations). However, this approach provides a way of integrating international developments in a coherent account, and to interpret recent developments in discussions of tact in the light of ones occurring earlier (e.g., before and immediately after WWII)—a task that, to my knowledge, has not yet been undertaken.

7   For the remainder of this paragraph, the passages quoted are from Kant (1793/1974, p. 41) and Herbart (1802/2022, pp. 31–32).

8   Fageth (2021) similarly describes two principal ways of conceptualizing pedagogical tact: 1) "As a mediating principle between the theoretical-general and the practical-concrete" and 2) "as an ethical-normative conceptualization of antinomies for the formation of pedagogical relationships" (p. 16).

9   I owe a debt of gratitude to Karsten Kenklies (Strathclyde University) for pointing out this source.

10   For Dewey and for many progressives today, the "inquiry" and "problem-solving" processes that constitute learning are simultaneously natural and cultural, social and individual, as well as practical and natural-scientific. It is this "intellectual process" of testing and validating knowledge that provides Dewey with the organizing principle for theory and practice in education. In distinction to the theories referenced in scholarship on tact, Dewey's understanding of theory tends to be positivistic: Like any theory in the natural sciences, it claims to provide certain, valid, verifiable knowledge of its subject—including education. On this understanding, which still dominates much English-language educational discourse, pedagogical practice becomes the immediate implementation of theory, rather than its mediation through interpretation and adaptation.

11   Nohl's "role in National Socialism remains controversial" as Dollinger (2008) explains in his historical overview of pedagogy (p. 247): On the one hand, "the key points of Nohl's pedagogy contradicted National Socialist propaganda on education, and he himself was forced into retirement" during the Nazi era (p. 248). On the other hand, Nohl gave a series of lectures titled "The Fundaments of National Education" in 1933–34, and (as above) he seemed later to take issue with the overthrow of the Nazi regime.

12   Left untranslated here, the term *Gelassenheit* (serenity, letting go, releasement) was later adopted as a philosophical term by Martin Heidegger who in fact corresponded with Blochmann regularly from 1918 to 1969 (see Storck, J. [1990]. *Martin Heidegger–Elisabeth*

Blochmann. Briefwechsel. 1918–1969. Deutsche Schillergesellschaft). Nonetheless, there is no trace of the transmission of this from Blochmann to Heidegger (or vice-versa) in their correspondence.

[13] One exception is: Bernfeld, S. (1925/1973). *Sisyphus or the limits of education.* University of California Press. Also, one of Nohl's students, O. F. Bollnow, addressed the educator's fallibility very directly in: Bollnow, O. F. (1959/2022). Risk and failure in education. In N. Friesen (Ed. Trans.), *Tact and the pedagogical relation: Introductory readings* (pp. 137–152). Peter Lang.

[14] Discussed in Prairat 2017 on pp. 91–92. Fink's works on philosophy are readily available; his writing on education are gradually appearing in English, for example, Fink, E. (1960/2016). *Play as symbol of the world: And other writings.* Indiana University Press; and Fink, E. (1959/2022). The questionableness of the modern educator. In N. Friesen (Ed. Trans.), *Tact and the Pedagogical Relation* (117–136). Peter Lang.

[15] For example, see Bollnow, O. F. (1944/1989). The pedagogical atmosphere. *Phenomenology + Pedagogy* 7, 5–77; Koerrenz, R. (2017). *Existentialism and education. An introduction to Otto Friedrich Bollnow.* Palgrave.

[16] This is not to say that other works on pedagogical tact did not appear between 1962 and 1991. These include: Müssener, G. (1977). Begriff und Funktion des Pädagogischen Takts in Herbarts System der Pädagogik. *Zeitschrift für Pädagogik, 14,* 259–269; Pleines, J.-E. (1980). Die logische Funktion des Taktes im Anschluss an das Kantische System der Philosophie betrachtet. *Kant-Studien, 71,* 469–487; and Suzuki, S. (May, 1988). Die Bedeutung des Herbartschen "pädagogischen Takts" für die Lehrerausbildung. *Studies in the Philosophy of Education, 58,* 15–27.

[17] See Fageth, 2021, p. 14, for a somewhat more extensive set of texts. There are a number of other relatively recent publications related to pedagogical tact not included in this overview: Suzuki, S. (2010). *Takt in modern education.* Waxmann. Despite the title, only two of the six chapters of this short monograph discuss pedagogical tact. A number of edited collections have also appeared: Gödde, G & Zirfas, J. (2012). *Takt und Taktlosigkeit. Über Ordnungen und Unordnungen in Kunst, Kultur und Therapie.* transcript; Burghardt, D. Krinninger, D. & Seichter, S. (Eds). (2015). *Pädagogischer Takt: Theorie – Empirie – Kultur*; Friesen, N. (Ed.) (Trans.) (2022). *Tact and the pedagogical relation: Introductory readings.* Peter Lang. Also, at least one report and a more informal account of have been published: Gastager, A. & Patry, J.-L. (Eds. 2017). *Pädagogischer Takt: Analysen zu Theorie und Praxis.* Leykam; and Vollmer, J. (2019). *Taktvolle Nähe: Vom Finden des angemessenen Abstands in pädagogischen Beziehungen.* Psychosozial-Verlag. Other texts, more tangentially related to the tradition of pedagogy and pedagogical tact include: Steeg-Thornhill, S. M. & Badley, K. (2020). *Generating tact and flow for effective teaching and learning.* Routledge. Finally, there are two Ph.D. studies of note: Sipman, G. (2021). *Enhancing teacher pedagogical tact through intuition: A design study* <https://ris.utwente.nl/ws/portalfiles/portal/268201560/Thesis_G_Sipman.pdf> and B. Fageth. (2021). *Pädagogischer Takt in der Elementarpädagogik.* Juventa.

[18] Specifically in 1896, 1904, 2006, and again in 2017.

[19] For a hermeneutic treatment of the exemplary in education, see Buck, G. (1981). *Hermeneutik und Bildung: Elemente einer verstehenden Bildungslehre.* Fink. See especially Chapter 9: „Thesen über das Exemplarische" (pp. 199–224).

[20] *Aisthesis* refers to that which is perceptual and/or sensuous.

[21] Müller explains further: "By 'pedagogical logic' I mean the specific language games, 'vocabularies,' 'grammars,' patterns of interpretation, or forms of interaction and intervention that define pedagogy in theory and practice, that is, the modern pedagogical habitus [i.e., the mode or style of an individual's engagement] as a whole, which, in view of the strangeness

and otherness of the Other (the child, the adolescent, the student), must always also limit itself (or acknowledge its limitation)" (H.-R. Müller, private communication, August 29, 2023).

[22] Mollenhauer (1983/2014) concludes his modern educational classic, *Forgotten Connections*, by referring to the need of adults to provide justification "for the audacity that lies at the heart of any efforts in the upbringing and *Bildung* of a child" (p. 129). Reichenbach (2001), meanwhile, emphasizes that the uncontrollability of pedagogical situations means that the educator can ultimately only fail or be a "dilettante": "Because education is so rich in incompetence and dilettantism, so rich in situations where one side or both in this process 'fall out of their roles,' it is also rich in feelings of shame. ...This failure is built into the structure of the educational situation. The educator sees herself as responsible for something she cannot control: the freedom of the child [who is also a] subject" (p. 368).

[23] Again quoting Gauchet, Prairat continues: "Teaching always requires the co-presence of the actors. 'Proximity speaks,' writes Gauchet... the most abstract things of the mind, those that are the pure exercise of reason, in principle, become more accessible and clearer to us when they come to us through the medium of another, of his or her voice, his or her body, his or her life, of that aura called presence" (p. 61). See also: Friesen, Chapter 7 in this volume.

Bibliography

Adorno, T. (1951/1974). *Minima moralia: Reflections on a damaged life*. (E. Jephcott, Trans.). Verso.

Adorno, T. (1969/2005). Marginalia to theory and practice. In T. Adorno (Ed.), *Catchwords II: Critical models* (H. W. Pickford, Trans.). Columbia University Press.

Arendt, H. (1958/1968). The crisis in education. *Between past and future* (pp. 173–196). Penguin.

Beiser, F. C. (2022) *Johann Friedrich Herbart: The grandfather of analytic philosophy*. Oxford University Press.

Biesta, G. (2011). Disciplines and theory in the academic study of education: A comparative analysis of the Anglo-American and Continental construction of the field. *Pedagogy, Culture & Society 19*(2), 175–192.

Blochmann, E. (1950). Der pädagogische Takt. *Die Sammlung: Zeitung für Kultur und Erziehung, 5*, 712–720.

Blochmann, E. (1951). Die Sitte und der pädagogische Takt. *Die Sammlung: Zeitung für Kultur und Erziehung, 6*, 589–593.

Buber, M. (1923/1970). *I and thou*. (W. Kaufmann, Trans.). Free Press.

Burghardt, D. & Zirfas, J. (2019). *Der Pädagogische Takt. Eine erziehungswissenschaftliche Problemformel*. Beltz/Juventa.

Canguilhem, G, Humberto P. L., Madkour, I., Fink, E., Nikam, N. A., Guido N., MacKinnon, D., Moore, M. H., McKeon, R. (1953). *The teaching of philosophy:*

An international enquiry of UNESCO. UNESCO. <https://unesdoc.unesco.org/ark:/48223/pf0000090083>

Castells, M. and Cardoso, G. eds. (2005). *The network society: From knowledge to policy.* Johns Hopkins Center for Transatlantic Relations.

Dewey, J. (1897). My pedagogic creed. *The School Journal, 54*(3), 77–80.

Dewey, J. (1904). *The relation of theory to practice in education.* University of Chicago Press.

Dollinger, B. (2008). *Klassiker der Pädagogik: Die Bildung der modernen Gesellschaft.* Springer VS.

Fageth, B. (2021). *Pädagogischer Takt in der Elementarpädagogik.* Beltz Juventa.

Friesen, N. (2021). Atmospheres and understanding: Past, present, and future. In M. Brinkmann, J. Türstig & M. Weber (Eds.), *Emotion – feeling – mood: Phenomenological and pedagogical perspectives* (pp. 115–128). Springer VS.

Friesen, N. (2022). The antinomies of pedagogy and aporias of embodiment: A historical and phenomenological investigation. In A. Kraus, C. Wulf (Eds.), *Handbook of embodiment and learning* (pp. 91–106). Palgrave. <https://doi.org/10.1007/978-3-030-93001-1_6>

Friesen, N. (2023). Accentuate the negative: Schleiermacher's dialectic. In N. Friesen & K. Kenklies (Eds. Trans.), *F.D.E. Schleiermacher's outlines of the art of education: A translation & discussion* (pp. 177–213). Peter Lang.

Friesen, N. (Ed. 2022). *Tact and the pedagogical relation: Introductory readings.* Peter Lang.

Friesen, N. & Osguthorpe, R. (2018). Tact and the pedagogical triangle: The authenticity of teachers in relation. *Teaching and Teacher Education, 70*(June). <https://doi.org/10.1016/j.tate.2017.11.023>

Friesen, N. & Kenklies, K. (2023). "Continental Pedagogy & Curriculum." In R. Tierney, F. Rizvi, & K. Ercikan (eds.), *The international encyclopedia of education* (4th ed) (pp. 245–255). Elsevier.

Gauchet, M. (2003). Démocratie, éducation, philosophie. In M.-C. Blais, M. Gauchet, & D. Ottavi (Eds.), *Pour une philosophie politique de l'éducation.* Hachette.

Go, H. L. (June, 2017). Eduquer avec tact. *Recherches & Educations.* <https://doi.org/10.4000/rechercheseducations.5177>

Helsper, W. (2021). *Professionalität und Professionalisierung pädagogischen Handelns. Eine Einführung.* Barbara Budrich.

Hainschink, V. & Zahra-Ecker, R. A. (2018). Leben in Antinomien – Bewältigungsdispositionen aus arbeitsbezogenen Verhaltens- und Erlebensmustern. *Pedagogical Horizons 2*(2), 179–194.

Herbart, J. F. (1802/2022). Introductory lecture to students in pedagogy. In N. Friesen (Ed. Trans.), *Tact and the pedagogical relation: Introductory readings* (pp. 28–37). Peter Lang.

Heyd, D. (1995). Tact: Sense, sensitivity, and virtue. *Inquiry: An Interdisciplinary Journal of Philosophy 38*(3), 217–231. <http://doi.org/10.1080/00201749508602387>

Humboldt, W. von (1793/1999). Theory of Bildung. In Hopmann, S., Westbury, I. & Riquarts, K. (Eds. Trans.), *Teaching as a reflective practice: The German Didaktik tradition* (pp. 57–61). Routledge.

Kant, I. (1789/2007). *Anthropology from a pragmatic point of view.* (R. B. Louden, Trans.). Cambridge University Press.

Kant, I. (1793/1974). *On the old saw: That may be right in theory, but it won't work in practice.* (E. B. Ashton, Trans.). University of Pennsylvania Press.

Kraut, R. (2022). Aristotle's ethics. In N. Zalta & U. Nodelman (Eds.), *The Stanford Encyclopedia of Philosophy.* <https://plato.stanford.edu/archives/fall2022/entries/aristotle-ethics/>

Levinas, E. (1987). *Time and the Other.* Duquesne University Press.

Luhmann, N. (1977). Differentiation of society. *The Canadian Journal of Sociology / Cahiers Canadiens de Sociologie*, *2*(1), 29–53. <https://doi.org/10.2307/3340510>

McMurry, C. (1897). *The method of the recitation.* Public-School Publishing.

Meirieu, P. (1991). *Le choix d'éduquer. Éthique et pédagogie.* ESF.

Mollenhauer, K. (1983/2014). *Forgotten connections: On culture and upbringing.* Routledge.

Müller, H.-R. (2015). Zur Theorie des pädagogischen Takts. In D. Krinninger & S. Seichter (Eds.), *Pädagogischer Takt: Theorie – Empirie – Kultur* (pp. 13–24). Ferdinand Schöningh.

Müssener, G. (1977). Begriff und Funktion des Pädagogischen Takts in Herbarts System der Pädagogik. *Zeitschrift für Pädagogik, 14,* 259–269.

Muth, J. (1962/2022). Pedagogical tact: Study of a contemporary form of educational and instructional engagement (selections). In N. Friesen (Ed. Trans.), *Tact and the pedagogical relation: Introductory readings.* (pp. 85–117). Peter Lang.

Nohl, H. (1933/2022). The pedagogical relation and the formative community. In N. Friesen (Ed. Trans.), *Tact & the pedagogical relation: An introduction* (pp. 75–84). Peter Lang.

Nohl, H. (1958). *Erziehergestalten.* Vandenhoeck & Ruprech.

Oxford University Press. (1989). Tact. In *Oxford English dictionary.* <https://oed.com/view/Entry/232982>

Pleines, J.-E. (1980). Die logische Funktion des Taktes im Anschluss an das Kantische System der Philosophie betrachtet. *Kant-Studien, 71,* 469–487.

Prairat, E. (2017). *Éduquer avec tact.* ESF.

Problem. (2023). Online etymology. <https://www.etymonline.com/>

Rabushka, A. and Shepsle, K. A. (2008). *Politics in plural societies: A theory of democratic instability.* Pearson.

Reichenbach, R. (2001). *Demokratisches Selbst und dilettantisches Subjekt.* Waxmann.

Russell, D. (2018). *Tact: Aesthetic liberalism and the essay form in nineteenth century Britain.* <https://doi.org/10.2307/j.ctvc778wq>

Schleiermacher, F. D. E. (1826/2023). *F.D.E. Schleiermacher's outlines of the art of education: A translation & discussion.* N. Friesen & K. Kenklies (Eds. Trans.). Peter Lang.

Schleiermacher, F. D. E. (2000). *Texte zur Pädagogik. Kommentierte Studienausgabe,* vols. 1 & 2. M. Winkler & J. Brachmann (Eds). Suhrkamp.

Schlömerkemper, J. (2018). *Pädagogische Prozesse in antinomischer Deutung: Begriffliche Klärung und Entwürfe für Lernen und Lehren.* Beltz/Juventa.

Stewart, D. (1793/1864). *Outlines of moral philosophy.* Garland.

Suzuki, S. (May, 1988). Die Bedeutung des Herbartschen "pädagogischen Takts" für die Lehrerausbildung. *Studies in the Philosophy of Education, 58,* 15–27.

UNESCO. (1953). *The teaching of philosophy: An international enquiry of UNESCO,* 185–214. <https://doi.org/10.5840/tpenquiry195315>

van Manen, M. (1991). *The tact of teaching: The meaning of pedagogical thoughtfulness.* SUNY Press.

van Manen, M. (2015). *Pedagogical tact: Knowing what to do when you don't know what to do.* Routledge.

Voltaire. (1776/1879). *A philosophical dictionary.* Blackwell.

Ziller, T. (1876). *Vorlesungen über allgemeine Pädagogik.* Heinrich Matthes.

Chapter Synopses

Norm Friesen

Three Sections

As has been made clear in the previous pages, this collection builds on a 200-year history of pedagogical thought and related political and social developments. As such, it not only connects contemporary discourses on pedagogical tact to those of the last two centuries, it also reconnects abstract theory and concrete practice. The topic of tact itself is defined by a tension between these opposites, and their opposition is reflected both in this volume's sub-title (reconnecting theory and practice), and in the structure of its sections and chapters. Originally seen as a way of understanding the mediation of theory and practice, pedagogical tact has itself been subject to much theoretical reflection. This is indicated in the first section or set of chapters, which cover pedagogical tact from a number of theoretical perspectives.

The first chapter, by Eirick Prairat, represents the perspective of ethical theory (Prairat is an ethicist of education), taking also the vantage point of the French pedagogical canon (e.g., Montaigne, de La Salle, Rousseau). The second and third chapters undertake reconstructions of pedagogical tact from the perspectives of Hannah Arendt's political (and educational) theory and in relation to character and ethos as originally articulated by Aristotle. In doing so, these two chapters also broach the important question of the illustration or the example in both understanding and cultivating tactful pedagogical engagement.

The chapters in this volume's third section (Tact in Context) contextualize pedagogical tact in constructions of human community. "Pedagogical tact and the limits of community" references Helmuth Plessner's work on tact and diplomacy (Plessner, 1924/1999, pp. 149–170) in a discussion of the limits placed by pedagogical tact on the normative social contexts of institutional education. The chapter that follows, "Pedagogical tact and education in the family," considers pedagogical processes and their relationship to tact in modernity's most concrete and elementary form of community: the family.[1] For the family is the first and probably the most powerful educative unit—one in which tact is exercised, as this chapter shows, often in terms of the structure and boundaries between family and world.

The final section of this volume features chapters that address concrete practice by exploring the physically situated and embodied nature of pedagogical tact. The first looks to Merleau-Ponty's account of "the flesh" in *The Visible and the Invisible*, the second, to the question of the look, glance, or gaze (in German:

Blick) in tactful teaching. The third situates tact in the explicitly intercorporeal phenomenon of "resonance." Each brings into articulation aspects of social and pedagogical engagement that are at once deeply familiar but that evade attempts at description, explication, and formal analysis. These phenomena are associated with terms like "climate," "atmosphere," and "ambience," and apply not only to the ways that influence can be powerfully exercised in pedagogy, but also expand to include broader processes indispensable to personal development, such as the self-directed, growth designated as *Bildung*.

Individual Chapters

The paragraphs below provide more detailed overviews of each of the chapters in this volume, contextualizing terms and concepts that may be unfamiliar to those working outside of the continental pedagogical tradition.

"Reconsidering Tact," by Eirick Prairat, Professor of Philosophy of Education at the University of Lorraine, is appropriately titled as the opening contribution to a collection that itself reconsiders pedagogical tact from range of perspectives. Prairat develops a number of themes from his monograph, *Educate with Tact* (2017), as discussed in the introduction above. For example, Prairat begins his reconsideration by defining tact as a "virtue of relationships," and by discussing the UNESCO report authored by Eugen Fink and Georges Canguilhem (among others) that defines the tactful teaching of philosophy as the "meeting of two freedoms" (p. 52).

In tracing his own history of tact, Prairat's genealogy reaches further back than the one traced in the introduction, and includes figures active earlier than Voltaire or Herbart—such as Montaigne, Erasmus, and the French educational reformer, Jean-Baptiste de La Salle. Prairat also emphasizes the significance of two eminently French concerns: *civilité* (civility) and *savoir-faire* (know-how, finesse). *Savoir-faire* is particularly important for Prairat. He is unique in this collection in highlighting a technical, methodological component of tact. For Prairat, the technical refers both to the "what"—e.g., particular instructional skills or pedagogical expertise—and the "how"—the specific *way* that a "task" can be realized "according to the context and circumstances" (p. 53). It is through the inclusion of the latter, through a *savoir-comment-faire* that the otherwise technical tasks become specifically relational, and thus also ethical and potentially tactful. In this sense "ethics is immanent to the technical domain," Prairat says (p. 52). Pedagogical tact, of course, has much in common with Aristotelian phronesis, "the ability to choose the 'golden mean.'" However, "unlike phronesis… tact is [also] the ability to identify the point of convergence, the always fragile confluence between ethics and technique." The two are combined "in the pedagogical act" Prairat asserts, "precisely to give it its educational fullness" (p. 53).

Severin Sales Rödel follows Prairat in interpreting pedagogical tact in terms of virtue ethics. Reading Herbart's original 1802 account alongside Aristotle's *Rhetoric* and *Nicomachean Ethics*, Rödel develops an understanding of pedagogical tact specially as a character, disposition, or *ethos*: A "positioning [of] oneself in front of others, positioning oneself in a pedagogical situation" (p. 70). Such a situation, Rödel makes clear, is at once unique, relational, responsive, embodied, and normatively contingent—constituting a relational *disposition*. Rödel also follows Herbart (1802/2022) in referring to the cultivation of tact as a kind of preparation of one's "character," "mind," and "heart" (p. 33). He concludes by briefly outlining a way to cultivate pedagogical tact, again, by working with examples—asking student teachers for their responses to "different kinds of dilemmas and ambiguous situations"

> In this work with examples… students can learn to distance themselves from preconceptions and prejudices and become sensitive to something new and different about the documented situations in relation to ethos and moral decision-making… This lets them become sensitive to the embodied act of positioning that goes along with living a certain ethos. (p. 73)

"These acts of positioning are embodied ones," Rödel emphasizes—involving not just forms of corporeal expression, but also "establishing distance or proximity to others who are also taking part in the situation" (p. 71).

The third chapter in this collection, by Morten Korsgaard, VIA University, engages with Hannah Arendt in addressing the question of exemplarity and tact: Examples are the focus of this chapter, and they also play an indispensable part in the unfolding of Korsgaard's argument. He makes the case that these examples are the principle means by which tact becomes a part of pedagogical practice. Korsgaard sees Arendt's notion of natality—discussed in this book's introduction—as indispensable to contemporary definitions of education and pedagogy. However, in a bold gambit, he also takes Arendt's notion of the *daimon*—the way one is seen by others, one's public aspect—as significant for tact. In a way, this resonates with Plessner's notion of excentricity introduced by Hans-Rüdiger Müller (Chapter 6): In both, we are other to ourselves; we seek to understand how we are seen by others. This is a question that our excentricity can be seen to compel us to ask. But it is also one which, Arendt reminds us, can never be fully answered. Arendt also provides the metaphor central for Korsgaard's understanding of the relationship between pedagogical tact and exemplification. This is to be found in Arendt's reply to Kant, namely that to think with an "enlarged mentality"—as Kant asks of the cosmopolitan individual—can be achieved by "training one's imagination to *go visiting*" (Arendt, 1982, p. 43; emphasis added). Here, examples are personified as an active force, and our encounter with them is cast as a kind of conversation and familiarization. As Arendt described it, these visitations can take place with persons dead or alive, real or fictitious, and through examples of lived incidents, past or present.

Tact also has sociological and anthropological dimensions: As emphasized, its reference point is social convention (whether broken or intact), and it is realized in and through human embodiment, culture, and collectivity. Both of these aspects of tact are the focus of the fourth chapter, "Pedagogical Tact and the Limits of Community" by Hans-Rüdiger Müller, professor emeritus at Osnabrück University. Helmuth Plessner's philosophical anthropology—anthropological in the sense of a philosophical exploration of the human—is central to Müller's examination. Of particular importance is Plessner's notion of "excentric positionality": We are aware of ourselves in the world, we take a position in relation to ourselves. We can imagine ourselves as others see us; we can doubt, develop, surprise, or transcend ourselves. Our sense of "selfhood," in other words, is consequently not positioned egocentrically at our core; instead, our capacity for self-awareness, to take on our "selves" as a project, means that the self is peripheral. While this constitutes our essential brokenness and fundamental vulnerability, it is our own reflective self-awareness that allows us to engage with others' brokenness and vulnerability. This can be seen as the basis of tact itself, a subject with which Plessner engaged in the context of a broader discussion of diplomacy and community. Müller outlines three interpretations of pedagogical tact (mentioned above): First, as the mediation of theory and practice; second, it is a way of navigating conflicting pedagogical demands; and third, a limitation of active pedagogical intervention. Of these, it is the third, the self-limitation of pedagogy, that appears as most relevant to Plessner's portrayal of the modern human as broken and decentered. As Müller says, it "points to the problems of unreflectively demanding authenticity and self-transparency, closeness and immediacy—including in pedagogical contexts" (p. 109). Our individuality, Müller continues, can never "be subsumed without remainder into… the educational context" (p. 109); and it is arguably this remainder that constitutes both our fundamental vulnerability and our interpersonal capability.

As indicated at the beginning of this introduction, pedagogy—as the word is used here—refers to the influencing of one group by another, often an older generation's influence on one younger. This means that parents and the family, which are the focus of the chapter by Krinninger and Kesselhut, are also objects of analysis in German educational studies. (In addition, given the increasing interpenetration of home and school environments—e.g., via digital communication, in pandemic conditions, or through social programs—the effective "pedagogization" of home and family is of increasing importance for English-language research, too.) The authors (both from the University Osnabrück) begin by pointing out that in typical families, tact does not mediate practice and pedagogical theory as much as it regulates the flexible boundaries and structures that constitute the family and its connections to the world. For example, in the processes of setting up and navigating rules for children's TV viewing, tact can be said to be manifest in a family-specific sense of what constitutes a suitable environment for childhood development. The construction of a symbolic dimension, an ordering family narrative, a family's stabilizing conception of themselves, allows for further flexibility and mediation. "Tact is manifest" in these contexts "as a pragmatic, but not arbitrary tolerance of the difference between familial aspirations and familial reality" (p. 124). Ultimately, pedagogical tact in families is made "visible… as a practical knowledge that preserves the functionality of the family" and that is responsive to the "ideas, attitudes, and intentions of the parents, the children and the family as a community" (p. 126). As a prolegomenon to investigating such a pedagogy in the future, Krinninger and Kesselhut conclude, researchers should work to "describe the conditions of possibility, scope and forms of education as social practice" (p. 126).

Norm Friesen, Boise State University, opens the fourth section of the book by writing of "The Reciprocal Ambivalence of Tact and the Body." This chapter takes as its starting point the understanding that tact offers the educator above all "a guide to action in the face of conflicting demands" (p. 106). Reflecting recent German discourses on teacher professionalization (e.g., Helsper, 2021), this chapter characterizes these conflicting demands not as isolated instances, but as representing (if not actually constituting) the structure of the field of pedagogical action itself. It is the capacity to tactfully effectively negotiate these opposites and the tensions between them that constitutes tact. Echoing Herbart, this way of defining professionalization affirms academic preparation and study, but it highlights values practical experience above all (see also this book's epilogue, "Pedagogical tact as a professional skill"). Understanding pedagogy as fundamentally embodied, Friesen references Merleau-Ponty's account of intercorporeity from *The Visible and Invisible* (1968). Like the pedagogical field itself, Merleau-Ponty sees the human body as itself fundamentally ambivalent and paradoxical:

> Our body is a being of two leaves, from one side a thing among things and otherwise what sees them and touches them; …it unites these two properties within itself, [as well as] its double belongingness to the order of the "object" and to the order of the "subject." (p. 137)

The dynamics of the body and the pedagogical field display a startling isomorphism. This similarity is subsequently taken as a basis for understanding the ways that pedagogical antipodes (like proximity and distance or support and counteraction) can be communicated simultaneously and thus brought in to balance by one's physical position, glance or voice. In addition, the physical presence of an educator and with those being educated can powerfully communicate an ineluctable message of commitment, availability, even vulnerability.

Phenomenologist Bernhard Waldenfels (2007) has written that, from the perspective of information theory, "the body can …function at the same time as sender, message, channel, and also as receiver" (p. 256). Our bodies signal and pick up on non-verbal information, and—in the case of pleasure or pain, for example—also effectively provide the content of what is communicated. Jörg Zirfas and Daniel Burghardt (University of Cologne and University of Innsbruck, respectively) consider the pedagogical dimension of some of this manifold reciprocity in "Tactful views: On forms of educational measure and precaution." In formulating their thesis on visual communication, the authors quote a 2012 dissertation on the "implicit logic of the pedagogical look" from Friederike Schmidt (2012): "*Bildung*"—the formative process writ large—constitutes "the overarching frame of every pedagogical gaze" (p. 15): Someone's glance, look, or glare can be formative in the sense that it can build another up; or conversely, tear another down. To truly "see" someone is not simply to register their presence, but to recognize and hold them in regard—with all of the evaluative, empathic, or affirmative significance that this might imply. The look also is reflexive, involving an awareness of one's own awareness: "The tactful pedagogical gaze," Zirfas and Burghardt explain, "links a movement of attention and invitation with a movement of distance and reflexivity" (p. 163). It is the often-overlooked relational power and depth of vision that can be said to lead Zirfas and Burghardt to emphasize the reflexive moment of measure, precaution, and forbearance in the pedagogical gaze. Also referencing Aristotle's ethics of virtue, they define the tactful person as one who combines "phronesis (practical prudence) with forbearance"—working to mediate the relationship between ethical universality and individual particularity.

In the final chapter in the section on embodiment (and in the volume as a whole) Jens Beljan (University Jena) works with the phenomenon of "resonance," defined literally as the sympathetic vibration of two bodies. German luminary Hartmut Rosa has made resonance a key term in his sociology to describe a quality, a tension, or an interplay that occurs in the relationship of self and world (see Rosa, 2018). This means that this chapter—like those from Prairat through Rödel to Zirfas and Burghardt—takes as its principal interest the question of relationships in pedagogy. As a positive relation with the world, resonance represents a phenomenon that is germane to *Bildung*, famously defined by Wilhelm von Humboldt (1793/1999) as "the linking of the self to the world to achieve the most general, most animated, and most unrestrained interplay" (p. 58). At the same time, this desirable experience of growth and attunement is *non-disposible, Unverfügbar*: It is not "at our disposal," and cannot be directly accessed, appropriated, or controlled. Resonance is also intercorporeal and inter-affective, and in these senses closely related to the phenomenon of lived atmosphere or climate, the shared manifestation of a kind of mood which is also beyond any one person's control. Resonance finds its dialectical opposite in the experience of alienation, a phenomenon which inhibits learning, but that is nonetheless necessary for resonance to eventually "flourish and be sustained" (p. 177). Beljan speaks of a "pedagogy of resonance" (pp. 169–173) which subordinates tact to resonance, but gives it a key role: Tact offers a practical sensitivity for the modulation of potentially resonant relational possibilities: "tact modulates the quality of the self-world-relation" (p. 172). In cultivating an atmosphere or collective mood, tact has the potential to adjust the emotional color of a specific space and time. In this context, a pedagogy of resonance would "not so much [be] concerned with the subjective experience of resonance, but with the intersubjective and objective preconditions for its appearance" (p. 187), Beljan concludes.

As a postscript, Senkbeil and Friesen offer a conceptualization of pedagogical tact as an essential component for the teacher professionalization process. This concept document focuses not only on the antipodal structures and tensions that teachers must responsively navigate, but also on ontological conceptions of reflection and reflexivity (*Reflexivität*) and of habitus (from Bourdieu). It also outlines a process model of the competencies constitutive of teacher professionalism, showing how they can be further developed. Professional knowledge, motivation, and skills are all shown to feed into ready action and (tactful) practice, and—through the medium of reflexivity and habitus—to "feed back" into the further development of disciplinary and experiential knowledge, and of active situational awareness. The document concludes by describing a range of reflective positions and processes that can be cultivated in formal teacher education, specifically in the context of post-practicum "reflective seminars."

Note

[1] The term "family" came to designate the nuclear family (one or two parents and their children) gradually and only well into the eighteenth century. Earlier, "family" designated a group of servants under one master, or those living under one roof—a body that could consist of those linked either by servitude or various forms of kinship (OED 1989).

Bibliography

Arendt, H. (1964/1982). *Lectures on Kant's political philosophy.* University of Chicago Press.

Helsper, W. (2021). *Professionalität und Professionalisierung pädagogischen Handelns: Eine Einführung.* Barbara Budrich.

Herbart, J. F. (1802/2022). Introductory lecture to students in pedagogy. In N. Friesen (Ed. Trans.), *Tact and the pedagogical relation: Introductory readings* (pp. 28–37). Peter Lang.

Humboldt, W. von (1793/1999). Theory of Bildung. In Hopmann, S., Westbury, I. & Riquarts, K. (Eds. Trans.), *Teaching as a reflective practice: The German* Didaktik *tradition* (pp. 57–61). Routledge.

Merleau-Ponty, M. (1968). *The visible and invisible* (A. Lingis, Trans.). Northwestern University Press.

Muth, J. (1962/2022). Pedagogical tact: Study of a contemporary form of educational and instructional engagement. In N. Friesen (Ed. Trans.), *Tact and the pedagogical relation: Introductory readings* (pp. 88–113), Peter Lang.

Oxford English Dictionary (1989). Family. In *The Oxford English Dictionary* (vol. V, p. 703).

Plessner, H. (1924/1999). *The limits of community: A critique of social radicalism.* (A. Wallace, Trans.). Prometheus.

Rosa, H. (2018). *Resonance: A sociology of our relationship to the world.* (J. C. Wagner, Trans.). Polity.

Schmidt, F. (2012). *Implizite Logiken des pädagogischen Blickes: Eine rekonstruktive Studie über Wahrnehmung im Kontext der Wohnungslosenhilfe.* Springer VS.

Waldenfels, B. (2007). *Antwortregister.* Suhrkamp.

PART II

Theorizing Tact

Reconsidering Tact

Eirick Prairat[1]

> Sometimes an expression has to be withdrawn from language
> and sent for cleaning—then it can be put back into circulation.
> —LUDWIG WITTGENSTEIN (1980, p. 39e)

Introduction

The issue of wellbeing at school can be approached from different perspectives. We have chosen to place ourselves at the heart of the pedagogical relationship and to defend a thesis: tact is not only a first-rate ethical disposition for the professions of relation but is also and above all a major pedagogical skill. The first section of this chapter shows that tact is not only a relational skill or quality (*habileté relationnelle*), as we like to say, but that it is indeed a virtue. The second section returns to the question of connection (*lien*). This is an essential question for the pedagogue. One must never lose sight of connection because it is the condition of all educational action. No matter the intention or the aim, if others do not respond, the most beautiful of educational projects are already compromised. This fear of rupture is a pedagogical constant; it is the educational anguish (*l'angoisse*) par excellence. Finally, the third and last section follows in the wake of Herbart's and Canguilhem's opening a new path and showing that tact is a pedagogical skill of prime importance. It is to pedagogical activity what phronesis is to moral action: a principle for deciding and acting.

An Ethical Disposition

An Invisible Virtue

Tact (*tactus* in Latin) comes from the verb *tangere*, to touch. Tact is originally the sense of touch. It is not only what we use to discover the tangible properties of a thing (its fluidity, softness, hardness, shape, temperature, dryness, or humidity); it is also sensitivity, that is, what we feel when we touch it. Unlike sight, touch is not a sense of distance. It requires contact so that touch is always touched and touch is inevitably touching. It is the most exquisite of our senses, Voltaire says, because, unlike the other senses, which "are limited to the satisfaction of the individual who possesses them," tact has this strange and marvelous power "to intoxicate at the same time two thinking beings," the one who touches and the one who is touched (Voltaire, 1837, Volume Six, Dialogue XXII, p. 711).

In a second, more topical sense, which is the one we are interested in in this chapter, tact can be defined as an art of judgment and a way of behaving. It is an art of judging that combines finesse and accuracy and a way of behaving that is attentive to nuances and circumstances. It is both the one and the other, an art of judging that extends into conduct and a way of being supported and guided by an appreciation of the situation. As a faculty of judgment, tact is a way of feeling that has been freed from physical sensation. As an attitude, it is attentive to what to do or not to do, to say or not to say. The philosophical tradition has given it little credit; the reasons are, evidently, numerous. Tact does not seem to have a political aspect like justice or tolerance. It is not spectacular and, therefore cannot compete with courage, nor does it have the greatness and prestige of generosity.

However, tact is virtue—"almost," says Renan (2011). That is what we would like to show in this first section. Certainly, it is barely a virtue, almost invisible, but we would be wrong to underestimate or neglect it. The philosopher David Heyd writes: "Tact is a typically social or interpersonal virtue. Its value does not lie in the internal harmony or excellence of the agent as a human being, but mainly in facilitating human relations ... It concerns the value of intimacy and expresses a personal attention to the singularity of the human situation" (Heyd, 1995, p. 227). Tact can be said to be an interstitial virtue insofar as it reveals itself and excels in the interplay of exchanges and interactions. It is concerned with connection, which is probably why the great Hungarian writer Imre Kertész (2012) does not hesitate to say that "in human relations, tact is the maximum that can be achieved" (p. 33).

Care Professions, Pioneering Professions

In the world of work, medicine was the first to make a place for it; tact was originally manifesting itself as a duty of discretion. "Whatever I see or hear in society during, or even outside the practice of my profession, I will keep silent what never needs to be disclosed, considering discretion as a duty in such cases," reads the last lines of the Hippocratic Oath. Professional secrecy, essential to the practice of medicine, finds here, as many commentators have pointed out, a founding word. But it seems to us that, beyond professional secrecy, the Hippocratic Oath calls for a sense of restraint and a way of behaving that prefigures precisely the virtue of tact. It suggests an attitude; it sketches out a form of conduct. Moreover, the virtue of tact will be found, much later, in the codes of medical ethics and, more broadly, in the various deontologies[2] concerning the health care professions.

Care of the body but also care of the soul: Nascent psychoanalysis had the almost immediate intuition that the work of analysis also requires an acute sense of relationship. It is the American psychoanalyst Rudolf Loewenstein who, as far as we know, first and most clearly formulated this idea, explicitly referring in his remarks to the word "tact." In a contribution in the early 1930s to the *Revue Française de Psychoanalyse*, Loewenstein drew his colleagues' attention to the importance of tact for analysis. He even gave it the status of a professional quality. For tact, Loewenstein (2007) says, makes it possible to give shape to interpretation and to anticipate when it is appropriate to engage in it. Intuition of the *kairos*, a grasping of the opportune moment, interpretation must occur at the moment when it can come to give meaning to what the patient is experiencing and, by the same token, relieve him or her (p. 188).

"The analyst," writes Loewenstein (2007), "must always pay attention to the latent meaning of the interpretation he gives and avoid that which implicitly contains a prohibition or a reproach against certain feelings or thoughts of the one being analyzed" (pp. 187–188). In other words, instead of blaming or hurting others, one must be attentive to them. And Loewenstein adds: "What seems particularly important to me is that the analyst should always be able to see clearly the latent meaning, that he should know the significance of his words" (p. 188). Knowing how to communicate without altering, how to say without slandering, in short, favors a form of contact that leaves the Other intact in his very being. We can draw from this analysis two lessons that have a general significance in the sense that they transcend the question of tact in psychoanalytic treatment. This is what we do in the following section.

A Relational Virtue

Tact is, in essence, a virtue of relationships. This means that having tact involves having a sense of timeliness and a sense of skill. This is what Jean-François Goubet rightly says when he writes:

> Tact is … a situated intelligence. *In* [the] situation rather than *of* it, since it is not a question of grasping oneself in a reflexive manner, contemplating oneself as an object, and thus ceasing to act and to be acted upon. In situation also by virtue of the encounter, of the joint presence of several people around a specific object. And in this respect, tact is defined as the ability to put one's finger on something, to be relevant. Relevance includes at least two aspects: a sense of appropriateness, that is to say of the word or gesture on the right occasion, and a sense of address, that is to say of the destination of the word or gesture in order for it to be effective. (Goubet, 2005, p. 18; emphases added)

A sense of appropriateness, because tact refers us to the idea of an adequate gesture, a right word, speech stripped of all dross; a keen awareness of what deserves to be said or done and how it should be said or done. Being tactful means knowing how to adjust to the particular situation one is experiencing.

If the sense of timeliness testifies to a sense of the situation, the sense of knowing to whom one is speaking attests to an aptitude to discern and recognize. Addressing Paul is not talking to James, and speaking to James is not addressing Pauline. Tact is an art of distinctions and individuation.

> What I would praise would be a soul with many floors… a soul at ease wherever fortune led it; which could chat with a neighbor about whatever he is building, his hunting or his legal action, or take pleasure in conversing with a carpenter or a gardener. I envy those who can come down to the level of the meanest of their staff and make conversation with their own servants. (Montaigne, 1580/1993, p. 925)

"A soul with many floors." The Montaignist formula is admirable; it is also tactful knowing how to "adapt" to the person you are talking to. Modulation and plasticity. The young Bergson would have subscribed to the Montaignist approach: "The person who is accomplished in the world," writes the philosopher,

> knows how to speak to each person about the thing that interests [them]. He enters into the viewpoints of others without always adopting them. He understands everything without however excusing everything. What pleases us in him is the facility with which he circulates among feelings and ideas. (adapted from 1892/2016, p. 5)

We said "plasticity," Bergson answers "flexibility."

To become wise, as we can see, is neither to adhere nor to excuse. There is no hypocrisy in this open and understanding attitude because "there will always be the same distance between this refined politeness and obsequious hypocrisy as between the desire to serve people and the art of using them" (Bergson, 1892/2016, p. 5). In hypocrisy, there is a desire to conceal. The hypocrite hides his character, camouflages his intentions, and simulates feelings and virtues to present himself in a favorable light.[3] Tact is not concealment but self-effacement. The tactful man does not appeal to appearance but always gives way, as it is not himself that interests him but the Other: the one who faces him.

Concern for Connection, Concern for Others
Tact and Civility

We would be mistaken if we were to hastily conclude that tact can be assimilated with civility. Both are certainly attitudes that show that others matter and, as such, deserve consideration. However, beyond this family resemblance, tact and civility seem distinct. Let us clarify the idea of civility. It was Erasmus who consecrated the term in our cultural landscape in 1530 by publishing his famous *De civilitate morum puerilium* (*A Handbook on Good Manners for Children*; 2008).

In this work, intended for children between the ages of 7 and 12, the humanist specifies the manners and bodily conventions (*externum corporis decorum*) to be respected in order to make oneself likable in society. Erasmian civility is synonymous with decorum. It is, to use the Montaignist formula of the *Essays*, "the science of interpersonal relationships."[4] Erasmus has many emulators. No fewer than about 50 treatises on manners were published in the seventeenth century. Several pedagogues will also try their hand at this difficult exercise by prescribing socially appropriate customs. *The Rules of Christian Decorum and Civility* of Jean-Baptiste de La Salle (1703/1990) deserve to be cited here as a model of this kind.

Closer to us, Ferdinand Buisson's *Dictionary of Pedagogy and Instruction*, the secular Bible of the black Hussars of the Republic,[5] reserves in its second edition two long pages for the question of civility and its importance in the educational process.[6] "Civility," notes the author of the article in the very first lines,

> is the set of conventions that govern the relations of men among themselves: in other words, the manner in which they should behave toward their superiors, their equals, and their inferiors. A tacit convention, to which usage has given the force of law, has determined for almost all possible cases in social relations a rule of conduct that cannot be broken or ignored without being considered rude and ill-bred, without upsetting those with whom one lives, without losing the material and intellectual benefits of social relations. Hence the obvious need to inculcate the precepts of civility especially in children. (Desprez, 1887, p. 396)

Civility connects individuals; it is a grammar intended to regulate and facilitate interactions by predefining certain behavior; knowledge that the honest person, always anxious to maintain a pleasant trade with his contemporaries, could not ignore or evade.[7]

When we speak about civility in educational debates, we think of pupils or children; when we evoke tact, we relate it more readily to adults or professionals. It is true that we can also talk about academic civility. Our intention is not to show that tact is a characteristic of the educator or the teacher, but to understand the difference between these two modes of being. And what immediately seems to set them apart is that civility is respect for established conventions and customs, whereas tact is manifested precisely where no such recommendation exists. If Loewenstein appeals to tact, it is because there are no predefined rules that should be followed methodically in order to conduct the clinical interview efficiently. Tact is precisely there to make up for this absence. It is the virtue of the interval, the quality of the in-between. Although one can make an inventory of the rules and prescriptions of civility and turn them into collections and treatises (for the use of novices and others), this is completely unlike tact, which is invented in its very performance. Just as we speak of a legal vacuum to evoke those situations where no rule of law comes to guide us, we could speak of a "social void" to signify those situations that escape all codification; tact manifests itself precisely in these moments of a normative vacuum. "By 'tact' we understand," writes Gadamer, "a special sensitivity and sensitiveness to situations and how to behave in them, for which knowledge from general principles as well as the capability to notice them does not suffice. Hence an essential part of tact is that it is tacit and cannot be formulated and expressed" (1960/2006, pp. 14–15).

Good Manners or Manners of Goodness?[8]

We can contest the very (or too) separative thesis that we have just defended and say that tact is the diamond tip of civility, its ultimate phase, its achievement: Civility beyond rules and prescriptions. If we intend to defend this thesis, and let us say that it is perfectly defensible, then it must be said that there is a civility of rules and a civility beyond rules. There are two stages in sum, the second of which (post-rule civility) would be the end and the overcoming of the first (civility of rules). Just as in Kohlberg (1958), the conventional moral stage, marked by respect for prevailing rules, is followed by a post-conventional moral stage governed by abstract principles of justice. It should be said, analogously, that there is a post-conventional stage of civility, a stage that is no longer governed by prescriptions but by a concern for the Other, by what might be called attentive intention. This is certainly what Bergson would say when he shows that beyond ceremonial civility can be glimpsed "a politeness of the spirit and the heart"[9] (Bergson, 2016, pp. 47–58).

Whatever the debate may be (tact: first cousin or big brother of civility?), it does not seem decisive to us. The two theses come together to affirm that to be tactful is to show fair attention to things and people by paying attention to our ways of saying and doing. It is less about having manners that are good than about "good manners," and it is not playing with words to say that. The man who has tact is the very opposite of the man with manners, the pedantic, the precious (Barthes, 2002, p. 64).[10] The latter mimics codes of good conduct, he "over-plays" them. Ironically, he can even use his knowledge of social customs to derive some benefit from them. An excess of good manners is always a little suspicious. The tactful man is opposed to the ethical attachment to form, opposed to the man who likes form for form's sake—formalism—in the sense that it is a way of approaching the Other. The American philosopher Robert Audi speaks beautifully of a "duty of manner" (Audi, 2004, p. 182).

The Touch of Language

We must return to the question of language to close this second section. To speak is certainly to send a message, but it is also to touch. There is a touch of language. This is undoubtedly what Jakobson means when he evokes its famous phatic function (Jakobson, 1960, pp. 209–248). Language, beyond the information it delivers, is a way of relating to people, of approaching them. Tact, through language, reconnects with the original touch that characterizes it. With malicious, abrupt, or brutal words, we can hurt the person we are talking to; with loose words, as we drop blows, we can dirty or damage what we are talking about. These words are, strictly speaking, "curses."[11] Conversely, there can be kind and caring words. "Words are deeds" (Wittgenstein, 1980, 50e). They can have the hardness of a blow that is struck as well as the softness of a caress that is lavished.

Here we are far from the rhetoric that always aims to lecture, far also from the eloquence that seeks to seduce when it does not aim to move. A tactful address does not have this ambition; it does not aim at any conquest; it is not assaulting any citadel. It seeks more modestly not to mishandle, not to rush. It also aims to stimulate, to give confidence, or to reveal in the Other unsuspected resources. Language not only has a descriptive vocation; it also has a performative function that allows it to shape a reality, to give substance to realities that would not exist without it. Tact gives itself to be seen in an ethos and is concretized in an art of speaking, in a form of address. It enjoins us not to desert the place of language. Even better, it invites us to inhabit our ways of speaking because "as soon as we speak, we have a responsibility toward others" (Lacroix, 2010, p. 47).

It is for this reason that we can never say that we have enough tact. Saying "I have enough tact" is precisely a way of showing that one lacks it. Tact, like modesty, like humility, is a virtue that is annulled as soon as one claims it. In the very moment when I testify to my satisfaction, I show an arrogance that betrays me. On the other hand, the person who is truly tactful always experiences lack, always feels that they have not had enough, that he or she could still improve, and that he or she could have done better in a given circumstance. For there are, admittedly, a thousand and one occasions in everyday life when one is not up to the task: a hasty action, something that escapes us in speaking, a word that is out of place, an attitude that is a little haughty. The great British philosopher Bernard Williams was very interested in moral life and its painful meanderings. For Williams (1982), there is no moral life without conflicts. But the tragedy is that these conflicts can neither be avoided nor entirely satisfactorily resolved so they always leave "a feeling of regret" (p. 27). I tend to think that persons of tact who have not been up to the task experience precisely this feeling, they feel the bitter taste of regret, regret for having unnecessarily offended their interlocutors.

A Pedagogical Skill

The Forgotten Lesson

Who remembers Johann Friedrich Herbart, professor of philosophy and pedagogy, in Göttingen and then in Königsberg, at the beginning of the nineteenth century? Who remembers the man who, together with Dilthey and Schleiermacher, inspired the current of humanist pedagogy (*geisteswissenschaftliche Pädagogik*)?[12] Herbart, Kant's successor at Königsberg, published his great treatise on pedagogy in 1806.[13] A forgotten, erased work, like Herbart's very name; yet it is the first and perhaps the only educational work to have made such an important place for the astonishing quality that is tact. This is not what immediately appeared to readers as most original in this work, but as time goes by, it is Herbart's true lesson. We will quote him abundantly because his words deserve to be heard again.

The pedagogue, Herbart remarks, always defies theory because it is too general. What help can it be for the practitioner confronted with particular situations? Action is by definition inscribed in original contexts determined by particular constraints. However, theory "passes over all details, over all circumstances that surround the practical teacher at any given moment. This is the reason why practical workers dislike mixing a rigid, thoroughly investigated theory with their art" (Herbart, 1802/2022, p. 31). Experience alone, in their eyes, is formative. We do not dispute that experience has formative virtues, but Herbart tells us that this formative power should not be overestimated because the experience in which I engage is, first and foremost, my experience. It is always taken from a unique point of view, my own. If experience teaches us something, it is in another way closed in on itself, often inciting us to repeat our ways of acting. Practice alone leads to routine because what it produces is "extremely limited and entirely indecisive experience" (p. 31). It cannot teach the practitioner

> what would have happened had his action been different or what proceeding with greater power or wisdom might have achieved… The teacher simply does not experience these things; instead, he experiences only his own self, his own relation to others, the failure of his own plans. He does not discover his basic failings. (Herbart, 1802/2022, p. 31)

Experience is only fully formative if what we take from it has been able to make the detour through theory. The latter, in fact, opens us up to general considerations that allow us to broaden the viewpoint of experience, which is always restricted. We form ourselves through practice and theory, by experience and general ideas. How then to articulate theory and practice? Let us forget the idea of an ideal, top-down application of theory: "Such a deliberate and complete application of scientific propositions would require a supernatural being" (Herbart, 1802/2022,

p. 32). The heterogeneous relationship between theory and practice requires the introduction of a third term. Teaching is an action oriented toward a precise goal (to make people learn). It certainly requires the mastery of knowledge and know-how; but to avoid missing its goal, it also requires a faculty that is as close as possible to action: tact.

Judge and Decide

Herbart defines tact as a "quick" faculty for "judgment and decision." More precisely, it is a skill capable of understanding how a student learns and at what pace. "Pedagogical tact," writes Herbart, "consists above all in discerning when it is necessary to abandon a student at his slow pace, and when it is appropriate, on the contrary, to go faster."[14] Herbartian tact attests to an ability to promptly grasp and appreciate a situation's characteristics. It is precisely for this reason that tact depends on feeling. It is a state of the spirit, an "emotional state" capable of reflecting how it "has been affected from the outside" (Herbart, 1802/2022, p. 32). Of course, tact does not protect us from misinterpretation; it is not infallible, for one certainly cannot find "a deliberate and complete application of scientific propositions" to "answer the true requirements of [each] individual case" (p. 32). However, it remains "the immediate director of our practice" (p. 32).

Tact is therefore a "quick" faculty of "judgment and decision," it allows one to perceive the relevant characteristics of a situation and then to decide. This is a far cry from Aristotelian deliberation (*bouleusis*), which requires time or even slowness because it depends on the rules of reasoning. Let us remember: good deliberation, writes Aristotle in one of his more famous works, is not "the readiness of a discerning glance, for this both involves no reasoning and is something that is quick in its operation, while men deliberate a long time, and they say that one should carry out quickly the conclusions of one's deliberation, but should deliberate slowly" (Aristotle, trans. 2006, V1.9, p. 111). Herbart's tact is far removed from the torments and meanderings of deliberation; it is very close to what Aristotle calls "a discerning glance" that is the mark of a "readiness of mind." A nuanced understanding of situations, backed by a form of empathy, Herbart's tact grasps a situation in its various facets with a clear awareness of the possible. What pedagogue would dare to say that this capability is not a major skill?

The Art and the Method

[After Herbart,] tact was not spoken about for almost 150 years. It was not until a UNESCO document entitled "Survey on the Teaching of Philosophy," written in November 1951, that the word "tact" reappears. This text, made public in August 1952, examines, through a major international survey, the place of the teaching of philosophy in the different educational systems, the way in which this teaching is given, and its importance for the formation of the citizen. But the most important thing in this thick document of 244 pages, is the final declaration of the experts.[15] They affirm from the outset that they do not ignore "the risks inherent in the exercise of free and autonomous thought" (UNESCO, 1953a, final declaration, point 3).

Consequently, here is the method they propose:

> On the one hand, it seems desirable that the teaching of philosophy should begin, especially at its first stage, with the clarification of lived experience. For example, problems such as certainty, evil or destiny do not belong only to the past but concern the man of today. Adolescents may have direct, and sometimes cruel experience of this... On the other hand, in adhering too closely to the description and expression of a particular experience, philosophy would lose its meaning as a search for universal principles of intelligibility and valorization... Direct trade with the works of philosophers seems indispensable. (UNESCO, 1953a, final declaration, point 5)

From personal experience to universal principles, philosophical teaching must proceed according to the ascending dialectic dear to Plato.

But the committee of experts does not remain with a discourse on method, because a method without instructions for its use is an inoperative one. Hence its recommendation of tact is understood as an art of doing, a delicate and sensitive way of implementing the recommended method. "Tact, a fundamental pedagogical virtue, imposes itself on philosophy teachers, because of the average age of the students ... and the human importance of the problems dealt with ... tact is the contact of two freedoms" (UNESCO, 1953a, final declaration, point 3, adapted).[16] A meeting of two freedoms, one of which is still in its infancy; meditations on important questions whose gravity the students sometimes glimpse; tact is no longer a quick faculty of apprehension and decision, it is a way of doing things, an art of "how to." Here it is elevated to the rank of pedagogical skill.

Tact and Pedagogical Savoir-Faire[17]

Let us start again. A good teacher is a teacher who masters not only a field of knowledge but also specific "knowings-how" that can be called pedagogical (e.g., knowing how to conduct an oral exam, to carry out a plan, to elaborate and administer an evaluation, to lead a debate, to conduct a didactic exchange). These pedagogical knowings-how (or pedagogical skills or expertise), insofar as they involve a relational dimension, are inseparably ethical and technical. Ethics is neither above nor beside; there is neither transcendence nor exteriority. Ethics is immanent to the technical domain; it is not in a position of "superstructure," nor is it a kind of extra that, in a second stage, would come to color axiologically neutral knowings-how. It is necessary to stop dissociating the registers of technicality and ethics.

In this respect, the reflections of the last few decades on evaluation are symptomatic. They have focused essentially, if not exclusively, on technical aspects: relevance and objectivity. Relevance: when we evaluate in this way, are we evaluating what we claim to evaluate? Objectivity: by what procedure do we keep the evaluator's subjectivity at bay? However, in the evening, in front of his stack of exercises, the teacher asks himself other questions, ones simpler and deeper at the same time: Should I take into account the admirable, persistent effort of this student in assessing his work? Shouldn't I be a little more lenient with this troubled student right now? These decisions, as we can see, are as much ethical as they are technical. To reduce evaluation to a simple procedure is to damage it as a pedagogical gesture. Let us add that these pedagogical knowings-how can be implemented in different ways. There is not only one way to conduct an oral exam or to organize remedial work. Certainly, a pedagogical skill mobilizes invariant elements, but it can nevertheless be realized in different ways according to the context and circumstances.

Tact defies rules and principles; it is of the order of perception in its most immediate form. Tact is the rapid ability to appreciate the characteristics of a situation and to decide. However, the pedagogical decision does not only point to what is important to do, it also signals the "how to." It is through tact that a skill becomes "knowing-how-what," *savoir-comment-faire*, that a technical skill becomes a pedagogical gesture (Spranzi, 2013). We can legitimately relate pedagogical tact to the Aristotelian *phronesis*, which is the faculty of holding forth, and as such is also distinct from reason (Aristotle, 2006, 1140b25.). Like tact, it is contingent and relates to action. Like tact, which requires and presupposes know-how, *phronesis* is conditioned by skill (Aristotle, trans. 2006, 1 VI, 9, 1142a10). But unlike *phronesis*, which is the ability to choose the "golden mean," tact is the ability to identify the point of convergence, the always fragile confluence between ethics and technique. For ethics and technique do not oppose each other in the pedagogical act; they are combined precisely to give it its educational fullness.

In this sense, pedagogical tact manifests the expertise of the teacher, and it is not a matter of having the final word; for expertise is guaranteed by the automation of certain procedures. "In an expert's own know-how, the rules fade in favor of situational elements that take over: the more expert an agent is, the less he needs to deliberate and make conscious decisions" (Spranzi, 2013, p. 1). Expert judgment is quick and immediate, it is not limited to perceiving the relevant characteristics of a situation because it apprehends at the same time what must be done and how it must be done. This is what Herbart had already glimpsed more than two centuries ago when he wrote that tact is nothing other than "the immediate director of our practice" (2022, p. 32).

Notes

[1] Translated by Norm Friesen, Etienne Vallée and Thomas Senkbeil from: Prairat, E. (2017). Reconsidérer le tact. *Recherches et Educations*, *17*(1). <https://doi.org/10.4000/rechercheseducations.3394>

[2] A deontological ethics (*deon*=duty, *logos*=science) is one that emphasizes duty and the fact that morality of actions inheres in the acts themselves rather than their consequences, as captured in phrases like "duty for duty's sake" or "virtue is its own reward." It is opposed to teleological or consequentialist ethics, which judge the ethical value of an action on the basis of its outcomes. [-trans].

[3] In the trial of hypocrisy made against civility, the famous definition of politeness given by Jean de La Bruyère (1645–1696) undoubtedly brings with it a heavy responsibility. La Bruyère celebrated politeness without restraint by saying that it was "a certain attention to ensure that by our words and by our manners others are pleased with us and with themselves" (La Bruyère, 1976, *De la conversation*). The idea of pleasing is too evident to not attract suspicion.

[4] "Science" is translated as "learning" in the edition of Montaigne referenced earlier. [-trans].

[5] Hussars are Prussian troops who fought fiercely against Napoleon's army, known for their black capes; here: authoritarian French pedagogues. Buisson's Dictionary, available online, includes articles by the likes of Durkheim, and is an invaluable conceptual and historical resource: <https://gallica.bnf.fr/ark:/12148/bpt6k24232h.texteImage> [-trans].

[6] On the importance of civility in the educational process, see Alain (Émile-Auguste Chartier; 1932), *Propos sur l'education*, chapter XXV (where Alain praises reading as the route to politeness) and Olivier Reboul *Les valeurs de l'éducation*, pp. 86 and 210–213 (where symbols and politeness are also brought into connection).

[7] On the history of books on civility, in addition to the work of Norbert Elias (1982, 1983), we can refer to Ariès, P. (1973). *L'enfant et la vie familiale sous l'Ancien Régime*. Seuil, pp. 120–124 and 429–441, and to R. Chartier, M.-M. Compère & D. Julia (1976). *L'éducation en France du XVIe au XVIIIe* (pp. 136–145). Sedes.

[8] This title echoes Prairat's earlier reference to "deontological" ethics (see footnote 2), raising the question whether manners are intrinsically good (or ethical) or only extrinsically so. [-trans].

[9] Bergson speaks of "spiritual politeness, politeness of manners, and politeness of the heart," which is the highest form of politeness, a virtue (2011, p. 7).

[10] The author is referring to Barthes' discussion of tact in *The Neutral* (2007) on pp. 29–36, 47. [-trans].

[11] On the violence of words and the wounds they can inflict, see Ali Benmakhlouf's (2016) book *La conversation comme manière de vivre*, p. 104. This risk of seeing language become violent is something that educators have been all too aware of. The teacher who follows the example of Jean-Baptiste de la Salle, for example, can speak in a firm manner to intimidate his students. However, he will not use "insulting words, or words that are even slightly insulting, to call out (…): rascal, naughty, ornery, scabby, snotty, etc." (p. 104). (La Salle, 1951, 2nd part, chapter V, article 4). "The tongue does not flagellate less than the rods," already remarked the Jesuit François Sacchini at the beginning of the seventeenth century. "Let us avoid words that express contempt: they damage the reputation like pamphlets [i.e.,

religious leaflets, e.g., attacking the Pope]. Let us not let slip a derogatory word about the child's family, his country, his natural defects if by chance he had any" (Sacchini quoted by Charmot, 1943, p. 362).

[12] For example, see Friesen, N. (2020). Education as a *Geisteswissenschaft*: An introduction to human science pedagogy. *Journal of Curriculum Studies, 52*(3), 307–322 <https://doi.org/10.1080/00220272.2019.1705917> [-trans].

[13] Note: A 2022 translation of Herbart's "Introductory Lecture" into English is provided in this text: Herbart, J. F. (1802/2022). Introductory lecture to students in pedagogy. In N. Friesen (Ed. Trans.), *Tact and the pedagogical relation: Introductory readings*. Peter Lang. -trans. The full title of the book [from which Herbart's text on tact is taken] is *Allgemeine Pädagogik aus dem Zweck der Erziehung abgeleitet* which has been translated as "General pedagogy deduced from the purpose of education." Herbart's pedagogical work was translated into French in 1894 by the Germanist Augustin Pinloche. Since then, only a partial edition of his *Allgemeine Pädagogik* has appeared thanks to Johan Tilmant.

[14] Prairat attributes this phrase to the 2007 French translation of Herbart (p. 29). The translators are not able to find an equivalent or analog in German. [-trans].

[15] Inspector General [and philosopher] Georges Canguilhem represented France on this small committee, which included Eugen Fink, professor at the University of Freiburg, director of the Husserl Archives, and an eminent figure in the early development of phenomenology. [Although a version of this report is available in English, it does not correspond closely to the French quoted by Prairat. -trans].

[16] The English version of the UNESCO document reads as follows: "This idea of *tact* provided a starting point for the detailed study and definition of this virtue in the teacher; the committee of experts felt that tact, in the broadest sense of the term, is a reconciliation of two freedoms, and agreed to draw the attention of teachers to its importance" (UNESCO 1953a, p. 201). [-trans].

[17] Prairat is using "know-how" in the plural, that is, "knowings-how"; this is reflected in the use of the term that follows. [-trans].

Bibliography

Alain. (1957). *Propos sur l'éducation*. Presses Universitaires de France.

Aristotle. (2006). *The Nicomachean ethics*. (D. Ross, Trans.). Oxford University Press.

Ariès, P. (1973). *L'enfant et la vie familiale sous l'Ancien Régime*. Le Seuil.

Audi, R. (2004). *The good in the right: A theory of intuition and intrinsic value*. Princeton University Press.

Barthes, R. (2007). *The neutral: Lecture course at the College de France (1977–1978)* (R. Krauss & D. Hollier, Trans.). Columbia University Press.

Benmakhlouf, A. (2016). *La conversation comme manière de vivre*. Albin Michel.

Bergson, H. (2016). Politeness. *Journal of French and Francophone Philosophy - Revue de la philosophie française et de langue française, XXIV*(2), 3–9. <https://jffp.pitt.edu/ojs/index.php/jffp/article/view/767/729>

Buisson, F. (1882–1887). *Dictionnaire de pédagogie et d'instruction primaire*. Hachette. <https://gallica.bnf.fr/ark:/12148/bpt6k24232h.texteImage>

Charmot, F. (1943). *La pédagogie des jésuites. Ses principes, son actualité*. Editions Spes.

Chartier, R., Compère, M.-M. & Julia, D. (1976). *L'éducation en France du XVIe au XVIIIe*. Sedes.

Desprez, A. (1887). Civilité. In F. Bussion (Ed.), *Dictionnaire de pédagogie et d'instruction primaire*. (pp. 396–398). Hachette.

Elias, N. (1982). *The history of manners*. (E. Jephcott, Trans.). Pantheon.

Elias, N. (1983). *The court society*. (E. Jephcott, Trans.). Pantheon.

Erasmus. (2008). *A handbook on good manners for children*. (E. Merchant, Ed. Trans.). Preface Publishing.

Gadamer, H.-G. (1960/2006). *Truth and method* (2nd ed. rev.) (J. Weisenheimer & D. G. Marshall, Trans.). Continuum.

Goubet, J.-F. (2005). *Qu'est-ce que le tact pédagogique? Essai d'une définition philosophique*. Actes du colloque de la journée d'étude du 25 mai (pp. 17–22). IUFM Nord-Pas de Calais.

Heyd, D. (1995). Tact: Sense, sensibility, and virtue. *Inquiry, 38*(3), 217–231.

Jakobson, R. (1960). Linguistics and poetics. In T. Sebeok (Ed.), *Style in language* (pp. 350–377). MIT Press.

Herbart, J. F. (1802/2022). Introductory lecture to students in pedagogy. In N. Friesen, (Ed. Trans.), *Tact and the pedagogical relation: Introductory readings* (pp. 25–38). Peter Lang.

Herbart, J. F. (2007). *Tact, expérience et sympathie en pédagogie*. J. Tilmant (Ed. Trans.). Economica.

Kertész, I. (2012). *Sauvegarde. Journal 2001–2003*. Actes Sud.

Kohlberg, L. (1958). *The development of modes of moral thinking and choice in the years 10 to 16*. Doctoral Thesis. University of Chicago.

La Bruyère, J. de (1690/1976). *The morals and manners of the seventeenth century, being the character of La Bruyère*. (H. Stott, Trans.), David Stott.

Lacroix, M. (2010). *Paroles toxiques, paroles bienfaisantes. Pour une éthique du langage*. Robert Laffont.

La Salle, J.-B. de (1703/1990). *The rules of Christian decorum and civility*. (R. Arnandez, Trans.). Christian Brothers Conference.

Loewenstein, R. (2007). Remarques sur le tact dans la technique psychanalytique. *Figures de la Psychanalyse, 15*(1), 181–189.

Montaigne, M. de (1580/1993). *The complete essays*. (M.A. Screech, Trans.). Penguin.

Reboul, O. (1992). *Les valeurs de l'éducation*. Presses Universitaires de France.

Renan., E. (2011). *La réforme intellectuelle et morale*. Editions Perrin.

Spranzi., M. (2013). Décider et faire (2). *Implications philosophiques: Espace de recherche et de diffusion*, 1–7. <https://doi.org/10.3917/eslm.154.0105>

UNESCO. (1953a). *L'enseignement de la philosophie. Une enquête internationale de l'Unesco*. UNESCO.

UNESCO. (1953b). *The teaching of philosophy: An international enquiry of UNESCO. Conclusions of the enquiry and suggestions for the development and improvement of the teaching of philosophy* (pp. 185–214). UNESCO. <https://doi.org/10.5840/tpenquiry195315>

Voltaire. (1837). Œuvres complètes. Avec des notes et une notice historique sur la vie de Voltaire Vol. 6. Furne Libraire-Editeur.

Williams, B. (1983). *Moral luck*. Cambridge University Press.

Wittgenstein, L. (1980). *Culture and value*. University of Chicago Press.

A Matter of "Character, Mind, and Heart"?
On the Role of Ethos in Preparing the Tactful Teacher

Severin Sales Rödel

Introduction

Pedagogical tact, as Daniel Burghardt and Jörg Zirfas (2019) state, is a term that might seem a little antiquated at first glance. And what is more, it is a concept notoriously underdefined in pedagogical theory, and at the same time highly charged with meaning and emotional, social, and moral expectations. Still, Burghardt and Zirfas argue that it is a concept that has become indispensable for pedagogical theory and practice, as its opacity corresponds to a central problem of modern pedagogical theory: The tension between definiteness and indeterminacy, between certainty and uncertainty, or between necessity and contingency in pedagogical practice (Burghardt & Zirfas, 2019, p. 9). By offering a horizon for reflecting on these challenges, the concept of tact has become a helpful component in acquiring and further developing pedagogical professionality (Burghardt & Zirfas, 2019).

Tact, as it is understood in this chapter, is a theoretical-practical skill that both gives orientation in everyday pedagogical practice and offers possibilities to reflect, criticize, and transform this very pedagogical practice. Given this fundamental relevance for pedagogical theory and practice, it is no wonder that the phenomenon of pedagogical tact has a long history:[1] The beginnings of the discourse on tact can be traced back to Johann Friedrich Herbart's writings in the late eighteenth and early nineteenth centuries (Herbart, 1802). The theory of tact was further developed by Herman Nohl, who defined it as a "stance [that] gives the educator a singular distance to his subject as well as to his student"[2] (Nohl, 1957, p. 137) and by Jakob Muth, who argued that tact was to be found in the character of the language used in education, in authenticity, in interaction, in the avoidance of any violation of the child's dignity, and in the preservation of the distance necessary within pedagogical relationships (Muth, 1967, p. 5). Nohl and Muth, both representatives of *geisteswissenschaftliche Pädagogik*,[3] underline the personal and relational components of pedagogical tact; according to them, it is part of the "pedagogical relation" (Nohl, 1957, p. 169). The discourse on tact, which, for a long time was mainly restricted to the German-speaking academia, was opened for an international community by contributions from Max van Manen (1991, 2015). van Manen renders tact as a kind of normative, personal and intuitive knowledge, which he sees best reflected upon in phenomenological theory and methodology (van Manen, 1991). In contrast to Nohl and Muth, van Manen conceives tact more as a matter of knowledge and skill than of intuition, as something that can become a matter of research, in order to develop and improve "pedagogical sensitivity." Recent publications on pedagogical tact[4] reframe the classical problem of theory and practice by pointing out the aesthetic and ethical dimensions of tact (Burghardt & Zirfas, 2019) and its fragility and fluidity (Senkbeil, 2020). With these perspectives, the subject of tactful interaction, that is, the teacher or educator, also becomes questionable in the light of aesthetic and poststructuralist theories: Tact is not 'exercised' by a pedagogical expert or genius; tactful practitioners themselves are subject to contingency and situative atmospheres which makes tact into a "balancing act" (Senkbeil, 2020, p. 131) within the repetitive structure of pedagogical interaction (Senkbeil, 2020, p. 129). Norm Friesen and Richard Osguthorpe (2018) even see tact as a means of maintaining the authenticity in teacher-student relations, which is at stake when education and schooling are regarded solely under a means-ends rationality (p. 262). This definition of tact can be regarded as including a critical-political stance, if we assume that the means-ends rationality is a main feature of the output-oriented models of new governance and of current educational politics.[5]

In the following, I will try to draw on some of these notions and add a new perspective to the discourse on pedagogical tact. I will suggest that the phenomenon of pedagogical tact is closely linked to the question of (pedagogical) ethos, both in what concerns its inner structure and the process in which pedagogical tact can be acquired. I will expand on this by presenting two examples of classroom interaction recounted by student teachers and developing four central questions in a brief phenomenology of tact. I will then relate these questions to Johann Friedrich Herbart's work and the "blueprint" of the concept of pedagogical tact which he presents in his lectures from 1802. I will argue that Herbart's answer to the question of how tact is acquired uses a concept very similar to classical notions of ethos. However, because Herbart constructs his concept of the acquisition of tact on a theory-based preparation of future educators, two major points of criticism arise. To address these, I will introduce a concept of ethos that takes both the normative elements of tact and its intersubjective and reciprocal structure into account. I will argue that by adopting such an ethos, teachers and pedagogical professionals are provided with the preconditions of acquiring tact in specific situations. Unlike tact, the specific ethos I am suggesting here (Brinkmann, 2017) can also be acquired in situations outside of practice, that is, in university level teacher training. Accordingly, the last section of the chapter briefly sketches suggestions for practicing an ethos that prepares the acquisition of tact in the context of teacher training.

A Brief Phenomenology of Tact:
Two Examples from Classroom Research[6]

Example A: The students in my English class seemed rather restless and upset. I had already admonished them once and asked them to be quieter and pay attention. But the effect only lasted for a few minutes and the noise level in the class rose again. I had known this class for a while now and this behavior puzzled me, so I simply asked what was going on today. One student explained to me that two hours ago, they had a math test and that was why they just couldn't concentrate properly. I then decided to postpone the (rather dry) grammar topic I had prepared for the day to the next lesson and instead play a round of "Vocabulary Champ" with the students. We had done this playful exercise a few days ago, and it seemed to me that they had a lot of fun doing it, but still took it seriously and engaged with the topic of the lesson. This seemed like a good compromise, and it worked that day for me and the students: Everyone settled down, and we practiced vocabulary.

Example B: The topic of yesterday's lesson was the meteorological phenomenon of "inversion." I explained to the students that this weather phenomenon can be observed on some days in our region and how such a weather situation occurs. One student didn't seem to understand my explanations and asked me why the clouds stayed exactly at the altitude at which they stayed. At that moment, I no longer knew how to respond—the answer might have slipped my mind or I hadn't known it in the first place. I immediately noticed that I became very nervous and didn't know what to answer anymore. Therefore, I simply said: "That's not really important for you. You just need to know that such a thing as inversion exists in the South Tyrolean Alps."

When we look at these two examples, we might find them quite different. I would argue that the first one clearly shows what can be called "tactful pedagogical interaction," while the second one doesn't. However, a negative example of pedagogical tact can also teach us something about tact and the basic problems connected to it:

1. First, one could argue that these descriptions are classical examples of the so-called "technological deficit" (Luhmann & Schorr, 1982, p. 11) in education: Pedagogical interaction does not follow causal rules, is always fallible, and teaching and learning are very different processes, separated by an unbridgeable gap.[7] This basic fact leads educators to ask for a skill or technique that bridges the gap between the two spheres, even though they can never be fully congruent. In example A, we see the teacher bringing his concept of teaching (he prepared a certain lesson) to the learning needs of the students (or rather: the challenge to learning presented by the students). He somehow manages to do the right thing at the right time. In example B, we find a similar situation: The teacher presents a topic and introduces new knowledge; however, this does not lead to the students learning exactly what he had in mind. We could even say that he doesn't teach in a tactful

way as he refuses to engage with the "logic of learning." In both examples, we can see different ways to deal with the "technological deficit" and the absence of causality in education. From this perspective, tact would be *the ability to act as if there were causality while knowing from experience that there is no causality*. Teachers have to act as if the students learned through and with them, while knowing that it is absolutely uncertain (if not highly unlikely) that they actually always learn what teachers want them to learn.

2. This leads us to the second problem: *The incongruence of theory and practice*. Even though I tried to interpret and thus to theorize the practical experience which we find in the short descriptions, the richness of a tactful situation and the embodied atmosphere of a situation that enables tactful teaching can never be fully accounted for in theory. And vice versa: A theory of pedagogical tact will always be too complicated and too abstract for a person having to practice tact. A tactful teacher would thus be one who on the one hand does not fully rely on "knowledge," but on the other hand does not deny it completely and is dependent on the routines, habitualizations, and the "we've always done it that way"-mindset. In example A, the teacher breaks with routines and his lesson planning, but he also admits his insecurity and the fact that he doesn't know what will happen. In example B, the teacher relies both on "textbook knowledge" (a certain plan for the lesson or perhaps even a plan for the whole school year) and on his routines, in which he is used to considering himself the omniscient teacher.

3. The third problem is centered around *pedagogical dilemmas or challenging situations that provoke tactful interaction*. In example A, the teacher has to decide whether he can discipline the students (i.e., sanction them) sufficiently to allow him to go on with his lesson plan—which will still present the danger that the students might settle down but are still not really following his lesson. Or he can change his lesson plan, take away a bit of the tension and "buddy up" with the students—at the cost of his long-term lesson schedule. In example B, the student teacher has to decide whether to openly admit his lack of knowledge and maybe turn this situation into a collective task for seeking the answer to the question together with the students. Or he can try to keep up the façade of the omniscient teacher by simply exercising his authority and deciding what is important to know and what is not—maybe at the price of demotivating a student who was actually interested in the problem of inversion. Tact in the first example shows itself as a way of dealing with such dilemmas that is sensitive to students and their needs, that is learning-oriented, and that leads to a pedagogical outcome for a situation which can be considered "good" educational practice.

4. And finally, there is *the problem of learning how to act tactfully*. The two examples are taken from the notebooks of student teachers, giving an account of their experiences in their first teaching internship. These teachers are at the beginning of their pedagogical career, which means that they still have not yet acquired what we call pedagogical tact. The question of how exactly the process of acquiring tact can be theorized in order to design settings in which tact can be learned in a purposeful and structured way remains open. Tactful pedagogical interaction does not seem to be covered by theory-informed lesson planning, as the first example shows, which means that tact cannot be learned in a university seminar. The second example, however, shows that practice alone is not enough: A teacher who always goes with his gut feeling or "instinct" will not become a tactful practitioner—unless we assume that there is something like a "natural-born teacher" (see Spranger, 1960).

Of course, this very brief analysis of tactful and non-tactful teaching has at its core a certain normative assumption about teaching and tact, and allows the author to interpret and define the situations from a position of power (Derrida, 1984). However, my point here is not so much that the reader agrees or disagrees with my interpretation, but that the questions I am raising in this context are relevant for a reflection on the phenomenon of tact and its further discussion in the context of educational theory. In the following, I will address the four topics or questions presented above and briefly integrate them into the context of Herbart's theory of pedagogical tact as he sketches it in his introductory lectures on pedagogy.

Lines of Tradition

Herbart's Understanding of Tact

Looking at what was earlier called the "technological deficit" (Luhmann & Schorr, 1982, p. 11) through the lens of Herbart's theory, we need to differentiate between what he calls "Wissenschaft" (theory or theoretical reflection) and "Kunst" (art) (Herbart, 1802/2022, p. 30): Theory on the one hand aims to establish concepts and models, to explore the foundations and reasons for various phenomena. Art on the other hand shows itself in skills, in (inter)action, and in an ability to decide quickly while in a difficult situation. Art is always directed at a certain purpose or telos. If educational practice is rendered as "art," as Herbart suggests, the problem of technology does not arise in the first place: art is not to be (fully) grasped by the logic of a systematic theory of education, which means that the impossibility of technology is at the core of what is at question here.

Herbart argues from a pedagogical logic, defining "the pedagogical" first, and then tries to find a suitable instrument to explore the phenomenon in question. The perspective of the "technological deficit" presupposes that there has to be a technological grasp or causal take on education before actually asking what education is. Tact, we could say with Herbart, can never be technological, because the inner logic of education does not allow for such a thing as technology.

If we look at the second point, the incongruence of theory and practice, we get closer to Herbart's understanding of tact: He calls tact the *"Mittelglied"* (1802, p. 285)—the mediator or middle link—between theory and practice. Theory and practice need to be mediated, as theory (or science) can only teach the practitioner either "too much and too little" (2022, p. 31). Theory teaches "too much," as it covers a broad field of experience. The teacher or educator will only touch a very small part of this field in his daily practice. At the same time, it teaches "too little," as theory cannot answer the questions and problems arising from the given, specific situation that teachers find themselves in—this of course is only true if theory claimed to be universal.

This leads us to the third point, in which we will find a more definite answer to the question of what tact actually is and how it helps to deal with dilemmas or challenging situations which are not covered by "textbook knowledge." Tact is characterized as quick judgment and decision, based not on a theoretical plan or routine, but on a feeling for the "true requirements of the individual case" (2022, p. 32). This ability to read pedagogical situations, as challenging or dilemmatic as they might be, and to respond to them very quickly, should lead the educator to "know what has to be done, to do it right and with vigor" (1802, p. 290). This ability is based on a feeling for the situation and the "expression" of "inner movements," rather than in reflection or knowledge. Tact replaces theory if we take into account that theory teaches the educator/teacher "too much" and "too little" at the same time.

The last question—how can tact be acquired?—is solved by Herbart in a way that underlines the relevance of both theoretical and practical teacher education. Tact itself can only be learned in practice (Herbart, 2022, p. 32), it has to be practiced (*Übung*; Herbart, 1802, p. 285). By interacting pedagogically or, in other words, by gaining pedagogical experience, teachers become tactful teachers. However, experience itself is not enough (2022, p. 31), as it does not tell us what a "good" pedagogical interaction is (in the sense of tactful interaction), and what isn't. In order to have meaningful experiences in teaching and educating, teachers have to engage with theory and reflection prior to their practical phase, not to prepare for specific situations, but to prepare their "character[8], their mind and their heart" (Herbart, 1802, p. 286; Herbart, 2022, p. 33) in order to "to correctly receive, perceive, feel, and judge the phenomena awaiting him and the situation in which he will be placed" (2022, p. 33). The tactful teacher/educator thus has prepared for the "art of education" (2022, p. 33) by engaging with theory, an engagement that enables him to learn from his own practical experiences and "attunes" (p. 33) his mind and heart for situations that both require and foster tactful interaction.

This last point shows quite clearly that tact is not a matter of knowledge, motivation, or will, but rather of competence, skill, and knowing-how. To acquire tact, teachers have to show a certain attitude of openness to their surroundings, that is, to the students or children and the topics, goals, or "contents" of educational processes, as well as to themselves as practitioners who might fail.

"Preparation of Character, Mind and Heart" as Ethos?

Given the above, we have to assume that before educators can acquire tact (as a skill), they have to adopt a certain attitude or stance toward the field of practice they might acquire tact in. Even though Herbart does not use the term "attitude" or *ethos*, and only speaks of "preparation of the character, mind and heart," the concept of tact or rather, *the prerequisites for learning tactful interaction* has a lot in common with the concept of ethos. If we are interested in the question of how teachers become tactful teachers, we would thus have to look first at the specific attitude or stance that lets teachers have meaningful practical experience which eventually leads to the acquisition of tact. In the following, I will outline the parallels and differences between Herbart's "preparation of the character and heart" and an Aristotelian concept of ethos, referring to the *Nicomachean Ethics* (Aristotle, 1925) and *Rhetoric* (Aristotle, 1924).

In addition to this, I will also identify two points of criticism—one stemming from the question of the "good" or the normative component in concepts of ethos and tact, the other from the fact that Herbart at one point sees tact as a matter only of sound knowledge in the field of *Bildsamkeit* (or perfectibility). I will first sketch out these problematic constellations and then point out how they might be addressed when enriching Herbart's theory of tact (or theories of tact in general) with elements from a theory of pedagogical ethos.

Herbart's "Preparation" and a Theory of Ethos: Parallels and Differences

First of all, we have to take a closer look at the concept of ethos. In the *Nicomachean Ethics*, Aristotle introduces the term "ethos" by dividing all virtues in two categories: On the one hand, there are virtues of the mind or intellect which can be acquired by being taught, by reflection and contemplation (Aristotle, 1925, Book II 1103a). On the other hand, there are virtues which can only be acquired through practical activities, that is, they have to be practiced or exercised. These are virtues of the character, that is, each represents a specific ethos, such as "bravery." They are acquired through practical activities that aim at "the good" (1103a)—such as playing the guitar in order to become a good guitar player. The virtues of the character thus always involve a judgment (or at least the ability to be judged by another person), and feature an entelechial structure, as they comprise the aim of the specific practice in the practice itself: the warrior becomes brave by facing danger (1103a).

If we compare the concepts of "preparation of character, mind and heart" (Herbart) and ethos (Aristotle) as I sketched above here—albeit all too briefly—we will find a few similarities: *Both Herbart's "preparation" and ethos are notions that relate to the character or personality* of teachers. They are closely tied to the way a person interacts, thinks, and perceives. Also, *they comprise reflective elements*: Demonstrating an ethos does not only mean to be oriented toward certain customs or conventions, but to reflect these customs from an ethical perspective and to chose to act accordingly. Herbart's "preparations" aim at a similar goal; they are meant to enable practitioners to reflect on their own pedagogical interactions. And finally, *both concepts comprise normative elements*. Ethos aims at a (more general) good, and Herbart's "preparation" aims at "grasping situations correctly" (1802, p. 286), "knowing what has to be done," and "doing it right" (p. 290).

Looking at these similarities, we could argue that the "preparation" for acquiring pedagogical tact (as described by Herbart) and ethos are actually very much alike, and that Herbart's "preparation of the character, mind and heart" is only tailored to a more specific field—the field of education—while Aristotle's concept of ethos applies to all forms of practice. However, we can also note a few differences between the two concepts: Firstly, ethos *is not to be acquired through theoretical knowledge* or by simply being taught by someone. It has to be acquired and refined in the field of practice itself and by actually doing something, creating something, or interacting with someone. As a consequence, *the corresponding form of the acquisition or learning of ethos is practicing*, that is, a repetitive kind of learning that aims at fostering a certain knowing-how (Brinkmann, 2012). Herbart argues that *the preparation of character, mind and heart is based in the study of educational theories* (see also next section). Secondly, *ethos features an entelechial structure*, as argued above, whereas *"preparation" is not both means and ends*. It is instead a means to acquire something different; it is an attitude that serves as the starting point to learn the skill of tact.

In the following, I would like to argue that the benefit of seeing ethos and Herbart's concept of "preparation" as two interrelated concepts not only lies in recognizing the similarities in definition, but in some additional thoughts that the Aristotelean concept of ethos brings along with it and which can fill a gap in Herbart's theory of tact. To show this, I will briefly refer to the preconditions of acquiring tact as conceptualized by Herbart, or more precisely, to the specific knowledge that prepares the tactful practitioner. Going back to Herbart's central argument concerning the acquisition of tact—that it can only be acquired after theoretical studies that prepare the "character, mind and heart" of a teacher—we could raise the question about how exactly theoretical preparatory work can lead to building a certain "character." Further, we could ask about the kind of theories and abstract knowledge that would prepare teachers' "hearts." Herbart himself suggests focusing on a theory of Bildsamkeit (Herbart, 2022, p. 35) to foster a practical attitude that enables teachers to become tactful. Bildsamkeit is based on the assumption that all humans are characterized by a certain "plasticity," providing them with the ability to shape their own character, their skills and more generally, their relations to world and to self. Herbart argues that Bildsamkeit is part of the nature of humankind and that man "is a creature who transforms itself, who changes from one state to another" (Herbart, 1802, p. 290). Bildsamkeit thus stands for the radical openness of humans and makes us unlike animals, which are determined by nature. In other words: To be human is to determine what and who humans are and to establish in which relation one stands to the world and to others (Benner, 2015, p. 84). Being prepared by a sound theoretical, systematic knowledge of "Bildsamkeit" and of its relation to educational processes—that is, both as a prerequisite and goal—should provide teachers with "character" and "heart" to develop and refine their excercise of tact (Herbart, 1802, p. 288). Herbart, in other words, attempts to transfer the *theory* of Bildsamkeit directly into related practice.

Critical Remarks

Besides expressing general doubt about the congruency of theoretical knowledge and practical knowledge, I would like to emphasize two more critical points about Herbart's thoughts on preparing teachers to become tactful.

Focusing on the concept of Bildsamkeit when trying to define the content of scholarly preparation for acquiring tact makes it difficult to grasp pedagogical tact normatively. The concept of Bildsamkeit, precisely because of its openness and its quality as a "category of possibility" (Schäfer, 2009, p. 187), offers little opportunity for normative definition.[9] The question of what is good or bad education, that is, what is desirable or undesirable in terms of the student's Bildsamkeit, remains open. But this very question should actually be answerable;

for Herbart's theory of tact demands that the teacher "knows what has to be done," that he does it "right and with vigor" (Herbart, 1802, p. 290). The problem, then, is that the concept of pedagogical tact tries to address the problem of normativity with purely pedagogical vocabulary: What is pedagogically tactful is what is appropriate in the sense of Bildsamkeit—which, however, must remain open and indeterminate by definition (Benner, 2015, p. 78). A reference to norms and values that do not stem from the sphere of pedagogy and education is missing in this concept.

By focusing solely on theories of Bildsamkeit and the pedagogical/educational interactions that support Bildsamkeit, Herbart presents a bifurcated concept of teaching and learning, of inner psychological processes (Bildsamkeit and Bildung on the side of the student) and a separate outside world that somehow needs to penetrate and influence these inner psychological spheres. He thus neglects the relational and situative character of pedagogical interaction (Meyer-Drawe, 2010). The relational character of pedagogical interaction becomes obvious when we take its embodied, reciprocal structure into account. Pedagogical interaction is not limited to the execution of certain actions by a teacher or educator and the results or effects on the side of students or children. It can rather be described as a phenomenon of reciprocal influences from both sides and shows a strong dependency on the quality of the relation between the protagonists (Friesen, 2017; Meyer-Drawe, 1996; Waldenfels, 2007). The situative character is reflected, for example, in the fact that pedagogical interaction takes place in a certain setting (i.e., a classroom, kindergarten, youth club), in a certain atmosphere (Rödel, 2020), and in certain spaces that include certain materials and artifacts. Both the relational and situative traits suggest that pedagogical interactions are inescapably embodied processes (Brinkmann, 2017). In more general terms, we find a precursor to such a relational and responsive theory of ethos already in Aristotle's *Rhetoric*: the ethos or credibility of an orator is always in close interaction with the logos, that is, the argument or content of the speech, but also with the emotions of the audience or the pathos (Aristotle, 1924, I:3; for a pedagogical perspective see Agostini, 2020). Ethos as a practical attitude is never limited to the performance or the impersonation by an individual, but always refers to others and the embodied relations speakers find themselves in. This aspect of pedagogical ethos—and, in Herbart's terms, the "preparation of the character"—may be overlooked when focusing too much on the concept of Bildsamkeit, as teachers or educators may only become concerned with how the student's process of Bildung is influenced by his or her actions, and neglect the reverse effect, namely, how the teacher, as an agent, is influenced by the student.

Beyond *Bildsamkeit*
Opening new Perspectives on Ethos and Tact

Having shown that there are some problems associated with a focus on the concept of Bildsamkeit in the training of prospective (tactful) educators, and that these problems might impede the acquisition of a certain attitude of "character" or "heart" (Herbart), I will take up the two preceding criticisms to argue for a combination of the concepts of ethos and pedagogical tact. On the one hand, I will draw on Herbart himself (on a source other than the *Lectures on Pedagogy*). On the other hand, I will bring in suggestions from my own research on ethos in teacher education.

Practicing Ethos Aesthetically

Let us turn to the first problem, the question of normativity. In another lecture on the subject of education (Herbart, 1804), Herbart proposes to solve the question of teaching what is "good" and "bad" to students, and thus of this aspect of the normativity of education, with the formation of a certain ethos in *students*. He leaves open the question of what exactly "the good" is or from which authority it is to be derived (e.g., divine or secular authorities). Also, he argues that the good cannot be imparted to the student in the form of knowledge or certain guidelines; rather, it is a matter of getting the student to "find himself as choosing the good, as rejecting the evil" (Herbart, 1804, p. 108). According to Herbart, this process is the only path to "character formation" (p. 108). So we have to think of "the good" in contexts of education as an appeal that elicits specific reactions in those who have developed a sensitivity for it and who thus "find themselves" as answering to it. The sensitivity to this appeal is of an aesthetic quality similar to sensitivity to the beautiful; it cannot be taught or passed on directly but must be practiced. Herbart, like Aristotle, introduces an *entelechy of the good* in the *experience of the good* at this point. He proposes that through the "aesthetic representation of the world" (p. 112), that is, a confrontation of students with the most plural and diverse contents, values, methods, techniques, and cultures of knowledge, a sense of what "the good" is (or could or should be) is gradually awakened in students. According to Herbart, "this elevation to a self-confident personality should [...] take place in the mind of the student himself and be accomplished by his own activity" (p. 108). The role the teacher plays in this remains obscure in Herbart's work, but it can be assumed that teachers carefully curate the "aesthetic representation of the world," smuggling a conception of the good into the educational process through the back door, as it were (p. 114).

Given my focus up to this point, however, I do not want to pursue this question further. Rather, I would like to raise the question of how we can introduce normative elements into the formation of an ethos that enables tactful action and the formation of pedagogical tact by realigning an "aesthetic representation of the world." We could argue that through the confrontation with a plurality of moral and ethical positions, future educators can develop a reflective attitude toward the question of "good" or "right." Dealing with as many different normative alternatives from as many different fields as possible (pedagogy, psychology, philosophy, political theory, jurisprudence, science, perhaps even economy and religion) enables teachers to distance themselves from preconceptions and prejudices and lets them notice something new and different about questions of tact, that is, questions of "what has to be done?" Only by considering and identifying with many different normative positions can our own positions be relativized and an attitude of openness be established that lets educators and teachers accept the contingency[10] of guiding norms in pedagogical interactions, but at the same time raise the question of "the good" anew. At this point, I would suggest a concept of *phronesis* (Brinkmann & Rödel, 2021, p. 43), that is, a kind of practical wisdom. In such an understanding of reflective practice (Schön, 1987), the distancing movement mentioned above would not lead future teachers to derive the lowest common denominator from all norms and values and to build an "intersection" of good practice that is then transferred into one's own repertoire of teaching skills. On the contrary: Teachers could acquire the ability to let their daily practice surprise them in terms of their own normative assumptions, values, and routines and to be open to the question that is central to the training of pedagogical tact: What is "the good" in my specific practice, and what could "the good" in the future be? Such an attitude or ethos of insight in the contingent structure of pedagogical situations can be considered as a starting point for cultivating pedagogical tact.

Ethos as an Embodied Phenomenon

As mentioned above, one can criticize Herbart for neglecting the situative, intersubjective, and reciprocal elements of educational processes when it comes to preparing a fruitful environment for acquiring tact. In the first findings of an ongoing international research project, we can find some possibilities for addressing this neglect in traditional theories of tact and its acquisition. A pedagogical ethos, as Brinkmann and Rödel suggest (2021), only becomes manifest in certain actions or practices of positioning oneself in front of others, of positioning oneself in a pedagogical situation. If we look back at the examples mentioned above, the teacher in the second narrative description engages in such an act of positioning when he shows himself as an omniscient teacher.

These acts of positioning are embodied ones, that is, a combination of acts of speech, gestures, a certain posture and facial expression, but they are also ones of establishing distance or proximity to others who are also taking part in the situation. In phenomenological terms, acts of positioning that indicate a certain ethos can also be seen as "responsive acts" in a structure of inter-relatedness. Phenomenological theory suggests that when we respond to others and to situations, we are already connected to the others and our response to them and to their appeal or "call." All of this is situated in an in-between (Waldenfels, 2007), i.e., it is neither completely "ours" nor "theirs" but is an act between activity and passivity. This assumption is based on a notion of the lived body, that is, a body that serves as a medium of expression and communication beyond the use of language. This also means that participants in a (pedagogical) situation are related to each other through an embodied sphere, a kind of common space that is opened by the presence of different lived bodies. Given such a theory of embodied inter-relatedness, we would have to assume that within an act of positioning in pedagogical contexts, teachers or educators do not simply express a certain, willfully chosen standpoint or moral value, but that they are themselves subject to situative, intersubjective relations and that their positioning is (partly) also a positioning of others through the person of the teacher. In consequence, ethos is not to be considered a solipsistic skill or competence, but a social and embodied phenomenon. If we argue that developing sensitivity for tact has to rely on a pedagogical ethos that recognizes the social, reciprocal, and embodied foundations of pedagogical interaction, we can suggest an addition to Herbart's theory of preparing teachers for tactful interaction. If we assume that at the beginning of acquiring pedagogical tact there has to be a certain pedagogical ethos that becomes manifest in embodied acts of positioning, we can draw a richer picture of the actors and relations defining a pedagogical situation, and thus gain a more differentiated approach to questions of tact.

Ethos as a Facilitator for the Acquisition of Tact

I will briefly sum up the thoughts presented above and also point out some practical implications of my attempt to combine the classical theory of tact with elements of (pedagogical) ethos. As for one of the central questions in the context of tact—how can it be acquired by future teachers or educators?—I would like to sketch out an approach to "teaching" a pedagogical ethos that can foster an attitude in which tact can be recognized as a field of professional development.

In the first part of this chapter, I pointed out the relevance of tact in pedagogical discourse. Tact can be seen as an answer to the problem(s) of the tension between definiteness and indeterminacy, between certainty and uncertainty, or between necessity and contingency in pedagogical practice. As a "soft skill" of educators and teachers, tact can fill the gap between the technological fantasy (Karcher, 2020) of causally regulated pedagogical interaction and a purely habitual pedagogical practice by offering the possibility of reflecting on this tension and by acquiring and further developing pedagogical professionality.

In a brief phenomenology of tactful and non-tactful pedagogical practice I have pointed out four central questions that are constitutive for tactful pedagogical practice: Pedagogical tact addresses the central problem of the so-called technological deficit of pedagogy. From this perspective, tact would appear as *the ability to act as if there were causality while knowing that there is no causality*. The concept of tact also addresses the *incongruence of theory and practice* in the field of education and allows us to become sensitive to *pedagogical dilemmas or challenging situations that ask for tactful interaction*. And finally, it can be said that tact presents a major challenge for the training of future teachers, as *the question of how tact can be learned or acquired is still unsolved*. It cannot be learned in a (theory-based) university seminar, but it also seems that it cannot be acquired purely through practice in the field.

As I have shown, Herbart renders tactful educational practice an art, thus removing it from the sphere of the technological fantasies of education. Also, he identifies tact as the mediating link between theory and practice. As for pedagogical dilemmas, tact offers an affectively-based repertoire for interacting and reacting without relying on textbook knowledge. These three points are also echoed in the final question of how tact is acquired. Here, Herbart's understanding of tact is based on its practice in pedagogical situations, which, however, first requires the acquisition of a certain attitude or ethos—or, as Herbart says, demands a sound preparation of "character, mind and heart" (Herbart, 1802, p. 286).

This leads to the question of the similarities and differences between classical understandings of ethos and Herbart's quasi-ethos that would enable teachers and educators to practice tactful teaching. Both ethos and Herbart's "preparation" relate to the character or personality; they are both comprised of reflective and normative features. They differ in the following two ways: Ethos is not to be acquired through theoretical knowledge. It has to be practiced, while the preparation of character, mind and heart is based in the study of educational theories. Also, ethos features an entelechial structure, while "preparation" involves practices or means that are notably different from their ends. I have also pointed out a basic problem in Herbart's concept of tact that arises from the preparation of character being grounded in a theoretical knowledge of the concept of Bildsamkeit. According to Herbart, this kind of knowledge enables teachers to act tactfully concerning the recognition of each human's Bildsamkeit as an anthropological precondition for education. However, the focus on Bildsamkeit makes it difficult to address normative issues; at the same time, the relational structure of education is neglected.

To address these shortcomings, I have referred to a concept of ethos that is based on Herbart's theory of an "aesthetic representation of the world" (see Herbart, 1804, p. 105) and argued that through the experience of confronting many different normative perspectives on educational situations, future teachers can relativize their own positions and establish an attitude of openness. This attitude or ethos lets teachers and educators accept the contingency of certain norms and values in pedagogical interactions. At the same time, it challenges these pedagogues to repeatedly raise the question of what might be good educational practice. Through reference to Bernard Waldenfels' theory of embodied responsivity, I have pointed out that ethos and its accompanying (moral) positionings must always be thought of in social, embodied, and reciprocal terms. This means that tactful interaction that is structured intersubjectively and responsively can only be acquired via an attitude, an ethos, a developed moral position.

To close, I will try to illustrate these last points by referring to a "didactic of ethos," which has been developed in a research project in Berlin, Vienna and Innsbruck. The project *Ethos im Lehrberuf–Manual zur Übung einer professionellen Haltung* aims at introducing exercises of ethos as exercises in moral decision-making into teacher training on university level. Very much in the sense of Herbart's "aesthetic representation," students are confronted with a textbook featuring a broad set of examples from pedagogical practice which represent different kinds of dilemmas and ambiguous situations. These situations all require tactful pedagogical interaction and thus act as stimuli for discussion and reflection on different ways of judging situations, on different moral values which could guide appropriate actions, and on the ambiguity of pedagogical situations in general. In this work with classroom examples, students can learn to distance themselves from preconceptions and prejudices and become sensitive to something new and different about these situations in relation to ethos and moral decision-making. By discussing different perspectives with their peers, future teachers also have to position themselves as they argue for one perspective or the other. This lets them become sensitive to the embodied act of positioning that goes along with living a certain ethos.

Working through various examples and perspectives is not to be seen as practice in pedagogical tact itself, but as a practice of a certain ethos, one that allows future teachers to see situations that require tactful interaction in different ways. In this sense, it can contribute to fostering pedagogical tact by first establishing an ethos that sensitizes beginning teachers and educators to questions of what good educational practice is, and to the role that they play in an intersubjective and embodied pedagogical situation and—perhaps most importantly—by showing that these questions can be answered only for a very specific pedagogical situation. A general answer to these important ethical questions always remains open and, in this sense, a tactful ethos would also mean to not force them to a final conclusion but instead to work on keeping them open.

Notes

[1] For a comprehensive history of pedagogical tact, see Müller (2015).

[2] Translation by Norm Friesen (Nohl, 2022, pp. 80–81). I would like to thank Norm Friesen for all the helpful comments on translations of German original texts for this chapter.

[3] For an English introduction to this specifically German field of educational theory, see Friesen (2020).

[4] For further reading on recent theories of pedagogical tact see the anthology by Burghardt et al. (2015). For an overview on the discourse of tact in therapeutic and aesthetic fields and its relation to educational theory, see the book by Günter Gödde and Jörg Zirfas (2014).

[5] Gert Biesta presents a very similar argument in his works on the nature of teaching, but without speaking explicitly of tact (Biesta, 2017a, 2017b).

[6] The examples quoted here are reflective accounts of student teachers, who describe situations from their teaching practice that they found difficult to handle.

[7] For this distinction, see also Klaus Prange's (2005) theory of the "pedagogical difference."

[8] Herbart uses the German word Gemüt (or *Gemüth* in old spelling), a term that is hard to translate as it has various meanings. In a nutshell, it can be rendered as the totality of the mental and spiritual powers of a person and the receptivity to impressions that appeal to the feeling and intellect (Grimm, 1999, Vol. 5, Col. 3293). Herbart uses the three terms "Gemüth, Herz und Kopf," with "Herz und Kopf" (direct translation: heart and head) covering the common, dualistic spheres of mind and heart, rationality and emotionality. So it seems likely that he uses Gemüt to cover another dimension of human experience and interaction with the world; he might want to emphasize the personal and receptive elements in his characterization of an attitude that enables the acquisition of tact. Thus, Gemüth is translated here as "character," in accordance with Kant's definition of Gemüt as a character trait that serves as a disposition to be open to aesthetic impressions as well as to (transcendental) ideas (Kant, 2002, Critique of Judgement, § 49).

[9] This is not to say that the concept of Bildsamkeit has lost its relevance for educational theory (see, e.g., Benner, 2015, p. 70ff.).

[10] I would like to clarify at this point that (pedagogical) contingency is not to be mistaken as arbitrariness. The former still is subject to reasoning and logical justification, while the latter is not and tends to produce result in what Herbart calls pedagogical "Schlendrian" (Herbart, 1802, p. 284)—a kind of sloppy routine, that is "habitual and eternally uniform" (Herbart, 2022, p. 32).

Bibliography

Agostini, E. (2020). Aisthesis – Pathos – Ethos. Möglichkeitsräume pädagogischer Achtsamkeit und Zuwendung. In B. Engel, T. Emke, K. Böhme, E. Agostini, & A. Bube (Eds.), *Wahrnehmen Beziehungs- und Erkenntnisräume öffnen. Ästhetische Wahrnehmung in Kunst, Bildung und Forschung* (pp. 139–155). Kopaed Verlag.

Aristotle. (1925). *The Nicomachean ethics*. (D. Ross, Trans.) Oxford University Press.

Aristotle. (1924). *The Rhetoric and Poetics of Aristotle*. (W. Rhys Roberts, Trans.) University of Virginia Press.

Benner, D. (2015). *Allgemeine Pädagogik. Eine systematisch-problemgeschichtliche Einführung in die Grundstruktur pädagogischen Denkens und Handelns*. Beltz Juventa.

Biesta, G. (2017a). *The rediscovery of teaching*. Routledge.

Biesta, G. (2017b). Education, measurement and the professions: Reclaiming a space for democratic professionality in education. *Educational Philosophy and Theory*, 49(4), 315–330. <https://doi.org/10.1080/00131857.2015.1048665>

Brinkmann, M. (2017). Leib, Wiederholung, Übung. Zu Theorie und Empirie interkorporaler Performativität. In C. Thompson & S. Schenk (Eds.), *Zwischenwelten der Pädagogik*. (pp. 155–172). Schöningh.

Brinkmann, M. (2012). *Pädagogische Übung. Praxis und Theorie einer elementaren Lernform*. Ferdinand Schöningh.

Brinkmann, M. & Rödel, S. (2021). Ethos im Lehrberuf. Haltung zeigen und Haltung üben. *Journal für LehrerInnenbildung*, 21 (3), 42–63.

Burghardt, D. & Zirfas, J. (2019). *Der pädagogische Takt. Eine erziehungswissenschaftliche Problemformel*. Beltz Juventa.

Burghardt, D., Krinninger, D. and Seichter, S. (Eds.) (2015). *Pädagogischer Takt. Theorie - Empirie - Kultur*. Ferdinand Schöningh.

Derrida, J. (1984). Guter Wille zur Macht (I). Drei Fragen an Hans-Georg Gadamer. In P. Forget (Ed.), *Text und Interpretation: deutsch-französische Debatte*.W. Fink.

Friesen, N. (2020). Education as a *Geisteswissenschaft*: An introduction to human science pedagogy. *Curriculum Studies*, 52(1), 1–16.

Friesen, N. (2017). Radicalizing the pedagogical relation: Passion and intention, vulnerability and failure. In M. Brinkmann, M. F. Buck, S. Rödel (Eds.), *Pädagogik - Phänomenologie. Verhältnisbestimmungen und Herausforderungen*. Springer VS.

Friesen, N. & Osguthorpe, R. (2018). Tact and the pedagogical triangle: The authenticity of teachers in relation. *Teaching and Teacher Education*, 70, 255–264.

Gödde, G. & Zirfas, J. (Eds.) (2014). *Takt und Taktlosigkeit. Über Ordnungen und Unordnungen in Kunst, Kultur und Therapie.* transcript.

Grimm, J. and Grimm, W. (1999). *Deutsches Wörterbuch.* Deutscher Taschenbuch Verlag.

Herbart, J. F. (1802/1907). Zwei Vorlesungen über Pädagogik. In K. T. Kehrbach O. Flügel (Eds.), *Sämtliche Werke Vol. I*, (pp. 179–200). Hermann Beyer & Söhne.

Herbart, J. F. (1802/2022). Introductory lecture to students in pedagogy. In N. Friesen (Ed. Trans.), *Tact and the pedagogical relation: Introductory readings* (pp. 28–37). Peter Lang.

Herbart, J. F. (1804/1965). Über die Ästhetische Darstellung der Welt als das Hauptgeschäft der Erziehung. In W. Asmus (Ed.), *Pädagogische Schriften* (pp. 105–121). Helmut Küpper.

Kant, I. (2002). *Kritik der Urteilskraft.* Meiner.

Karcher, M. (2020). Die kybernetische Bändigung des Zufalls. Dataveillance und Learning Analytics als Herausforderung erziehungswissenschaftlicher Reflexion: Versuch einer Technikfolgenabschätzung. *Neue Steuerung – Renaissance der Kybernetik? Die Deutsche Schule Beiheft,* (15), 151–170.

Luhmann, N. & Schorr, K. E. (1982). Das Technologiedefizit der Erziehung und die Pädagogik. In N. Luhmann (Ed.), *Zwischen Technologie und Selbstreferenz. Fragen an die Pädagogik* (pp. 10–18). Suhrkamp.

Meyer-Drawe, K. (2010). Zur Erfahrung des Lernens. Eine Phänomenologische Skizze. *Santalka: Filosofija, Komunikacija 18*(3), 6–17.

Meyer-Drawe, K. (1996). Vom Anderen Lernen. Phänomenologische Betrachtungen in der Pädagogik: Klaus Schaller Zum Siebzigsten Geburtstag. In M. Borrelli and J. Ruhloff (Eds.), *Deutsche Gegenwartspädagogik 2* (pp. 85–100). Schneider-Verl.

Müller, H.-R. (2015). Zur Theorie des pädagogischen Takts. In S. Seichter, D. Krinninger, D. Burghardt (Eds.), *Pädagogischer Takt. Theorie - Empirie – Kultur* (pp. 13–24). Schöningh.

Muth, J. (1967). *Pädagogischer Takt. Monographie einer aktuellen Form erzieherischen und didaktischen Handelns.* Quelle & Meyer.

Nohl, H. (1957). *Die pädagogische Bewegung in Deutschland und ihre Theorie.* Verlag Schulte-Bulmke.

Prange, K. (2005). *Die Zeigestruktur der Erziehung. Grundriss der Operativen Pädagogik.* Schöningh.

Rödel, S. S. (2020). Geste, Stimmung und Bewegung im Schulischen Lernen – Empirische Einsatzpunkte in der Videoforschung. In Malte Brinkmann

(Ed.), *Verkörperungen. (Post-)Phänomenologische Untersuchungen Zwischen Erziehungswissenschaftlicher Theorie und Leiblichen Praxen in Pädagogischen Feldern* (pp. 35–58). Springer VS.

Schäfer, A. (2009). Bildende Fremdheit In L. Wigger (Ed.), *Wie ist Bildung möglich?* (pp. 185–200). Klinkhardt.

Schön, D. A. (1987). *Educating the reflective practitioner: Toward a new design for teaching and learning in the professions.* Jossey-Bass.

Senkbeil, T. (2020). Die Fragilität des Takts. Eine Rekonstruktion eines flüchtigen Moments. *Vierteljahrsschrift für Wissenschaftliche Pädagogik, 96*(1), 120–137.

Spranger, E. (1960). *Der geborene Erzieher.* Quelle & Meyer.

van Manen, M. (1991). *The tact of teaching. The meaning of pedagogical thoughtfulness.* SUNY Press.

van Manen, M. (2015). *Pedagogical tact. Knowing what to do when you don't know what to do.* Routledge.

Waldenfels, B. (2007). *Antwortregister.* Suhrkamp.

Tact as Pedagogical *Daimon*?[1]
Arendt on Tact, Exemplarity, and Judgment

Morten Korsgaard

In this chapter, I present an Arendtian perspective on tact and how it can be shaped in the educator. Pedagogical tact is generally understood as an ability to act appropriately in pedagogical situations with a sensitivity to the individual child or student, as well as to the group and the demands of the particular situation. Building on Arendt's work on action, exemplarity and judgment, I argue that tact is similar in structure to the *daimon* in ancient Greek thought. It designates a guiding spirit that is an inseparable part of who we are, yet beyond our immediate control and visible only to others. Accordingly, tact is not something we can define, nor can we systematize the acquisition or development of it. Rather we are left with the rather elusive proposition of studying examples of tact. This is not because they can simply be imitated, but because they offer the only way of placing ourselves in the vicinity of the tactful.

I

This chapter attempts to tackle the question of what pedagogical tact consists of and how it develops in the individual through the lens of Hannah Arendt's thinking about appearance and exemplarity. I raise the questions of what processes and from what sources we can draw when seeking to act properly in pedagogical situations? What does it entail to embody tact in movements and words, and how do we become capable of movements and words that would be deemed tactful? This is of course not a task that can be accomplished in any finished form or with fixed conclusions, nor can it be answered only conceptually or philosophically which will be the attempt here. Nor is Arendt the most likely theorist with whom to think about these matters. There are at least three reasons for this. First, Arendt never spoke explicitly about tact; second, Arendt's focus in her educational writings was never specifically on the work of the educator; third, she has often been read as a thinker whose theory of action was overly cognitive and negligent of affective and bodily aspects. Nonetheless, I will in this piece try to tease out some central aspects of Arendt's thinking that I believe to be relevant for theorizing pedagogical tact. I will do this by first trying to outline how we can understand tact in relation to Arendt's ideas about action and appearance, and secondly by turning to her ideas about exemplarity and judgment. Exemplarity will be presented as a possible source for understanding how tact is formed in and by the educator. Judgment will be explored as a way of understanding how exemplarity and tact are connected through an ability to open oneself to the contextual nature of pedagogy and the perspective of "the other" of the pedagogical relation. I will connect these ideas to a perhaps unlikely literary example, drawn from the short story *The Mysterious Stranger* by Mark Twain. I do this to show how tact is an embodied phenomenon which is exceedingly hard to grasp in any strict methodological way, or through establishment of criteria, principles, or rules for action. It is something that is part and parcel not just of what a person says or does but is in fact a manifestation of "who" one is. It is not a skill or a set of competences and abilities that can simply be acquired through scholarly learning, practical exercises, or rote repetition. As such, tact is a fickle friend, or with an Arendtian analogy, a *daimon*, looking over our shoulder; visible to everyone but ourselves.

II

Etymologically, tact derives from two familiar sources. One is the Latin *tāctus*, which translates as "keen perception," the other is the Greek *Taxis* (from the verb *tassein*; to order, to arrange), which means "an arrangement." Tact began to emerge in scholarly literature around 1800 in diverse works in philosophy, musicology, the study of war, and pedagogy. Kant spoke of "logical tact" in his *Anthropology*, Clausewitz about the "tact of judgment" in *On War*, and Herbart coined the term "pedagogical tact" in his lectures on education. The term seems in all these works to function almost heuristically to connote that undefinable ability to do what is right in complex social situations, where there are no set rules or laws to guide us. The two different etymological origins of the term are clear in two distinct ways in which it has been used in musicology. With the introduction of the modern bar notation in the sixteenth century, the vertical bar-line [*Taktstrich*], tact became a fixed measure of time in music, and with the later invention of the metronome this was mechanized. As such, tact functions as an organizing principle in music, by providing an ordering of the different voices, an arrangement of the sequences and the different sounds that form a piece of music. However, the organizing principle or mechanism, tact, is independent of the voices and sequences that make up the piece of music, it is "an empty measure or abstract structure independent of the notes and voices it structures" (Engberg Pedersen, 2018, p. 355). For music to be an aesthetic experience, following the order is not enough. In his wonderful article on tact in the early nineteenth century, Anders Engberg-Pedersen uses an example drawn from

E. T. A. Hoffmann's *Der Sandmann*, where Olimpia, an automaton, performs two pieces of music with absolute rhythmic precision. Her performance, however, leaves her audience unmoved.

> In her unpleasant, soulless correctness, Olimpia appears at once as the epitome and the perversion of the musical notion of Takt. On the one hand, Olimpia is the acoustic and visible manifestation of a musical principle that was invented some two hundred years earlier, viz. the invention of the modern measure or Takt. On the other hand, it is just this ordering principle that appears in perverted form in Olimpia's senseless performance. (Engberg-Pedersen, 2018, p. 354)

What Olimpia is missing is not the technical skill to follow the arrangement, rather it is the much more elusive sense of tact present in the Latin *tactus*, a keen perception or ability to sense the world around us. It is an aesthetic sense or capacity based on our ability to use our senses to "touch" the world around us.

According to Gadamer (1960/2006), tact is a kind of elasticity of the mind which permits us to maintain the appropriate distance to the objects and events of the world. This distance allows us to remain open to the world and the other, while not imposing our self-interest and preconceptions on the world or the other person.

> By "tact" we understand a special sensitivity and sensitiveness to situations and how to behave in them, for which knowledge from general principles does not suffice. Hence an essential part of tact is that it is tacit and unformulable. One can say something tactfully; but that will always mean that one passes over something tactfully and leaves it unsaid, and it is tactless to express what one can only pass over. But to pass over something does not mean to avert one's gaze from it, but to keep an eye on it in such a way that rather than knock into it, one slips by it. Thus tact helps one to preserve distance. It avoids the offensive, the intrusive, the violation of the intimate sphere of the human person. (pp. 14–15)

Gadamer uses the word tact as an umbrella term for formation (*Bildung*), common sense (*sensus communis*), judgment (*Urteilskraft*), and taste (*Geschmack*), all of which are not only elements of a person's character, but the very building blocks of hermeneutic science. In this way, our ability to interpret aspects of the world is intertwined with the elements that make up our character. This might seem obvious, but it is crucial to Gadamer to make it explicit, and to show it as a fact from which science cannot escape, however objective it strives to be.

Arendt had a different, yet related way of putting it; "the answers of science will always remain replies to questions asked by men; the confusion in the issue of 'objectivity'" was to assume that there could be answers without questions and results independent of a question-asking-being" (Arendt, 2006, p. 49). This problem is made quite apparent when it comes to the notion of tact and made even more complex by the fact that the version of tact that is closest to me, that is my own, is not something I can put at a distance, and hence it is not amenable to study. It is, however, visible to those around us, and they will quickly see if we are merely "following the arrangement," and not fully sensitive to the aesthetic and personal aspects of the situation we find ourselves in.

III

In her seminal work, *The Human Condition*, Arendt wants to examine what it is we (as humans) *do*. What kinds of activities do we engage in, and how have these changed over time? In a peculiar revival of Kant's philosophical anthropology, Arendt charts the different spheres of human action and engages with the question of what makes us human. One crucial aspect of this is that we appear before others. "With word and deed we insert ourselves into the human world, and this insertion is like a second birth, in which we confirm and take upon ourselves the naked fact of our original physical appearance" (Arendt, 1998, pp. 176–177). Arendt calls this "naked fact" of our appearance in the world *natality*. This is the fact that we are born into the world as a specific somebody, in a specific time and place, which no one else could occupy. It is this "miracle" of being born that provides us with a "who," as distinct from a "what," and the potentiality to remanifest the miracle of our singular birth by acting in the world.

> In acting and speaking, men show who they are, reveal actively their unique personal identities and thus make their appearance in the human world, while their physical identities appear without any activity of their own in the unique shape of the body and sound of the voice. This disclosure of "who" in contradistinction to "what" somebody is—his qualities, gifts, talents, and shortcomings, which he may display or hide—is implicit in everything somebody says and does. It can be hidden only in complete silence and perfect passivity, but its disclosure can almost never be achieved as a willful purpose, as though one possessed and could dispose of this "who" in the same manner he has and can dispose of his qualities. (p. 179)

This means that unlike my qualities and abilities, such as playing the violin, doing complex math, or reciting poetry by heart, which can be consciously put on display, "who" I am, is not something I can consciously hide away or put on display, and most importantly it is not visible to myself.

> On the contrary, it is more than likely that the "who," which appears so clearly and unmistakably to others, remains hidden from the person himself, like the *daimon* in Greek religion which accompanies each man throughout his life, always looking over his shoulder from behind and thus visible only to those he encounters. (1998, pp. 179–180)

A daimon in Greek mythology was a divine power or guiding spirit that followed each human throughout their life. And one who had a good daimon would also be able to attain *eudaimonia* (i.e., happiness or wellbeing). Socrates famously invoked his *daimon*, his inner voice, in his defense. Arendt seems to focus more on the aspect of the daimon which has to do with its elusiveness than on its role as guide. It is unmistakably ours, yet we cannot see it. It follows us wherever we go, yet we cannot make it do our bidding. How it is seen is always in the hands of others.

Who we are is a conglomerate of bodily and mental features. It is our Bildung, our physiognomy, our personal traits, our judgments, the way we move, our tastes, our sense of the world, our aesthetic sensibilities. In continuation of the way Gadamer used the term tact, I would say that it comes very close to being "who" we are. The trouble with getting at "who" we are is thus reminiscent of the trouble with defining and describing tact.

> The manifestation of who the speaker and doer unexchangeably is, though it is plainly visible, retains a curious intangibility that confounds all efforts toward unequivocal verbal expression. The moment we want to say who somebody is, our very vocabulary leads us astray into saying what he is; we get entangled in a description of qualities he necessarily shares with others like him; we begin to describe a type or a "character" in the old meaning of the word, with the result that his specific uniqueness escapes us. (1998, p. 181)

Although it is probably not viable to claim that tact is the same as who one is, or that who we are is reducible to tact, the two overlap sufficiently to say that just as the question of who we are constantly eludes us, so does tact. Once we try to pin down what makes a person tactful, we resort to descriptions of features or abilities that can never give the full picture. We resort to words and descriptions like empathic, eloquent, quick on her feet, sensitive, accommodating, and so on. All of these are aspects of one's personae which can be identified and even worked on. But tact and who we are is never just that. "It excludes in principle our ever being able to handle these affairs as we handle things whose nature is at our disposal because we can name them" (1998, pp. 181–182). If we could name our daimon, we could perhaps bring it to heel, and finally give the *cogito* the role that the Enlightenment envisioned for it. Alas, our daimon constantly eludes us.

IV

Yet as Zirfas reminds us, this might not be such a big issue, since "our concern here is not with such education or cultivation of the self by itself" (Zirfas, 2012/2022, p. 180). What we are talking about when we speak of tact is something inherently relational. Tact is the ability to maintain the proper distance to the other, allowing him or her to come into their own. To become. This entails that "[p]edagogical tact, in other words, is above all a principle of *mediation*." (Zirfas, p. 180). This is true in a double sense. It is on the one hand as Herbart (1802/2022) argued a "link intermediate between theory and practice... a quick judgment and decision that is not habitual and eternally uniform" (p. 32). On the other hand, it is also the mediation between the child as he or she is, and who they are to become.

Regarding the first sense of mediation, Zirfas is quick to add that it should not be understood rationalistically, as the cognitive and voluntary implementation of principles, the Enlightenment dream of rational and principled control of emotion and behavior. "It should be considered to what extent emotional qualities have always been included in rational considerations or to what extent tact is characterized not only by cognitive elements but also by aspects of sense, emotion and will" (2022, p. 181). Without wanting to get into a discussion of whether this is consistent with Herbart's own thinking, it is important, because it points to the previous point about how tact is always a fickle friend, and never fully in our control.

Regarding the second sense (the child as they are and who they are to become), this leads us of course directly to the paradoxical aspects of pedagogical practice. How can we possibly lead children in a way that mediates between who they are in the moment and who they will become. "Pedagogical tact remains embedded in this pedagogical paradox: of needing to encourage people to behave in a way that is self-determined, and of their simultaneous inability to achieve this on their own" (Zirfas, 2012/2022, p. 184). What remains then is the tactfulness that places one at the appropriate distance between the two states, the present and the future, just enough to allow the child to become self-determining in their own becoming. Hence, there is no escaping the paradox, nor any solution or finality to it. All we can do is to stay with and attempt to balance the paradox.

This has to do with the relation between the individual and general in the form of the world to come. On the one hand we lead children toward "who" they will become, on the other the "who" they will become remains open and undetermined. As Zirfas argues, quoting Schleiermacher, "Pedagogy must react tactfully to individuality in order not to destroy it: 'That which is directed toward the individual is what we call tact, a feeling for that which is unbecoming in each of us'"[2] (Schleiermacher, 1806/1981, p. 147, in Zirfas, 2022, p. 182). This is very close to Arendt's formulation of education's central concern; the fact of natality. This entails that "our hope always hangs on the new which every generation brings; but precisely because we can base our hope only on this, we destroy everything if we so try to control the new that we, the old, can dictate how it will look"

(Arendt, 2006 p. 189). However, and paradoxically perhaps, Arendt never makes the relation and responsibility toward the individual the center of her argument in "The Crisis in Education." Rather it is the relation to the world and the concept of plurality that she places at the center.[3] The reason for this is that there is much more at stake in education than the individual and the individual teacher's relation to the child. The world itself and human beings' ability to establish a relation to it is at stake. One could argue of course that this makes Arendt blind to the fact that oftentimes this very problem is played out precisely in the teacher's relation to individual children. However, it does seem to be at least implicitly present in her argument for the centrality of natality, which is precisely the appearance of the individual in plurality. The details of the relation however, Arendt wishes to leave in the hands of the educators (2006, p. 192).

Were she to have pursued this path, however, she would have had to confront the issue of the relation between judgment and action. And as we know she did not live to fully develop this central theme. Another issue she would have had to confront is the relation between who we are, and how tact forms itself in us. Tact, like our "who," is by necessity ours, even if it is manifested only in relation to another, yet it is never fully in our hands, because we can never cognitively grasp it, nor can we claim to always be fully in control of the actions that follow from our tact and who we are.

Tact, as Gadamer reminds us, is a conglomerate of formation, common sense, Judgment, and taste. Zirfas adds that we cannot exclude emotion and will. Nor can we exclude our body, and the central role it plays in how we appear in the world. Returning to Herbart's definition of tact as a mediator, we could perhaps say that tact mediates between our "who" and the way we act in the world. This does not, however, place us in control of tact, nor of who we are, nor of how these appear for others in the world.

V

Once again, we are left in the dark concerning how we can meaningfully speak about how we can develop tact and what it means for the relation between theory and practice. Whether we will get any closer by following Arendt remains to be seen, but in *Men in Dark Times*, she does state her own position on how to find guidance for troubling questions.

> Even in the darkest of times we have the right to expect some illumination, and that such illumination may well come less from theories and concepts than from the uncertain, flickering, and often weak light that some men and women, in their lives and their works, will kindle under almost all circumstances and shed over the time span that

> was given them on earth—this conviction is the inarticulate background against which these profiles were drawn. Eyes so used to darkness as ours will hardly be able to tell whether their light was the light of a candle or that of a blazing sun. But such objective evaluation seems to me a matter of secondary importance which can safely be left to posterity. (Arendt, 1968, pp. ix–x)

Arendt explicitly questions the ability of theory and concepts alone to guide us, and posits instead the stories and examples, in this case, of historical and contemporary writers, who in some way portray a relation to the world and others that can help us to (re)think our condition. It is of course not given which exemplars we should choose, and, as shall be elaborated later on, Arendt is not invoking an Aristotelian admiration-emulation model of exemplarism here.[4] Whether we consider an example to be exemplary cannot be settled in any final way, and each example must be open to revalidation and reinterpretation. This is so not only for practical, fictional, or anecdotal examples, but also for pedagogical literature and theory. Whether an example has any pedagogical force and resonance will also be dependent on the encounters with novel readers and the discussions that arise in response to it. That *Emile* still has an exemplary pedagogical force is verified by the way it continues to challenge and provoke us to reflection on its pedagogical insights. "Consequently, examples exist both in relation to communities of people who have repeatedly judged them to be exemplary, and in relation to the history of those judgments that have set certain objects and individuals above others as models" (DeCaroli, 2007, p. 378). What makes pedagogical examples relevant is thus not whether we can emulate them efficiently or successfully, but whether they force us to make use of our judgment.

Herbart spoke of the pedagogical force of the example in relation to the development of pedagogical tact, and of the importance of being able to make use of the right company, the right examples.

> To lead us back to the ideas of the previous lecture, take an illustration. Conceive of a man of character—of moral character, if you please—only do not think merely of what is called a good, honest, law-abiding man, but hold present to your minds a man in whom the moral element has grown into that decision, steadiness, and organized swiftness of execution which with especial propriety deserves the name of character. (Herbart, 1802/1896, pp. 25–26)

Our pedagogical tact is thus very much formed by the examples we choose to engage with. This is not a matter of mere mimicking or appropriation of a vocabulary. It is a matter of letting this tact grow into one's person. Tact has to grow into us and become embodied in our actions, not just our words. Tact must penetrate our whole person, and not just some professional personae or way of speaking, lest it become simple automation as was the case for Olimpia.

"[A]s there are not only moral, but very many species of characters, so also there are very many species of tact, manners, and ways among educators" (Herbart, 1802/1896, p. 27).

Before returning to the issue of what examples actually do, I want to turn now to an example that is the complete opposite of Olimpia. An example of someone not bound at all by the confines of order and automation. In *The Mysterious Stranger* by Mark Twain, three young boys meet an angel who introduces himself as Satan, a namesake of his infamous uncle.

> Soon there came a youth strolling toward us through the trees, and he sat down and began to talk in a friendly way, just as if he knew us. But we did not answer him, for he was a stranger and we were not used to strangers and were shy of them. He had new and good clothes on, and was handsome and had a winning face and a pleasant voice, and was easy and graceful and unembarrassed, not slouchy and awkward and diffident, like other boys. (Twain, 1916, p. 10)

The angel quickly beguiles the young boys with his demeanor and personality.

> He was bent on putting us at ease, and *he had the right art*; one could not remain doubtful and timorous where a person was so earnest and simple and gentle, and talked so alluringly as he did; no, he won us over, and it was not long before we were content and comfortable and chatty, and glad we had found this new friend. (p. 11, emphasis added)

Satan does not only use his looks and his manners to entice the boys, but he also uses his abilities to manipulate his surroundings and conjure things into existence. First, he conjures all manners of food and delicacies.

> He ate nothing himself, but sat and chatted, and did one curious thing after another to amuse us. He made a tiny toy squirrel out of clay, and it ran up a tree and sat on a limb overhead and barked down at us. Then he made a dog that was not much larger than a mouse, and it treed the squirrel and danced about the tree, excited and barking, and was as alive as any dog could be. It frightened the squirrel from tree to tree and followed it up until both were out of sight in the forest. He made birds out of clay and set them free, and they flew away, singing. (pp. 12–13)

The boys are enraptured by Satan's person and his abilities and knowledge of the world. His art of using just the right words when they begin to become anxious or afraid and withdraw from him, and his ability to place in front of them magical objects that entice them back into attention, show his pedagogical tact. He does it all seemingly effortlessly, yet with a presence and attentiveness to their every word (and thought).

> I should not be able to make anyone understand how exciting it all was. You know that kind of quiver that trembles around through you when you are seeing something so strange and enchanting and wonderful that it is just a fearful joy to be alive and look

at it; and you know how you gaze, and your lips turn dry and your breath comes short, but you wouldn't be anywhere but there, not for the world. (p. 15)

Theodor here gives voice to a familiar experience of being captured by a phenomenon or a person that draws our attention fully and makes us forget both time and place. Sometimes even at the cost of other responsibilities or even our sense of right and wrong. While talking with the boys, Satan has conjured a small village of living creatures made of clay. Then, much to the horror of the boys, he casually begins to kill some of them and finally to destroy the village. The boys are horrified and appalled, yet

> he went on talking right along, and worked his enchantments upon us again with that fatal music of his voice. He made us forget everything; we could only listen to him, and love him, and be his slaves, to do with us as he would. He made us drunk with the joy of being with him, and of looking into the heaven of his eyes, and of feeling the ecstasy that thrilled along our veins from the touch of his hand. (p. 18)

Even when revealing some of the darker aspects of his being to the boys, aspects that repulse and scare them, Satan is able to calm them and explain to them the reasons for his haphazard dealings with things and people. Of course, Satan has the great advantage of being able to read the boys' mind, something alas, mere mortal educators have not. A further hindrance in developing one's tact. Being immortal and omnipotent, Satan is little interested in the goings on in human life, but nonetheless takes a special interest in Theodor and begins to educate him about the world and the follies of humankind. Satan is an attentive and caring teacher. Yet at times he portrays a distinct arrogance and, in his omnipotence, has little time and care for the feelings and moral sentiments of humans. Nevertheless, he introduces Theodor to a much wider world than the one his small village life would otherwise have acquainted him with. There is thus no doubt that Satan portrays many aspects of what we could call pedagogical tact in his dealings with the boys. Sometimes he is less than caring when it comes to the ignorance of humans, and whether he is in fact educating or manipulating, Theodor is of course open to discussion.[5]

The reason I want to highlight this particular example here is once again to emphasize the ambiguity and risks involved in invoking the idea of pedagogical tact. We will not get straightforward answers about what to do in specific pedagogical situations, nor evidence for effective learning activities, even when studying an immortal being. What we will get, however, is a way of proceeding that is sensitive to the discontinuity of pedagogical practice, and the particularity of both how tact forms itself in the individual and how it is always context dependent and relational.

Where tact is not automated, as it was in Olimpia's failed attempt to move her audience, but rather attuned to the particulars of the individuals involved and the particular situation, it is always hard to determine where the borders between right and wrong, manipulating and educating, can be drawn. When are we leading the children where they should go, and when are we in fact leading them astray by drawing their attention in specific ways and directions?

VI

According to Arendt, judgment is the faculty by which we determine right and wrong. It is a backward-looking mental capacity that judges what has happened, and what has befallen us. Judging, Arendt informs us, "is a viewpoint from which to look upon, to watch, to form judgments, or, as Kant himself says, to reflect upon human affairs. It does not tell one how *to act*" (Arendt, 1992, p. 44; italics in original). How then is it connected to tact? Following Arendt, it can be connected only indirectly. Judging is "an unending activity by which, in constant change and variation, we come to terms with and reconcile ourselves to reality, that is, try to be at home in the world" (Arendt, 1994, pp. 307–308). So rather than being the ability to judge right from wrong in a particular moment of action, judging is a process of reconciliation to being in the world with others. It is a matter of making oneself at home in the events and the plurality of the world. This entails that when invoking the concept of judgment in relation to tact, I am not trying to turn it into a placeholder, but rather pointing to something that I believe to be prior to being able to enact tact in pedagogical relations. First comes the ability to reconcile oneself to and to make oneself at home in the "pedagogical world." It is a matter of gaining understanding of where I come from and what circumstances I find myself in the midst of. "Only an 'understanding heart,' and not mere reflection or mere feeling, makes it bearable for us to live with other people, strangers forever, in the same world, and makes it possible for them to bear with us" (Arendt, 1954/1994, p. 322). Coming to terms with the world by putting one's judgment to work on the events and people that make up this world is a first step toward becoming at home enough to enact pedagogical tact in pedagogical relations. Or as Herbart put it in the quote above, we need "a preparation of both the understanding and the heart before entering upon our duties, by virtue of which the experience which we can obtain only in the work itself will become instructive to us."[6]

In the end, Arendt tells us, our ability for judging does not come down to our deductive or intuitive abilities to foresee or sit in final judgment of the events of the world. Rather, "our decisions about right and wrong will depend upon our choice of company, of those with whom we wish to spend our lives. And again, this company is chosen by thinking in examples, in examples of persons dead or alive, real or fictitious, and in examples of incidents, past or present" (Arendt, 2003, pp. 145–146). It is the ability to go visiting; to visit the perspectives of others when assuming the position of judge, that will determine if we succeed or fail. What for Gadamer was a kind of elasticity of reflection, Arendt, borrowing from Kant, calls it *Erweiterte Denkungsart* or enlarged thinking. However, where Kant seemed to think that the validity of one's judgment rested on having tested it against all the possible viewpoints,[7] Arendt urged us to find the right examples to consult. "To think with an enlarged mentality means that one trains one's imagination to go visiting" (Arendt, 1992, p. 43). This brings us back to the role of the example, which is to facilitate a visiting of another perspective and a reconciliation to our being in the world with others. This process of enlarging one's ability to visit the perspectives of others is central to becoming at home in pedagogical practice. It not only provides us with ways of reflecting on our own practice, by visiting that of others, it also, and crucially, provides us with a potential sense of being at home in our practice, and with how we appear to others.

What good does a "sense of being at home" do for educators who are faced with having to make quick judgments on what to do in particular situations and relations, you wonder? Well, perhaps not much, but does this not simply lead us back to the paradoxical nature of turning to the *daimon* we call tact as a starting point for talking about what it means to be a good educator? We can never lay it bare before us and dissect it to see what it consists of nor whence it came. This does not mean we cannot learn from others and from examples how we might become more at home in pedagogical thought and practice, it just means we have no privileged access to the process, nor any means of determining in advance what should be done in each situation, nor how we become someone who will do what is right nonetheless.

VII

In this chapter, I have tried to engage with the idea of pedagogical tact, and how this is shaped in the pedagogue. I have focused on establishing an initial connection between tact, exemplarity, and judgment in order to point to ways of understanding how tact is developed in the individual. Even if this has been no easy task, and perhaps leads at least partly to inconsistencies, it is a way of speaking about what being a pedagogue entails, and how one can work toward becoming a better one. Also, it is consistent in its inconsistency with the discontinuity and indeterminacy of pedagogical situations. As Zirfas (2012/2022) acknowledges; "One can say that the 'essence' of tact is its indeterminability and its openness" (p. 182). Even in light of this, I do think the notion of pedagogical tact is better suited to the difficult task of speaking about good pedagogical practice, than some of the alternatives that are in vogue, such as educational leadership or evidence-based practice. Instead of aiming for (the illusion of) certainty and efficiency, the metaphor of tact reminds us of the fragility of pedagogical situations and relations. It reminds us to be humble in the face of the uncertainties and discontinuity of pedagogical action. We can never be sure of the results of our actions in pedagogical situations, but we can try to comport ourselves in a way that is conducive to establishing a relation between the child and the world. This relation hinges of course in the first instance on attention, and our ability to capture it—be it through the use of our person and skills or through magical tricks that draw the gaze of the child or through our sense of music's ability to capture the sensory, gathering attention on something common is the primary moment of pedagogy. And for this we need not only knowledge but also the ability to put our bodies and minds to work to tactfully draw the child toward the world.

The problem remains of course, that the way tact is manifested in what we do remains just as indeterminate and open to us as educators as does the question of how to act in particular situations. We cannot be provided with a manual, but we can study examples. Not in the crude form of exemplars to simply imitate, but rather, through presentation of different examples that invite students to go visiting and to judge the particular in recognition and discussion of general principles. Here fiction—in the form of literature, film, music, and art—is vital, since it offers the students an entryway (see Korsgaard, 2019) that speaks to their senses as well as their sensibilities. Fiction and anecdotal examples can capture the attention and imagination in a different way than theoretical literature does, and when brought together, they can give access to new understanding and ways of being (an educator). Whether the examples I have chosen here will resonate and bring about understanding remains to be seen of course, but what is beyond doubt is that there are innumerable examples to draw from in the cultural heritage of any given context that speak to and about what it is to stand in relation to a new generation.

Notes

[1] The author thanks the organizers and audiences of INPE 2022 at The Danish School of Education, Copenhagen, for the opportunity to present an earlier version of this chapter. This chapter is the outcome of said presentation, further enriched by responses from those present and subsequently the reviewers and editors of the anthology.
[2] Schleiermacher, F. D. E. (1981). *Brouillon zur Ethik*. Felix Meiner, p. 147.
[3] For an elaboration of this reading of "The Crisis in Education," see Chapter 3 in *Bearing with Strangers*.

4   See the recent discussions of Lynda Zagzebski's interpretation of this (Croce, 2019; Croce & Vacarezza, 2017; Korsgaard, 2019, Dahlbeck, 2021).
5   See Dahlbeck (2021) for an insightful discussion of the character and its educational implications.
6   This is why I also believe that the study of theory should go hand in hand not only with practical experience, but also the study of examples of pedagogical relations in the form of fictional portrayals or anecdotal illustrations.
7   The debate about whether he did in fact mean all possible positions is ongoing (see Hanna, 2018).

Bibliography

Arendt, H. (1968). *Men in dark times*. Harcourt Brace Janovich.

Arendt, H. (1992). *Lectures on Kant's political philosophy*. University of Chicago Press.

Arendt, H. (1994). *Essays in understanding (1930–1954)*. Harcourt Brace.

Arendt, H. (1998). *The human condition*. University of Chicago Press.

Arendt, H. (2003). *Responsibility and judgment*. Random House.

Arendt, H. (2006). *Between past and future*. Penguin Books.

Croce, M. (2019). Exemplarism in moral education: Problems with applicability and indoctrination. *Journal of Moral Education*, 48(3), 291–302. <https://doi.org/10.1080/03057240.2019.1579086>

Croce, M. & Vaccarezza, M. S. (2017). Educating through exemplars: Alternative paths to virtue. *Theory and Research in Education*, 15(1), 5–19. <https://doi.org/10.1177/1477878517695903>

Dahlbeck, J. (2021). The pedagogical importance of Ingenium: Exemplarism and popular narratives. In J. Dahlbeck (Ed.), *Spinoza: Fiction and manipulation in civic education* (pp. 43–60). Springer.

DeCaroli, S. (2007). A capacity for agreement: Hannah Arendt and the "Critique of Judgment." *Social Theory and Practice*, 33(3), 361–386.

Engberg-Pedersen, A. (2018). The sense of tact: Hoffmann, Maelzel, and mechanical music. *The Germanic Review: Literature, Culture, Theory*, 93(4), 351–372. https://doi.org/10.1080/00168890.2018.1507993

Gadamer, H.–G. (1960/2006). *Truth and method* (2nd ed. rev.) (J. Weisenheimer & D. G. Marshall, Trans.). Continuum.

Hanna, R. (2018). Kant's theory of judgment. *The Stanford Encyclopedia of Philosophy* (Winter Edition). (E. N. Zalta, Ed.). <https://plato.stanford.edu/archives/spr2022/entries/kant-judgment/>

Herbart, J. F. (1802/1896). Introductory lectures to students in pedagogy. In W. J. Eckoff (Ed.), *Herbart's ABC of sense-perception and minor pedagogical works* (pp. 13–28). D. Appleton.

Kant, I. (1803/1983). Über Pädagogik. In W. Weischedel (Ed.), *Werke in 10 Bänden* (vol. 10) (pp. 691–764). Wissenschaftliche Buchgesellschaft.

Korsgaard, M. T. (2018). *Bearing with strangers. Arendt, education and the politics of inclusion*. Routledge.

Korsgaard, M. T. (2019). Exploring the role of exemplarity in education: Two dimensions of the teacher's task. *Ethics and Education, 14*(3), 271–284. <https://doi.org/10.1080/17449642.2019.1624466>

Mollenhauer, K. (1991). *Vergessene Zusammenhänge: Über Kultur und Erziehung*. Juventa Verlag.

Muth, J. (1962). *Pädagogischer Takt: Monographie einer aktuellen Form erzieherischen und didaktischen Handelns*. Quelle & Meyer.

Muth, J. (1962/2022). Pedagogical tact: Study of a contemporary form of educational and instructional engagement (selections). In N. Friesen (Ed. Trans.), *Tact and the pedagogical relation: Introductory readings* (pp. 85–117). Peter Lang.

Twain, M. (1916). *The mysterious stranger*. Harper & Brothers.

van Manen, M. (2016a). *Pedagogical tact*. Routledge.

van Manen, M. (2016b). *The tact of teaching*. Routledge.

Zagzebski, L. (2017). *Exemplarist moral theory*. Oxford University Press.

Zirfas, J. (2012/2022). Pedagogical tact: Ten theses. In N. Friesen (Ed. Trans.), *Tact and the pedagogical relation: Introductory readings* (pp. 175–196). Peter Lang.

PART III

Tact in Context

Pedagogical Tact and the Limits of Community

Hans-Rüdiger Müller

Introduction

The term "pedagogical tact" has cropped up time and again in pedagogical scholarship over the past two hundred years yet has eluded systematic theorization and practical methodization. It can be regarded as a *Problematisierungsformel* rather than a formula whose main function is to provide instructions for pedagogical practice (Burghardt & Zirfas, 2019, p. 10): That is to say, it can be seen as a concept that "problematizes" certain basic pedagogical facts, revealing aspects of pedagogical practice that are problematic in certain respects and making it possible to address them (both theoretically and practically). In order that it can serve this role, we first need to define "pedagogical tact" more precisely. In everyday pedagogical contexts, the term is mainly used to describe pedagogical practice that considers not just general principles of action (based on professional knowledge or experience) but also the unique character of every pedagogical situation and of all those involved, and hence avoids schematically applying generalized pedagogical knowledge to a specific situation. Someone acting with pedagogical tact will spontaneously respond in an appropriate manner to challenges posed by the indeterminacy and unpredictability of concrete pedagogical situations. We encounter this sort of tact outside of pedagogical settings, too: it is a feature of human social interaction in general. It might therefore be helpful to begin by clarifying the concept of socially tactful behavior in general, asking why it is necessary and what its conditions of possibility are, before then turning our attention to the specific issues of tact in pedagogical contexts. How does pedagogical tact in particular differ from social tact in general? In what ways is pedagogical tact used as a *Problematisierungsformel*? What role do feelings/affects and understanding/cognition play in pedagogically tactful practice? And what distinguishes pedagogically tactful practice from the acquisition of *social* tact through pedagogical interaction?

These are the questions that the present chapter will seek to address. The argument is divided into four parts. The first section presents an outline of the nuanced theory of (social) tact set out in Helmuth Plessner's 1924 sociological treatise *The Limits of Community* (Plessner, 1924/1999). The second section then takes a brief detour into Plessner's philosophical anthropology so as to gain a deeper understanding of the dialectic of closeness and distance in societal[1] interactions that is connected to the concept of tact; in particular, it will examine Plessner's theorem of "excentric positionality" (*exzentrische Positionalität*; Plessner, 2019), which he uses to distinguish different perspectives by and on human subjects (and intersubjective relations). In the third section, Plessner's sociological theory is applied to pedagogical interactions, and discussions of pedagogical tact are elucidated through the lens of Plessner's concept of tact. The fourth and final section gives a summary of the pedagogical significance of Plessner's sociological understanding of tact.

"Tact" as an Element of Plessner's Sociology

In Plessner's anthropologically based sociology, social tact plays a key role in marking the "limits of community" (*Grenzen der Gemeinschaft*), as his 1924 treatise was entitled. The work was motivated by the phenomenon of "social radicalism," which was influential and widespread at that time. In Germanophone countries, support for radically communal modes of life could be encountered in youth groups, in the social reform (*Lebensreform*) movement and in communist and nationalist ideologies of community. In response, Plessner gave an analysis of human beings' societal (*gesellschaftlich*) existence that showed the dangers of extreme communal (*gemeinschaftlich*) relations that rejected the anonymity and artificiality of societal reality. He saw social radicalism as one-sidedly emphasizing either irrationalist values (blood, ancestry, nature) at the expense of rationality or rationalist ones (ideals, beliefs, morality) at the expense of irrationality, despite the reality of human existence consisting precisely in the intermingling of rationality and irrationality. In Plessner's theory, social radicalism is based on a dualistic conception of human beings, a separation of body and mind, in which one of the two aspects of human existence is posited as absolute in contrast with the other. As a result, either the natural, unadulterated power of life or the power of the mind or spirit (*Geist*), cleansed of the irrationalities of life, serves as the basis of a close-knit social cohesion. This radical position rejects the reality of modern societal life (in which rational and irrational intermingle, and body, mind, and soul all play a part) as an aberration: its formal institutions (which disguise the informality of social communication without eliminating it), its social roles (behind which the agents' subjective motives are concealed), its ceremonies (which cast a universal form over the singularity of social encounters), and its detached, impersonal modes of behavior (which stand in the way of authentic subjective expression). But according to Plessner, it is precisely in this ambivalence of social relations (alluded to here in the remarks in parentheses) that the reality and possibilities of modern social life, with its aspirations to autonomy and individuality, are grounded. For the anonymity, formality, and (to some degree) abstractness of social interactions in the public sphere is the condition of possibility for protecting individuals' private selves in such exchanges. Communities based on relations among particular individuals, such as those between romantic partners, between parents and children, between friends, or between people fighting for a common cause, are also relevant to the constitution and maintenance of social attachments. However, in their radicalized, exclusionary form, where they are antagonistically opposed to formalized social interactions in the societal public sphere and elevated to the sole ideal of shared social life, they destroy the functionality of society and its institutions, a functionality which transcends specific individuals and beliefs. These relations also fail to protect individuals' private selves and subjective needs and potentials from being infringed upon by the collective. If it arises in a radical form without an opposing sphere to balance it out, a community based on "blood-based connection" (*blutsmäßige Verbundenheit*; Plessner, 1924/1999, p. 86) or one based on shared beliefs, a "community of the ideal" (*Gemeinschaft der Sache*; p. 92) based on shared beliefs, will monopolize every aspect of a person and reduce them to whatever fits with its conceptions. By contrast, the structure of the societal public sphere, with its formalized social interactions, allows individuals themselves to strike a balance between those aspects of their private selves they wish to share with the outside world in the social roles they have adopted and those they do not. Role-taking is augmented by role-making, in which individuals shape their own social roles, for instance as a teacher or student in an educational institution. However, people do not have complete rational control over their self-presentation in public interactions. In a person's embodied appearance—in their expressions, their gestures, their voice—the irrational sides of the human soul, their human emotions and drives, will shine through to some degree, and social interactions would be fairly sterile if they did not. Interaction is always also an embodied phenomenon, rooted in expression, perceptions and emotional resonances between people. And concrete social situations likewise do not entirely match the universal norms society provides for them. The "open system of interaction between persons who are unattached to each other" (Plessner, 1999, p. 149) that characterizes the sphere of society (*Gesellschaft*) in distinction from the social community (*Gemeinschaft*) involves a twofold "brokenness" (*Gebrochenheit*) that must be bridged in social interactions: the contradiction between situation and norm, and the contradiction between the holder of an office or role and the private individual. This inescapable brokenness of societal interactions cannot be repaired, it can only be bridged. In the world of business, politics and government, where relations take place not between "natural persons" but between "unrealized persons, functionaries, 'officials,'" commercial people of some kind or another" (Plessner, p. 166), the brokenness is bridged by ceremony (in the sense of formalized patterns of behavior that transcend specific situations) or diplomacy (as the strategic art of reconciling divergent interests while respecting the freedom and dignity of other people). And in the world of free, unconstrained sociability between unattached persons in public settings, it is bridged by prestige (which allows acknowledgment without demanding full self-transparency) and by a tactfulness that respects people's unfathomability and otherness. According to Plessner, the ultimate foundation of social tact (just like diplomacy and its strategic calculations) is the existential requirement to protect the "sensitivity at the center of every soul" (Plessner, p. 159) in the face of the brokenness of social reality:

> Tact is the ability to perceive incalculable differences, the capacity to comprehend that untranslatable language of appearances that situations and persons speak without words in their constellation, conduct, and physiognomy and in accordance with unfathomable symbols of life. Tact is the ability to respond to the subtlest vibrations of the environment. It is the willing openness to see others and, in so doing, to remove oneself from the field of vision; it is the willingness to measure others according to their standards and not one's own. Tact is the eternally alert respect before the other soul; that is why it is the first and last virtue of the human heart. (Plessner, 1924/1999, p. 163)

This section has outlined the sociological framework within which Plessner developed his concept of social tact and which distinguishes the various social modes in which people form relations, in which they exist, in which they can both protect and injure each other. But while these different modes are neatly separated in Plessner's theoretical analysis, in actual societal reality we encounter them as complex, interlocking clusters. The pursuit of strategic interests and satisfaction of communicative needs are not solely confined to certain social situations. Even community-based interactions can involve strategic interests and diplomatic attempts to reconcile them, or an interest in the individual and respect for their privacy. Social tact is thus also necessary in interpersonal relations to sound out the limits between "sociability" (*Geselligkeit*), "transaction" (*Geschäftlichkeit*) (p. 164) and trusted community (*Gemeinschaft*), each with their own respective modalities. With a scope extending far beyond casual social interactions, tact responds to the "vulnerability of psychological life" and is "tuned to the incalculability of individual differences within the social milieu" (p. 164). It is tuned to the situated character of social encounters—to their "being bound to an unrepresentable and uncategorizable situation that will never come again" (p. 166). Tactful behavior is based on a kind of "feeling [*Fernfühlung*] and touch [*Ferntastung*] for the distance of unremarkable, but information-rich things in the permanent oscillations of the situation of the social milieu" (p. 167). This intuitive interweaving of keeping one's distance from other people while empathetically engaging with them allows us to act appropriately toward them.

Plessner's Philosophical Anthropology and "Excentric Positionality"

Tact and diplomacy can be regarded as modes of social conduct that are intended to prevent us overstepping the appropriate distance from other people in a way that injures or exposes their private self. These modes of behavior avoid direct personal expression, and refrain from demanding absolute transparency and authenticity from others. People acting tactfully or diplomatically keep their distance and respect other people's reserve. This means that in the public sphere, people are able to partially conceal their private selves behind social roles, which viewed from the outside gives their behavior an artificial appearance. Tact or diplomacy still run a risk of failure, as an excessive artificiality of social form undermines trust in the seriousness of the relationship. The social mask that veils the mental and emotional activity going on in the background is not an arbitrary masquerade but marks a limit that protects the person's inner world while serving as an external expression of their self: "The person generalizes and objectifies himself through a mask behind which he becomes invisible up to a point without fully disappearing as a person" (Plessner, 1924/1999, p. 133). Joachim Fischer interprets this idea of Plessner's as a "sociology of 'limits'" (Fischer, 2016) that describes societal conduct as an "artificial alienation of expressive life" in which body, mind, and soul work in concert: "The mask is a longing of the soul, but an invention of the mind [*Geist*] and an act [*Durchführung*] of the body" (Fischer, 2016, p. 97) Fischer thus connects Plessner's sociological theory to the principles of philosophical anthropology that he formulated around the same time in his magnum opus *Levels of Organic Life and the Human* (Plessner, 2019, originally published as *Die Stufen des Organischen und der Mensch* in 1928). Viewed through the lens of his anthropological theory, we can discern in Plessner's "sociology of limits" the fundamental doubleness of human existence, its "excentric positionality," that he describes using a variety of terms. Because of this special, double position that human beings occupy in the world, they cannot uninterruptedly live in, or relate to, their environment from the central point of their psychophysical constitution ("centric" positionality); rather, they are both able and compelled to peer at their life from a distance (excentric positionality), to act on every facet of it. In short, they do not just live their life but also to direct and shape it, to not just express their inner self but to detach themselves from and modulate that expression. This fundamental brokenness, in which the human being hovers between living out their life and reflecting on it—without being able to shift at will from one to the other—forces them constantly into new forms of behavior and expression that interweave both aspects:

> To the human, the transition from being within his own lived body to existing outside of his lived body is the irreducible dual aspect of existence, a true split in his nature. He lives on both sides of this split as body and psyche *and* as the psychophysically neutral unity of these two spheres. (Plessner, 2019, p. 271; emphasis in original)

This idea marks a fundamental departure from the philosophical tradition of a mere dualism or hierarchy of body and mind/soul (which can still be observed in modern studies of the brain).

The society of embodied human beings, in which an always unstable, dynamic balance is sought between soul, body, and mind, constructs humans as "naturally artificial" (*natürlich künstlich*) beings. These are beings whose nature has by some means been transformed by culture, without depriving them of their individual embodied existence, their physicality, which is at the same time the expressive field of their psychophysical constitution. This is also where communities come up against their limit. Recognizing and respecting this inner limit—whose precise location will depend on the social situation and the people involved—requires tact. Communities that systematically overstep this limit tend toward totalitarianism. This applies also, and indeed especially, to pedagogical communities. These can be found in pedagogical institutions (the history of pedagogy is littered with examples, from the controlling pedagogical practices of the German Enlightenment to totalitarian regimes in residential education and boarding schools) or in familial settings (where unhealthy structures can form that isolate family members from the outside world while exerting all-encompassing control over, and demanding complete transparency of, their inner worlds).

Pedagogical Interaction: Community or Society?

What ideas and recommendations can pedagogy take from Plessner's anthropological and sociological writings on social tact? Can his theory be directly applied to the field of education? And how might it enrich the theory of pedagogical tact and related research?

To clarify these questions, it would seem helpful to begin by defining where precisely education fits in the different spheres of social reality. Does its logic of practice belong to the domain of societal, functional relations? Or is it more concerned with communal relations that focus on the *whole* individual? In other words, does education take place in a community or as part of a functionally differentiated society? Plessner himself alludes in passing to the latter possibility when he divides society into several functional spheres, with the sphere of "ethics and education" (*Sitte und Erziehung*) sitting alongside "the sphere of right" and "the spheres of the state, economy, and 'interaction' [*Verkehr*]" (Plessner, 1999, p. 149). He was probably thinking here primarily of the education system that over the last 200 years has developed as a subsystem of modern society (Luhmann & Schorr, 2000; Tenorth, 2000) or as an institutionalized subset of "overall human practice" (*menschliche Gesamtpraxis*) (Benner, 2012, pp. 27–43). But in the time since this development began in the latter years of the eighteenth century, we can also find examples that emphasize the need for an education based on personal or communal attachments and set apart from a society undergoing a process of formal differentiation, in order to meet the challenges of modernity. This strand can be traced from Pestalozzi's 1799 "Letter to a Friend on his work at Stans" (Pestalozzi, 2022) to the *Landerziehungsheime* (literally "rural educational homes") of reform pedagogy (Lietz, 1970), from "new education" (Dewey, 1968) and human science pedagogy (*geisteswissenschaftliche Pädagogik*) with its core theorem of "pedagogical relation" (*pädagogischer Bezug*; Herman Nohl, 1933/2022) to the pedagogical reception of attachment theory in the present day, an idea taken from evolutionary psychology (Mooney, 2010; Keller, 2011). Viewed this way, it is not so easy to decide which social structure education should be classified under. Schools are institutions embedded in society's functional organization, where teachers and students act in their social roles; but the classroom community and (especially in the younger year groups) the personal relations between teachers and students are also significant. Meanwhile, the family is a community where people live and are raised together, explicitly involving relations to particular individuals and strong personal attachments (Parsons & Bales, 1964)—and yet it stands in relations of functional (economic, governmental, legal, cultural) interdependence with its societal environment (economy, state, laws, culture) (Claessens, 1979; Elias, 1978), the employment and education systems, its social milieu and the local neighborhood (Müller & Krinninger, 2016). The family is regarded as a private sphere that is relatively autonomous from the societal public sphere, but even the parent–child relationship, despite its private nature and the emotional attachment it involves, requires respect for the limits of the other person's psychological and physical intimacy. And if a third person (e.g., another parent or a sibling) is added to the pedagogical dyad, this can create a kind of "familial public sphere," which sometimes demands that people treat each other with greater tact than is necessary in cases where the communication is solely between a single parent and a single child.

These examples show that the boundaries between the public, societal sphere and the private, communal one are fluid, even if these boundaries assume a different form in the public education system than in the private space of the family. But what makes social tact into pedagogical tact is not primarily the social site of interaction, but its pedagogical structure: the structural fact of the difference in development between child and adult, the fact that younger children differ from older ones (and from adults) in terms of their emotional attachments, vulnerability, need for protection and lower capacity for formalized interaction. Acquiring the ability to shift from a private to a public mode (or simply to distinguish between the two modes) and mastering societal roles, the diplomatic reconciliation of interests and social tact is a cultural learning exercise that is only gradually completed over the course of the developmental process. It requires both attentiveness to the particular vulnerability of the child, depending on their stage of development, and a carefully measured introduction to the challenge of "playing a role" in a socially appropriate, individually successful way on the stage of public interaction. Structurally, this learning program is reflected in the various stages of the public education system, marked by transitions from the largely informal relations in the family to the first experiences with professional educators at nursery, from nursery to the moderately formalized teaching interactions in primary school, from primary school to the definitive role-based relations between teachers and students at secondary school. In the end and at the level of concrete pedagogical practice, this result corresponds to a pedagogical tact that is responsive to a child's individual state of development and the specific situation at hand, that accommodates the child's need for attachment with an "attitude of inwardly limited and outwardly demonstrated 'kindliness' [*Wohlwollen*]" (Brumlik, 2015, p. 56) without rigidly fixing the child in that need. It is also a tact that, as far as possible, demands finely judged, socially detached, role-based behavior. From a certain perspective, education as a whole might be described as a work of "transitions" (see on this point Müller, 2004): the transition from a behavior motivated by spontaneous bodily and emotional impulses to one that is more cognitively structured (in terms of the interplay of body, mind and soul), the transition from situationally bound to institutionally shaped behavior (the interplay of interaction and institution) and, of course, the transition from dependence on others to self-determination (the interplay of heteronomy and autonomy). However, it would be overly simplistic to understand these transitions merely as linear transformations running in a single direction without referring back to their starting point. It seems more apt to describe them as expanding the domain of action, as differentiating forms of "expression" and "embodiment," as structuring the field between a psychophysical "living out" of life on the one hand and reflection on that life from an "excentric position" on the other.

If education can thus be understood as work on a "transition" that is never definitively completed but must, due to the essential "brokenness" (Plessner, 2019, p. 287) of human existence, be grappled with anew in every situation, then it is at the same time work on the contradictions, aporias and paradoxes that beset pedagogical interactions in the modern age and which have been a frequent topic of discussion in the literature on educational theory in German (Benner, 2012; Helsper, 2002; for a general summary see Burghardt & Zirfas, 2019, pp. 149–191). This pertains in particular to modern pedagogy's "paradox of autonomy" (Burghardt & Zirfas, 2019, p. 161), famously formulated by Kant in the early nineteenth century with his question "How do I cultivate freedom under constraint?" (Kant, 2007, p. 447). How can education comply with the Enlightenment demand to respect other people's freedom if its intended end is to cultivate the use of freedom that is autonomous (morally grounded) rather than merely capricious?

Johann Friedrich Herbart responded to this paradox by distinguishing three forms of pedagogical practice corresponding to different stages of a child's development (see Benner, 2018, p. 48):

1. "Discipline" (*Kinderregierung;* child governing) in which children are not yet given autonomy but rather protected from doing harm.
2. "Instruction" (*Unterricht*) that allows students to gain greater "experience of the world" (*Welterfahrung*) and introduces them to different, competing worldviews and systems of knowledge.
3. "Guidance" (*beratende Erziehung*) that allows young people "making the transition to autonomous action" (*im Übergang zu selbstverantwortetem Handeln*) to independently explore the different spheres of societal activity.

But developing theories of pedagogical practice is one thing; actually implementing them is another. If a kind of reflectivity rooted in scholarly research does gain a foothold within education and break the cycle of educational practices that are simply passed down unquestioned ("learned-by-doing") or are reflected on solely through the self-referential lens of practitioners' own experiences, this will create a gulf between theory and practice that requires theoretical clarification and practical remedy. Herbart's (1802/2022) famous answer to this problem was "pedagogical tact," which as a "faithful" servant of "theory" (*wahrhaft gehorsamer Diener der Theorie*) and an "immediate director of our practice" (*unmittelbarer Regent der Praxis*), he claimed, is able to bridge this gulf in concrete pedagogical practice (p. 32). On this view, practice is governed not by theory but by pedagogical tact, which mediates, on a case-by-case basis, between professional knowledge and general strategies on the one hand and the concrete development needs of a given learner on the other. Based on more recent discussions, we can distinguish three aspects to this mediating role (see Müller, 2015, pp. 15–22); pedagogical tact can be understood respectively as:

1. A teaching or instructional methodological principle that requires educators, within the bounds of general theoretical prescriptions, to consider the particular features of pedagogical situations in their concrete practice;
2. A guide to action in the face of conflicting demands;
3. A self-limitation of pedagogical rationality and pedagogical goals.

The first aspect relates most directly to Herbart's distinction between theory and practice. An instructional, methodological conception is based on general considerations that must be adapted to the specific features of a given pedagogical situation in order to help the learner tackle the subject matter independently. This requires educators to operate at a distance from both their knowledge of theory and professional experience, and from their immediate impressions of the specific situation. Too strong an attachment to general conceptions (for instance, of what a lesson should be like) is just as great a hindrance as being too caught up in the concrete situation. The transformative process runs in both directions, from the universal to the particular and from the particular to the universal, and so demands that educators stray neither too close to nor too far from either pole. Structurally speaking, this is the only way to create a space where pedagogically tactful practice is possible, though by no means guaranteed. The only way to use such a space productively is through a performative process that is open to the unpredictability and indeterminacy of pedagogical situations and that is shaped by pedagogical reflectivity without being wholly dictated by it (see on this point also Parmentier, 1991). Institutional rules in the public education system and the structure of everyday familial life can accommodate pedagogically tactful practice by enabling spaces of this kind.

The second aspect of these broadly contemporary roles of tact concerns the essentially aporetic structure of the modern project of education, as alluded to earlier with the reference to Kant's question about how to cultivate "freedom under constraint." How can the educational process address a person's instinctual drives and developing powers of understanding in a way that brings the physical, sensuous side of their existence into a productive relationship with their cultural and intellectual needs, rather than being a process of simply dominating the other? Friedrich Schiller, a contemporary of Kant's, criticized the notion of a theoretically or practically "determinative" (*bestimmend*) judgment of reason in contrast to Kant's "reflective power of judgment" (*reflexiver Urteilskraft*) serving as a rigid guide to action. In his 1794 text, *On the Aesthetic Education of Man*, Schiller (2016) formulated the idea of a balance between sensuous and analytic powers as the ideal of human existence. Although this state of balance is only a utopia, it is intimated in the particular spheres of play and art. The determinative power of judgment is indispensable to tactful practice in everyday pedagogical contexts. Nonetheless, a practical and theoretical perspective could emerge out of an attempt to interpret pedagogical tact as an expression of an "inner mobility" of judgment (between determinative and reflective judgment), an interpretation which acknowledges the sensuous, embodied aspect of pedagogical practice without falling into aestheticization or mystification.

Another pedagogical aporia resides in the contradiction between the goal of education and the principle of self-development or self-formation (*Selbstbildung*). Education is a specific social practice that cannot be separated from the expectation that it be "effective" at achieving its goals. To this end, it develops models, concepts and strategies (i.e., forms) to ensure that it will in fact (at least probably) be effective (Tenorth, 2003). On the other hand, however, there is no fixed mechanism for effective pedagogical practice; it is dependent on the learners' participation and their motivations and intentions, to which educators have no direct access. A child's *Bildsamkeit* (another term Herbart introduced to modern pedagogical scholarship, meaning "educability" or "adaptiveness"), their transition from "indeterminate" to "fixed" personhood (Herbart, 1965, p. 165), is set in motion from the outside but essentially depends on the self-forming activity of the subject themselves (Mollenhauer, 2014, pp. 64–66; Benner, 2012, p. 79). The principle of "negative education" advocated by Rousseau in his 1762 treatise *Emile* (Rousseau, 1979)—whereby a child is left to discover and learn things for themselves (albeit in an environment selected or structured according to pedagogical criteria)—is one possible response to this paradox of educational practice. However, it does not eliminate the contradiction between education's own goals and the processes of self-formation. For on the one hand, it confronts the self-forming subject with a pedagogically arranged environment that pre-structures their experiences; thus, even negative education does address the subject in a certain way, with a greater or a lesser degree of tact. On the other hand, meanwhile, it cannot wholly control what the self-forming subject makes out of this experience. Any "external demand for self-activity" (*Fremdaufforderung zur Selbsttätigkeit* Benner, 2012, pp. 78–92) involves both an aspect of external imposition and an aspect of active contribution by the subject. Given the tension between these two aspects, to act tactfully requires a suitable balance between structuring a pedagogical situation and leaving it open; it also requires dialogue and a sense for the other person's responsiveness.

There is also a constant tension between two other goals of modern pedagogy. It is supposed to help a person develop their individuality while simultaneously socializing them, that is, educating them in accordance with their culture's general expectations of education. Schleiermacher (1862/2023), writing at the time when modern societal forms were first emerging, saw these as two sides to education that can only be productively reconciled in a never-ending dialectical movement. On his view, this requires that an unstable balance be struck between distance from, and closeness to, both the individual and the societal aspects of education. Educators are always agents of societal expectations of education and cultivation which must be tactfully moderated with respect to a child's individual development needs and personality.

An examination of the history of pedagogy and of its theory up to the present day will allow us to identify further paradoxes besides the three just mentioned (see Helsper, 2002; Burghardt & Zirfas, 2019, pp. 149–191). But these three already point to the need, inherent to the modern concept of education, to strike a suitable balance in pedagogical practice between a plethora of immanent contradictions in a manner responsive to the concrete situation, or at least to tactfully gloss over those contradictions so that the pedagogical interaction can be continued even if one can only hope to achieve balance further down the line (Gödde & Zirfas, 2012, p. 11; Reichenbach, 2007, pp. 179–193).

In addition to addressing the theory–practice distinction and the inherent contradictions of modern pedagogy, there is also a third aspect of pedagogical tact to be considered, namely the need to strike an external balance between pedagogical practice and intentions on the one hand and on the other, the myriad non-pedagogical goals of individual lives and of society as a whole. Children are far more than just learners or subjects of educational expectations. And they live (to an increasing degree as they get older) in societal spheres shaped by different logics of action than that of pedagogical practice. The more "person-centric" an approach pedagogy takes to children and young people, the more it subjects all their impulses and activities to a pedagogical gaze that follows a pedagogical logic, the greater the danger (even if it is done with the best of intentions) of pedagogical colonization of children's (and families') day-to-day lives. The growing sensitivity to children's development needs that has come with the increasing professionalization of pedagogy in modern times and the greater expectations society now places on education have created a tendency to strive for optimization, which reduces children (and the adults responsible for them) to subjects of pedagogical expectations. Pedagogical tact thus also requires a deliberate self-limitation of pedagogical rationality and respect for the integrity of each individual, whose personality cannot be subsumed without remainder into their role in the educational context.

Conclusion

This chapter has shown pedagogical tact to be a key concept of modern pedagogy. Tact mediates the tensions and contradictions, antinomies, and antagonisms of pedagogical practice. It specifies the relation between pedagogical reflection and embodied pedagogical practice. And it expands our view beyond a pedagogical theory of action to a sociological theory of education that allows an interpretation of pedagogical interaction in the broader context of interpersonal conduct in the public and private spheres. Just like social tact, pedagogical tact works on the insoluble fragility of social reality and the vulnerability of the person (Burghardt et al., 2017; Senkbeil, 2020). A century ago, Plessner was already keenly aware that technical, industrial society, with its impersonal, "alienated" forms of interaction, its abstract rules and its competing worldviews and systems of knowledge, has created a countervailing longing for personal intimacy and authenticity. Expressions of this longing that are inimical to society—reactionary myths of a community where people's whole selves are included (even aspects they might wish to keep private)—threaten a totalitarian disrespect for people and their privacy and individuality. Plessner's theory of the "brokenness" of human existence (rooted in his theorem of "excentric positionality"), of humans' "natural artificiality" speaks directly to these contemporary concerns. Together with his notion of humans' "mediated immediacy" and the "embodiment" of their personhood in expressive social behavior that both reveals and conceals their inner self, Plessner points to the problems of unreflectively demanding authenticity and self-transparency, closeness and immediacy—including in pedagogical contexts. Not just crude educational techniques but also excessive intrusion into a child's individual personality can do harm and result in the failure of pedagogical efforts.

Note

[1] While "social" carries connotations related to the widest range of collective phenomena (including social gatherings and socialism as ideology), "societal" refers less ambiguously to the sphere of society and its organization.

Bibliography

Benner, D. (2012). *Allgemeine Pädagogik: Eine systematisch-problemgeschichtliche Einführung in die Grundstruktur pädagogischen Denkens und Handelns* (7th ed.). Beltz Juventa.

Benner, D. (2018). Pädagogischer Takt nach Herbart: Ein Dauerthema pädagogischer Theoriediskurse, ein Faktum im Prozess pädagogischer Professionalisierung, ein Gegenstand erziehungswissenschaftlicher Forschung. In A. Gastager & J.-L. Patry (Eds.). *Pädagogischer Takt: Analysen zu Theorie und Praxis* (pp. 43–58). Leykam Buchverlagsgesellschaft.

Brumlik, M. (2015). Pädagogische Taktlosigkeit. In D. Burghardt, D. Krinninger & S. Seichter (Eds.), *Pädagogischer Takt: Theorie – Empirie – Kultur* (pp. 53–57). Ferdinand Schöningh.

Burghardt, D., Dziabel, N., Höhne, T., Dederich, M., Lohwasser, D., Stöhr, R., & Zirfas, J. (2017). *Vulnerabilität: Pädagogische Herausforderungen*. Kohlhammer.

Burghardt, D. & Zirfas, J. (2019). *Der pädagogische Takt: Eine erziehungswissenschaftliche Problemformel*. Beltz Juventa.

Claessens, D. (1979). *Familie und Wertsystem: Eine Studie zur 'zweiten, soziokulturellen Geburt' des Menschen und der Belastbarkeit der 'Kernfamilie'* (4th ed.). Dunker & Humblot.

Dewey, J. (1916/1968). *Democracy and education: An Introduction to the Philosophy of Education*. Free Press.

Elias, N. (1978). *What is sociology?* Columbia University Press.

Fischer. J. (2016). Panzer oder Maske: "Verhaltenslehre der Kälte" oder Sozialtheorie der "Grenze." In W. Eßbach, J. Fischer, & H. Lethen (eds), *Plessners "Grenzen der Gemeinschaft": Eine Debatte* (2nd ed.) (pp. 80–102). Suhrkamp.

Gödde, G., & Zirfas, J. (2012). Die Kreativität des Takts: Einblicke in eine informelle Ordnungsstruktur. In G. Gödde & J. Zirfas (Eds.), *Takt und Taktlosigkeiten: Über Ordnungen und Unordnungen in der Kunst, Kultur und Therapie* (pp. 9–29). transcript.

Helsper, W. (2002). Lehrerprofessionalität als antinomische Handlungsstruktur. In M. Kraul, W. Marotzki, & C. Schweppe (Eds.), *Biographie und Profession* (pp. 64–102). Klinkhardt.

Herbart, J. F. (1802/2022). Herbart: Introductory lecture. In N. Friesen (Ed. Trans.), *Tact and the pedagogical relation* (pp. 25–38.). Peter Lang.

Herbart, J. F. (1835/1965). Umriss pädagogischer Vorlesungen. In W. Asmus (Ed.), *Pädagogische Schriften*, vol 3. Küpper

Kant, I. (1803/2007). Lectures on pedagogy. In G. Zöller & R. B. Louden (Eds. Trans.), *Anthropology, history, and education* (pp. 434–485). Cambridge University Press.

Keller, H. (2011). *Kinderalltag: Kulturen der Kindheit und ihre Bedeutung für Bindung, Bildung und Erziehung*. Springer.

Lietz, H. (1970). *Schulreform durch Neugründung: Ausgewählte pädagogische Schriften*. Ferdinand Schöningh.

Luhmann, N., & Schorr, K.-E. (1979/2000). *Problems of reflection in the system of education*. (R. Neuwirth, Trans.). Waxmann.

Mollenhauer, K. (2014). *Forgotten Connections: On culture and upbringing*. (N. Friesen, Trans.). Routledge.

Mooney, C. G. (2010). *Theories of attachment: An introduction to Bowlby, Ainsworth, Gerber, Brazolton, Kennell and Klaus*. Redleaf Press.

Müller, H.-R. (2004). Übergänge: Bildungsbewegungen im Geflecht symbolischer Ordnungen. In G. Mattenklott & C. Rosa (Eds.), *Ästhetische Erfahrung in der Kindheit: Theoretische Grundlagen und empirische Forschung* (pp. 61–76). Juventa.

Müller, H.-R. (2015). Zur Theorie des pädagogischen Takts. In D. Burghardt, D. Krinninger, & S. Seichter (Eds.), *Pädagogischer Takt: Theorie – Empirie – Kultur* (pp. 13–24). Ferdinand Schöningh.

Müller, H.-R., and Krinninger, D. (2016). *Familienstile: Eine pädagogisch-ethnographische Studie zur Familienerziehung*. Beltz Juventa.

Nohl, H. (1933/2022). The pedagogical relation and the formative community. In N. Friesen (Ed. Trans.), *Tact and the pedagogical relation: Introductory readings* (pp. 15–24). Peter Lang.

Parmentier, M. (1991). Selbständigkeit, pädagogischer Takt und relative Autonomie. *Vierteljahrsschrift für wissenschaftliche Pädagogik*, 67, 121–135.

Parsons, T., and Bales, R. F. (1964). *Family, socialization and interaction process*. Free Press.

Pestalozzi, J.-H. (1799/2022). Letter to a friend on his work at Stans. In N. Friesen (Ed. Trans.), *Tact and the pedagogical relation: Introductory readings* (pp. 15–24). Peter Lang.

Plessner, H. (1924/1999). *The limits of community: A critique of social radicalism*. (A. Wallace, Trans.). Prometheus.

Plessner, H. (1928/2019). *Levels of organic life and the human: An introduction to philosophical anthropology*. (M. Hyatt, Trans.). Fordham University Press.

Reichenbach, R. (2007). *Pädagogische Autorität: Macht und Vertrauen in der Erziehung.* Kohlhammer.

Rousseau, J.-J. (1762/1979). *Emile or on education.* (A. Bloom, Trans.). Basic Books.

Schiller, F. (1795/2016). *On the aesthetic education of man.* Penguin.

Schleiermacher, F. D. E. (1862/2023). Outlines of the art of education. In N. Friesen & K. Kenklies (Eds. Trans.), *Outlines of the art of education: A translation & discussion* (pp. 21–86). Peter Lang.

Senkbeil, T. (2020). Die Fragilität des Takts: Eine Rekonstruktion eines flüchtigen Moments, *Vierteljahrsschrift für wissenschaftliche Pädagogik, 96,* 120–137.

Tenorth, H.-E. (2000). *Geschichte der Erziehung: Einführung in die Grundzüge ihrer neuzeitlichen Entwicklung* (3rd fully revised and expanded ed). Juventa.

Tenorth, H.-E. (2003). *Form der Bildung – Bildung der Form.* Beltz.

Pedagogical Tact and Education in the Family

Dominik Krinninger and Kaja Kesselhut

Introduction

The main focus of the classical motif of pedagogical tact is how to grasp the intertwining of theoretical reflection and practical action. On Herbart's (1802/2022) view, the "routine" of a practice left to its own devices can be captured by a theory. This would be a theory that has previously given order to situational impressions and experiences and that thus prepares the way for well-informed action. Such action is not, however, bound by rules, but rather is sensitive to the particularity of the moment. This insight—of the inadequacy of theory to pedagogical practice—is of unquestionable value for a theory of pedagogical action.[1] But the dichotomous differentiation between scientific theory and spontaneous practice places greater focus on pedagogical action whose methodological and professional quality is improved by transcending unreflected routines.

In light of its rootedness in everyday life, the family does not really seem to fit into this dichotomy. For parents certainly do not educate their children in an arbitrary fashion or as part of a hermetic, self-referential practice; nor do they do so on the basis of a systematic theory. But parents and children *do* have experience in dealing with each other, and out of this experience, they develop a deep familiarity with their shared everyday life. For the purpose of a heuristic treatment of the concept of pedagogical tact in a description of education in families,[2] we need to pose the question of whether this tact can also grow out of the experiential knowledge of the family. Embeddedness in everyday life is characteristic of pedagogical action in the family here not only in the sense that it has no structured relationship to theoretical concepts of child-raising and education, but also in the sense that in the family, actions marked both explicitly and implicitly as pedagogically relevant are always embedded in other action contexts. The family is precisely not only a pedagogical community, but also a common household with daily tasks, a community devoted to mutual care and provision, and a complex of social relationships (between the parents and among the siblings) that cannot be grasped exclusively as pedagogical constellations. When and how do parents act pedagogically in their families, then? When and how does the family as a community behave pedagogically?

In light of the specific conditionalities and practical logics of pedagogical action in the family, the "problematizing formula" (Burghardt & Zirfas, 2019) that pedagogical tact represents can help to address these questions. Precisely the ambiguity of the concept—which was meant, in Herbart's classical version, to connect the practical business of education with what was taking on the contours of a "scientific" (i.e., scholarly, philosophical) pedagogy—proves helpful here: This concept's ambiguous character is helpful also for describing the pedagogical relevance of non-professional parental and familial practices which do not take place in the context of scientific reflection proper to them. This is the aim of the present chapter, which refers to two research projects on the family and uses the motif of tact to systematize empirical findings. The first part of the text highlights current pedagogical and education policy discourses about the family in which a skeptical view of the family is apparent. In the second part—and against this view—we present a fundamental theoretical model of education in the family. Then, in the last part of the text, we outline four registers of pedagogical tact in the family. The overall aim of our theoretically grounded and empirically supported arguments is to acknowledge the importance of the family's practical knowledge, which plays an essential role in the tactful structuring of the familial order and the promotion of childhood development amidst the coexistence of generations that takes place within it.

On the Need for a Positive, Systematic Look at Education in the Family

The present chapter is not the place for an extensive analysis of the current shifts between public and private instruction. Nonetheless, the outlining of a specifically familial pedagogical tact that is undertaken here has also to be seen against the background of a tendency to the standardization of families, which is apparent in a range of phenomena and processes. These phenomena and processes include education policy's singling out of so-called *"bildungsfern"* families—literally families that are "distant," alienated, from education. However, it is in fact the distance taken by public educational institutions from families that this label indirectly expresses (Reichenbach, 2015). It invokes the focus of middle-class parents on education as decisive resource for assuring that their children lead comfortable lives and may therefore lead their parents into a "panic" if such education is jeopardized (Budde, 2011). The significant increase in the number of children and young people taken into public custody, which has risen by around 100 percent in the last 25 years (*Statistisches Bundesamt*, 2020), should also be mentioned here. The expansion of institutions for preschool-age children and the reorientation of such institutions toward education (rather than care) as a key function is also part of the same context. Finally, the elementary school level plays a role here, which, in light of the prospect of a legal claim to daycare for school-age children, is about to undergo a massive expansion in Germany.

Moreover, the policies in question by no means refer to local German peculiarities but must be considered rather in the light of global transformations in the relationship between family and state (Betz et al., 2017). Above all in English-language discourse, the notion of "intensive parenting" has become a dominant motif of modern parenthood since around the mid-1990s (Deppe, 2018). On the one hand, this is associated with a strong focus on optimization, making, for example, early cognitive stimulation of children a sort of obligation for parents. On the other hand, the prevention of potential (educational) risks plays a major role (Macvarish, 2014). According to the discourse in education policy, children have gone from being "the invisible member of the family to [being] a source of hope for society" (*Kompetenzteam Wissenschaft*, 2013). At the same time, the social demands on parenthood have become considerably denser, but not all families are placed equally "under observation" as a consequence. Instead,

> what exactly is perceived as a danger or a risk largely depends on the contexts in which they [the children] grow up, on the level of educational attainment and the status of the parents, on public discourses on risks or on governmental norms and the norms of civil society. Furthermore, social contexts are to a large degree associated with normative ascriptions: this is to say that a childhood with unemployed parents counts as a risk, not because unemployment gives rise structurally to inequality, but rather because the behavior of unemployed parents is viewed critically. (Andresen, 2018)

Even if there are unquestionably good reasons, in terms of preschool, scholastic and social pedagogy, for many of the measures taken in the contexts referenced above, and even if the concerns of parents are likewise understandable, the overall impression given is that in society's view of child raising and education, the family tends to lag behind public institutions. In light of the skepticism vis-à-vis the pedagogical qualities of the family that is evident in this discursive situation, it seems worthwhile to put forward a pedagogically appreciative perspective on the family. What is at issue here is not only the substantive need for criticism of socially dominant views, but also a practical imperative for research. Without a positive perspective on familial practices and the pedagogical possibilities that are inherent to them, research in education runs the risk of spontaneously supporting the standardizing tendencies between institutional and private educational and care practices, instead of depicting them as social norms and thus making them available for critical analysis.

In this sense, it is not only necessary to expose the public "moral panic" with respect to the family as the rhetoric that it is. It is *also* necessary to work at contrasting this rhetoric with a positive picture of what it hides, a picture that is both empirically dense and systematically differentiated and that is also appreciative. In transferring the motif of pedagogical tact to the family as part of this critical approach, we must also, finally, avoid the mistake of viewing the public discourses on the family and its educational contributions (as well as its contributions to children's health as a public good) as the functional equivalent of a theoretical basis for familial *instruction*. For the debate is not about how families can educate children, but rather, above all, about the extent to which they should do this better or differently. The related appeals to parents are highly relevant for families. But they principally correspond to practices of "displaying families" (Finch, 2007), by means of which the family displays its familial competence vis-à-vis its social environment. Pedagogical action in the family is also related to the changing cultural models of child raising—for instance, the frequently described shift from "giving orders" to "negotiating" (Ecarius, 2002) or from "negotiating" to "advising" (Ecarius, 2018)—that families encounter in their overall generational positioning in society. Because these models represent patterns of the flow of social "educational mentalities" (Göppel, 2010), they are more likely to enter into habitual background knowledge—knowledge which frames the basic tendency of familial practices—than they are to represent a standard to which reference is actually made in concrete situations. We thus have to look for other sources of knowledge when it comes to familial pedagogical tact. As suggested at the outset, in order to find these sources, we turn to the experience that family members have in dealing with one another and that the family has as a community. Nonetheless, an intermediate step is required for addressing the questions thus raised. These are questions about how and in what form parents and families develop their models of pedagogical action in dealing with one another and with their environment. These are also questions of how they use these models to relate to situational problems of action. For there is a lack of systematic modeling of education in the family, of its conditions of possibility and scope of action, all of which could be used as theoretical frame in this context.[3]

The following reflections do not claim to meet the need for an updated theory of education in the family. Within the framework of this chapter, they serve to outline a basic motif of familial instruction in order to then establish the contours of a specifically familial logic of tact based on this motif. The related demarcations of the object of study are guided by concepts of theories of practices (e.g., as derived from sociologist Karl Mannheim), which allow us to include the social conditioning of what goes on in the family as well as the important dimension of family sociality. It is not only individuals who act in the family; the familial community as constellations of actors engaging with specific practice has also to be taken into account. This community is only sometimes the result of explicit intentionality, while it is embedded in overarching familial practices and their heterogeneous contexts. Taken together, this represents the essential characteristics of pedagogical action in the family. These moments of complexity in the family—i.e., its social prefiguration, the intertwining of individuality and sociality, and the overlapping practices—will be covered in a practice-theoretical model in what follows.

Education in the Family as Practical Reflexivity

The differential structure of the family represents a fundamental condition of possibility of education in the family. Grasping the family as a heterogeneously structured community provides a counterpoint to an influential social scientific view of the family as an agent of reproduction of social relations. Bourdieu can be regarded as the most prominent representative of such a view. Although it is never made a direct object of investigation, the family occupies a central place in his studies of the "physics" of social space. The effect of binding individuals to their origins that Bourdieu attributes to the family has to be seen against the background of a unifying or collectivizing picture in which the family appears as "the main 'subject' of reproduction strategies" (Bourdieu, 1998, p. 69). In this context, which remains highly influential today, the family appears as an accomplice of social relations and not as an actor constellation that is capable of critically reflecting on its members' and its own relationship to society. By contrast, the systematic-pedagogical perspective should try to reveal the family as the space and constellation of differentiation that it is precisely capable of this critical reflection (Müller, 2007). Even if, above all, homologies become visible when using a wide sociological focus, the family is thus always shaped by cultural differences resulting from the cultural origins of the parents, which never entirely coincide. Moreover, the family has to cope with a fundamental dialectic resulting from the fact that it is, on the one hand, a community of care and that on the other hand, it functions as an institution and mediates social recognition. These social logics are not mutually exclusive and neither takes precedence over the other (say, in the sense that the production of social norms gradually gets superimposed on a primordial, pure parental love). However, they cannot be easily or readily harmonized (Krinninger, 2015). And, finally, the developmental differences in the family as an intergenerational community have also to be taken into account. For even if the family were only about the transmission of cultural ways of life, the cultural contents that are imparted to the children are at first new for them, so that they cannot be regarded as self-evident, but rather require a targeted process of learning. As a result of this differential structure, families have to rework their order repeatedly, and this reworking cannot only be expected, say, once the family has sufficient economic resources or education (however "sufficient" is defined here).

A further structural moment of the family is decisive for theoretically modeling education in the family. What goes on in the family, what the members of the family do and how they relate to one another is embedded in overlapping contexts. As touched upon at the outset, at the very least the contexts of providing for the family, of running the household, and of family relationships play a role, whether directly or indirectly, in all family processes. This pragmatic interweaving of familial practices also pervades the pedagogical relations in the family. This suggests not principally looking for distinct or "pure" pedagogical forms of action and intentions when conducting a pedagogical analysis of the family but focusing rather on the everyday intertwining of routines and intentionality. In this context, intentionality should not be understood as limited to the rationality of a sovereign subject, but rather as also inherent to the performance and the materiality of practices (on the spectrum of pedagogical intentionality, see also Nohl, 2018). Theoretical guidance in this respect is to be found in Reckwitz (2003) and Alkemeyer (2013), who point to aspects that are also of significance for education in their discussions of the process of subject formation that takes place in social practices. On the one hand, Alkemeyer notes that successfully taking part in practices requires a certain "participation competence" (Alkemeyer, 2013, p. 59) which subjects not only integrate into an existing practice, but rather, at the same time, that puts them in a position " ... to help shape the course taken by the practice in an intentional and reflexive manner or to comment upon it critically" (p. 59). On the other hand, he underscores a specific type of practice, which aims at making "dispositions ... available" (p.60) and hence relates reflexively to those practices in which the dispositions in question are relevant. The two moments of the practical-guiding competencies (which are formed in participating in a practice) and of an explicitly reflexive relationship between social practices (which structures explicit pedagogies) can be brought together in a motif that helps to increase awareness of and make visible the pedagogical character of familial practices. This motif of practical reflexivity is not, in the first instance, directed toward explicitly communicative forms of knowledge in which such a relationship is produced. It also draws attention to practical knowledge about practices, which is formed by taking part in them and which can, as it were, *en passant* make these practices thematic in the very course of their performance. In this way—without having to be restricted to actions that are explicitly marked as, say, correctives or admonishments—pedagogical relevance of familial practices can be uncovered. This relevance is attributed to them in as much as they can reflexively relate both to themselves and to the world that is made an object in them. This point is of decisive importance for a perspective in educational theory that is based on theories of practice. It is only the possibility of theories referring—whether explicitly or implicitly—to practices that creates a scope for pedagogy. In this approach, a pedagogical analysis of family practices looks at forms of practical reflexivity in the coexistence of the different generations. Our view of education in the family is thus broadened, beyond interactions in parent-child constellations corresponding to the classical image of a pedagogical relationship and beyond an explicit mode of instruction, to include the pedagogical content of practices that are carried out in the family as a community of action. At the same time, this approach is distinguished from the perspective of theory of socialization inasmuch as it looks for a specific form of participation in familial practices and not just mere participation in the practices as such.

This pedagogical emphasis is thus based on a broadened spectrum of reflexivity, which stretches between the pole of practical knowledge inherent in social practices in their corporeality, and that of relatively stable trans-situational structures of order, which also draw on discursive forms of knowledge. In terms of practically embodied knowledge, reference to practice-theoretical positions that reveal the openness of the body to a social meaningfulness of physical actions can help us to progress further. Thus, Schatzki writes:

> By way of the body, mind is present in experience. Bodily doings and sayings are the realities in which psychological conditions consist in particular circumstances. This does not, however, reduce life conditions to bodily activities. Bodily activities are simply what there is in the (experiential) world to such conditions. The conditions themselves maintain, so to speak, a notional existence beyond the phenomenal expressing them. (Schatzki, 1996, p. 41)

In his conception of corporeally situated "life conditions," Schatzki describes the body in its fundamental significance for a personal existence, and, at the same time, he depicts it as capable of experience: "That life conditions are so ascribable means that both behavioral and inner bodily episodes are, too. To be a body, consequently, is to be able both to perform bodily doings and sayings and to experience bodily sensations and feelings" (Schatzki, 1996, p. 43). In this view, the human body is tightly linked to the materiality of the social, without, however, entirely merging into it. In Schatzki and his attentiveness to the moment of experience, we are thus following a somewhat "mild" rather than a radical variant of materialist thinking. In doing so, we join his argumentation, which he also gains by recourse to conceptualizations of sociomateriality in social-geographical studies: "Materiality ... cannot be separated from the experience of (material phenomena) nor from the meaning we attach to the experiences of (them)" (Steinberg & Peters, 2015, p. 256; adapted from Schatzki, 2019, p. 52).

Whereas practice-theoretical considerations of this sort allow us to uncover the meaningfulness of individual practical actions in everyday family life, it is important to grasp reflexivity in the family not only on the practical level, but also on the discursive one (Krinninger & Müller, 2020). This applies especially to the concepts and discourses or—to employ Appadurai's expression—the pedagogical "ideoscapes" in the family's surroundings. This level of reflexivity is based on the fact that familial actors—regardless of their socio-cultural situation—are not "judgmental dopes" (Garfinkel), but rather reflect on their family life and, to some extent, always also shape it in accordance with conceptual considerations. In light of the fact that families are embedded in a dense network of pedagogical institutional contexts, Dencik (1989) outlines a model of "dual socialization." In so doing, he opposes the idea that the family—even just at the beginning of socialization processes—has an autonomous, primordial function. It is, from the very start, inserted into institutional relationships. Reflexivity in the family thus also relates to how families develop their respective pedagogical order in their socio-ecological embedding in pedagogical institutional contexts. Griesemer and Star (2017) serve as a further useful reference here. They demarcate a concept of the ecological that focuses on processes of transformation of relations between social worlds by actors respective to each. If we transfer this view to the family, it becomes clear that the constitution of a pedagogical order in the family is not an exclusively intra-familial process. Rather, it is woven into a web of pedagogical orders that is constantly being established between the family and the pedagogical institutions in its social environment. The family as pedagogical space thus also acquires its form in adapting to the expectations addressed to it from the institutional side. Its reflexivity, moreover, is also apparent in a related familial "translation work" (Krinninger, 2020).

Registers of Pedagogical Tact in Families

On the basis of the foregoing theoretical reflections on the object of our inquiry and drawing on observations from two research projects, different varieties of a familial pedagogical tact will be presented in this section. The first research project looked at forms of instruction and educational potential in everyday family life.[4] Family scenes from the everyday life of eight families, as well as their own descriptions of familial events and family history, were documented by way of videographies, interviews, and photographic self-documentation. In assembling the material, special attention was given to the domains of playing, watching television, and family meals. These domains were not only chosen because it could be assumed that they play a role in almost all families, but also because they are not marked as pedagogical per se and allow for both intra- and intergenerational constellations. The second research project dealt with children's transition to elementary school.[5] Using 12 families as a sample, this study represents a qualitative-empirical study of how the community of parents and children actors handles the child's transition in their everyday lives. The project thus overcomes the "hyper-focus on parents" (Waterstradt, 2015) that often predominates in research on the family. It addressed the question of how the challenges involved in starting school are taken up, both in familial intergenerational relationships and in familial practices, and that of the role assigned to the children as actors in this connection. By adopting this broader perspective, the project tried resolutely to avoid the "normative narrowness" (Müller, 2007, p. 143) that "essentially [measures] the quality of the *good family* by how capable it is of producing a child who is educated and an achiever" (Andresen, 2012, p. 78, emphasis in the original). Both projects involved families that had at least one preschool-aged child in order to ensure that they were in comparable phases or that the transition to elementary school was imminent. Access to the families was obtained by way of kindergartens that the children attended and the participating families were recruited through a combination of two strategies. The pedagogical staff, functioning as "gatekeepers" (Merkens, 1997), put families in contact with the research team; at the same time, families were addressed by flyers and notices posted in the kindergartens, which invited them to take the initiative themselves. The assembled material shows how families deal with their specific conditions in socio-structural, cultural, and family-biographical terms—among other things. The practice-theoretical perspectives sketched out above and the observed familial practices converge in several registers, which emerge in different empirical contexts and with respect to which the families exhibit tact.

Connoisseurship and Fingerzeige

The family can be regarded as a paradigmatic constellation of an experiential space. Karl Mannheim's sociology of knowledge distinguishes between communicative (explicit, discursive, and secondary) knowledge and conjunctive (implicit, enacted, and "primordial") knowledge.[6] But we also find allusions in his work to a referential function that enables a degree of communicability of this knowledge among the members of an experiential community. According to Mannheim (1982), the common, enacted, or practical understanding that develops in an experiential space can also coalesce into a particular "connoisseurship" (p. 216):

> By "connoisseur" we mean a person who can take his experiential knowledge that relates to qualitative features, that is specialized and intensively concentrated upon a single field, and make it evident to a circle of individuals who are associated with him through a specific experiential community, directed toward the same subject-matter-field and bound by tradition. Making such knowledge evident may succeed through bare indications, unarticulated gestures, the merest hints. (Mannheim, 1982, p. 216)

What is rendered here as "merest hints" in the English translation of Mannheim's text is in fact *Fingerzeige* in the German original, suggesting physical "hints" such as a slight raising of the index finger. The basis for making experiential knowledge evident to others is "a capacity for intuition, which has been specifically formed and cultivated and which is present in all members of the experiential community" (Mannheim, 1982, p. 216). Such connoisseurship and its communicability address dimensions of the familial experiential space in which reflexive and regulatory references to familial practices by family actors are made possible by these forms of practice themselves. Even if it is not communicated as explicitly and discursively available knowledge, the practical knowledge of familial actors does not stay mute and anonymous as a consequence. More specifically, gestural commenting on the action can become insistent, but also mimetic structurings of action sequences serve as signposts for subsequent physical movements. Families know their routines, they know about the idiosyncratic peculiarities of their members, and they are well-versed in a form of interaction with each other that develops within the framework of each family's unique style. These things do not have to be made explicit; they are undertaken and taken into consideration in the family's joint action. But when there are disruptions—or disruptions are expected—the *"Fingerzeige"* serves as an important tool. Thus, in one family, the research project on "Family as a Cultural Milieu of Instruction" was able to observe a recurring and, for the family's style, significant look of a mother of four children. It was used, for instance, for the three youngest children during the complicated process of eating porridge and for regulate the actions and interactions of the five-year-old daughter and the eight-year-old son while the 10-month-old baby was being fed. In this respect, tact appears as a feeling for possible conflicts between the functionality of the familial practice and countervailing impulses of individual actors. It is important here that in the medium of the attention-directing *"Fingerzeig,"* the practice does not have to be abandoned or interrupted for the purpose of shifting to a different mode—say, to that of explanation or admonition.

Drawing and Dissolving Boundaries

One of the key categories that was elaborated in the above-mentioned project is that of the family's "educational configuration." This category relates to the social, economic, and cultural framework conditions in which the family is situated, but at the same time, it also asks about the specific familial order into which these conditions are brought by the family. In developing its categories, the project has recourse to the figurational concept of Norbert Elias.[7] Elias tries to grasp the relationship between individuals and society in a way that avoids a dichotomous opposing of the individual and society, and instead stresses the constitutive interdependencies that connect them to each other. He looks at both the subjects' activity in shaping social relations and at the power of the existing relations to affect the actors. By using Elias' figurational concept, we can avoid drawing rigid boundaries between family and society. The family can also be reconstructed as a social (con-)figuration, which is connected in turn to other social figurations like the working world and the educational system or the residential environment and the neighborhood. A modeling of the family as an educational configuration can thus incorporate both the conditioning of the family by social relations and the active participation of the family in shaping its situation. The specific form of the relationships between the external social world and the family's inner world is one dimension in which these connections are concretized in the family. The aforementioned shifts between public and private instruction represent an important development, providing a background against which it becomes relevant to look at how scholastic and familial instruction intertwine. But neighborhood networks and networks of friends also play a role here, as does a family's integration into a church community. Besides the specific forms of participation in the social environment, the shaping of the family's inner world is also an area in which the relationship of the family to its environment is thematized. Here, the internal family milieu can be structured more in the spirit of openness to social demands and contents or in the spirit of a familial appropriation or transformation of these demands and contents. These alternatives become particularly apparent, for instance, in how families deal with media. In the research project on "family styles," almost all of the families we studied had developed rules for their children's screen time. Nonetheless, television-watching practices proved to be very different from one family to another. The spectrum ranges from the 5-year-old watching television alone in the living room, while the mother cooks in the kitchen, to the organization of television-watching as a communal event for the whole family, followed by discussion with the 9-year-old daughter to reflect on the children's news she has just seen. Pedagogical tact is not principally directed here toward direct regulation of children's behavior; rather, it becomes apparent in a family-specific sense of what constitutes a suitable environment for childhood development in both material terms and in terms of content.

Is and Ought

The family is a complex form of life which requires reconciling many different things. The coexistence of two (or more) generations brings together needs and interests that are not always compatible, and the same is true between parents and among siblings. Moreover, the organization of the family's everyday life also poses recurrent problems that families have to cope with continuously. Finally, society's demands—like running the household, providing for the family materially, cultivating family relationships and, last but not least, the parent's pedagogical program—create calls to action, which, overall and in their paradoxical relation to one another, cannot always be entirely satisfied. Consequently, as Michael Winkler (2012) points out, the phrase "but we still have to" (*wir müssen aber noch*), designates a key solution for families that, for structural reasons, can hardly ever completely achieve what they ought to. Susanne Weinert Portmann has developed an idea that is related to this. She describes the family as a "mythical form of life" (Weinert, 2009), since, in light of the latent proneness to crisis that is structurally inherent to families, it is crucial for them to maintain an ordering narrative—a stabilizing conception of themselves. In one of the families studied, we were able to document a pronounced discourse on rules in this connection. Who has to do or not do what, who is allowed to do what—these were key questions in the family discussions. Tellingly, the rules—like, for instance, either "stop it or go to bed"—were only applied in attenuated form, if at all. Talking about the rules was much more important. It was by talking about them, and thus constructing a symbolic dimension, that the family of seven captured the complexity of its everyday life. Tact is manifest here as a pragmatic, but not arbitrary tolerance of the difference between familial aspirations and familial reality.

Interpellation and Translation

In another research project, we examined how the relationship between the public and the private order gets reconstituted in the course of the child's transition from the family to elementary school. In the view of education policy, the contours of this relationship are clear: Under the heading of "educational partnership" (Dusolt, 2018), policy has been calling for almost 30 years for a close alliance been home and school. Among other things, communication between the two spheres has been conceived as dialogical and as focusing on agreement regarding educational goals. Per the main thesis of the program, there has been a general consensus supporting the success of the program (Betz, 2015). From the perspective of the social sciences, an "intensifying of appeals to parents" (Jergus et al., 2018, p. 6) can generally be noted. As "educational coaches" (Lange et al., 2018), parents are given considerable responsibility for translating and securing scholastic interests in the family environment. "Good parents" are thus "resources for and arrangers of the development and education of their children" (Betz, 2013, p. 78).

In the model we developed on how the family handles the transition to elementary school, we are able to show that families are continually performing translation work. The concept of translation points beyond the idea of a mere mediation between heterogeneous entities (Cappai et al., 2010). It draws attention to the question of how orders of knowledge are imparted and raises our awareness of the fact that the privileging or selection of particular stocks of knowledge is the subject of strenuous negotiations (Engel, 2019). Consequently, the intra-familial space is also an arena of strenuous translation activity in which agreement has to be reached about what proves functional, allowing it to be translated and integrated into the existing order. We were able empirically to observe how conflictual situations arise when parents attempt to translate the educational goals of the school "literally": for example, by insisting on the correct execution of a writing exercise and keeping the child at their desk, even by physical means (hugging the child tightly). In short, appealing to parents as "assistant teachers" and proxies for fulfilling public interests creates a pedagogical dilemma for them: unconditional solidarity with the norms of the school (disciplined work) abrogates the child's claim to autonomy (and, as suggested, also to physical integrity).

There is no getting around a broader, social, educational discursive appeal to the family. There is also no denying the heterogeneous and sometimes irreconcilable demands on the family that are associated with it. But in some families, we were able to observe a somewhat freer translation: i.e., a tendency to deal with the demands in a playful manner. With a wink, one father told us how they let their son, who was yearning for vacation and complaining about a "tummy ache," skip school one day; during a remote lesson, another mother prompts her son, who had obviously not done his exercises, with the correct answers from off-camera—with both being clearly amused by the ruse; or there is another child's objection that he does not want to read his bedtime story himself, since otherwise he will be better than his classmates, is something that is laconically accepted by his mother as a "good argument."

What is striking about these situations is that they are handled without any moralizing commentary on the part of the parents ("in fact it's not all right," ... etc.). It appears at first glance that parental educational goals have been renounced and that the recognition of scholastic interests has likewise been abandoned in favor of intra-familial solidarity. But this is not the case. The humorous touches serve as an important practical-reflexive tool of differentiation: on closer inspection, the parents turn out, namely, to be only "quasi-accomplices" of the child. Pedagogical tact is expressed, firstly, through the fact that the parents enable the child not only to save face vis-à-vis the school, but also to avoid having to put up with any further humiliation on account of displeased parents who only *nolens volens* share responsibility for their child's misbehavior. Secondly, by playing along and pretending, parents succeed in granting provisional justification to children's countervailing goals of private withdrawal, support, or social membership. And they do this without having to completely reject the legitimacy of the school's demands for performance, autonomy or competitiveness—a rejection that would again bring them into conflict with the appeals to be "good parents."

Conclusion

The registers outlined above make it clear that the motif of tact can also be used to grasp pedagogical action in a non-professional context. Pedagogical tact in families becomes visible here as practical knowledge that preserves the functionality of the family as a pedagogical setting and is related to ideas, attitudes, and intentions of the parents, the children and the family as a community. This "knowledge" is not made effective, however, as a reflexivity that is explicitly distanced from the situation. Instead, it comes to bear in the reflexive-practical treatment of everyday familial life and the familial order particular to each family. The fact that this tact "lacks" theoretical underpinning is not so much a problem for everyday family life, but rather plays a role in the systematic-pedagogical appreciation of education in the family. In grasping the primordial, practical-reflexive potential of the family, an updated theory of family instruction could make an important contribution to debates about the family by finding a third way between "moral panic" and social naiveté. To this end, such a third way would have to actively resist an overhasty application of dominant social policy perspectives. This is a matter that itself requires tact: the existing methodological tools for capturing practical, situated knowledge have to be refined if we are to uncover practical, pedagogical knowledge from a scientific or rigorous, scholarly perspective; at the same time, doing this demands a research approach that is conscious of its own field constructions and is constantly reflecting on its own limits. This would appear especially important with regard to complex constellations that have diffuse boundaries—such as the family—in order for us to be able to recognize what is pedagogical in them and how it is conditioned. But from this perspective, reconstructing or deconstructing orders would be insufficient for a systematic pedagogy of family education. Such a pedagogy should also demonstrate how actors in these orders can and do act and, in this sense, it should work to describe the conditions of possibility, scope, and forms of education as social practice.

The question of the tactfulness of action within the framework of this practice is a key aspect which can turn such a description into a pedagogical description.

Notes

[1] After a prolonged period in which the category of pedagogical tact was rarely the subject of extensive debates, it has recently been taken up again (see Muth, 1962/2022; Suzuki, 2010; Gödde & Zirfas, 2012; Burghardt et al., 2015; Burghardt & Zirfas, 2019).

[2] We remind readers that education and pedagogy in German are both understood as applying to familial and other social contexts outside of the school. As a result, the German word for education, *Erziehung*, is sometimes translated here as "upbringing."

[3] On the need for such modeling, see Müller and Krinninger (2015).

[4] The project ("Family as a Cultural Milieu of Education") ran from 2008 to 2012 and was led by Hans-Rüdiger Müller and Dominik Krinninger of the University of Osnabrück. It was funded by the German Research Foundation (DFG). The project has given rise to several publications (e.g., Krinninger & Müller, 2012; Müller & Krinninger, 2014; Müller & Krinninger, 2016).

[5] The "Shaping the Transition to Elementary School within the family" project was funded by the German Research Foundation (DFG) from 09/2014 to 01/2018. The project was led by Dominik Krinninger; Kaja Kesselhut and Richard Sandig were the other members of the research team.

[6] This distinction underlies Mannheim's "praxeological sociology of knowledge," and serves as the basis for the documentary method, which seeks to reconstruct or make explicit primordial, implicit, conjunctive knowledge.

[7] See Elias, N. (1991). *The society of individuals*. Continuum; Elias, N. (1992). Figuration. In B. Schäfers (Ed.), *Grundbegriffe der Soziologie* (pp. 88–91). Springer VS; Elias, N. (1984). *What is sociology?* Columbia University Press.

Bibliography

Alkemeyer, T. (2013). Subjektivierung in sozialen Praktiken. In T. Alkemeyer, G. Budde, & D. Freist (Eds.), *Selbstbildungen. Soziale und kulturelle Praktiken der Subjektivierung* (pp. 33–68). transcript.

Andresen, S. (2012). Die "gute Familie." Zur Herstellung von Familienbildern. In C. Aubry, M. Geiss, V. Magyar-Haas, & D. Miller (Eds.), *Positionierungen. Zum Verhältnis von Wissenschaft, Pädagogik und Politik* (pp. 66–79). Beltz Juventa.

Andresen, S. (2018). Kindheit. In K. Böllert (Ed.), *Kompendium Kinder- und Jugendhilfe* (pp. 365–379). Springer.

Appadurai, A. (1996). *Modernity at large: Cultural dimensions of globalization*. University of Minnesota Press.

Betz, T., de Moll, F., & Bischoff, S. (2013). Gute Eltern—schlechte Eltern. Politische Konstruktionen von Elternschaft. In L. Correll & J. Lepperhoff (Eds.), *Frühe Bildung in der Familie. Perspektiven der Familienbildung* (pp. 69–80). Beltz Juventa.

Betz, T., Honig, M.-S., & Ostner, I. (Eds.) (2017). *Parents in the spotlight. Parenting practices and support from a comparative perspective*. Barbara Budrich.

Betz, T. (2015). *Das Ideal der Bildungs- und Erziehungspartnerschaft*. Verlag Bertelsmann Stiftung.

Bourdieu, P. (1998). The family spirit. In P. Bourdieu (Ed.), (R. Johnson, Trans.), *Practical reason: On the theory of action* (pp. 64–74). Stanford University Press.

Bude, H. (2011). *Bildungspanik: Was unsere Gesellschaft spaltet*. Bundeszentrale für politische Bildung.

Burghardt, D., Krinninger, D., & Seichter, S. (Eds.) (2015). *Pädagogischer Takt: Theorie – Empirie – Kultur*. Ferdinand Schöningh.

Burghardt, D., & Zirfas, J. (2019). *Der pädagogische Takt: Eine erziehungswissenschaftliche Problemformel*. Beltz Juventa.

Cappai, G., Shimanda, S., & Straub, J. (Eds.), (2010). *Interpretative Sozialforschung und Kulturanalyse: Hermeneutik und die komparative Analyse kulturellen Handelns*. transcript.

Correll, L., & Lepperhoff, J. (Eds.). (2013). *Frühe Bildung in der Familie: Perspektiven der Familienbildung*. Beltz Juventa.

Dencik, L. (1989). Growing up in the post-modern age: On the child's situation in the modern family, and on the position of the family in the modern welfare state. *Acta Sociologica, 32*(2), 155–180.

Deppe, U. (2018). Stichwort "Parenthood." In K. Jergus, J. O. Krüger, & A. Roch (Eds.), *Elternschaft zwischen Projekt und Projektion: Aktuelle Perspektiven der Elternforschung* (pp. 237–254). Springer VS.

Diehm, I. (2018). Frühkindliche Bildung—frühkindliche Förderung: Verheißungen, Verstrickungen und Verpflichtungen. In C. Thon, M. Menz, M. Mai, & L. Abdessadok (Eds.), *Kindheiten zwischen Familie und Kindertagesstätte: Differenzdiskurse und Positionierungen von Eltern und pädagogischen Fachkräften* (pp. 11–23). Springer VS.

Dusolt, H. (2018). *Elternarbeit als Erziehungspartnerschaft: Ein Leitfaden für den Vor- und Grundschulbereich*. Beltz Juventa.

Ecarius, J. (2002). *Familienerziehung im historischen Wandel: Eine qualitative Studie über Erziehung und Erziehungserfahrungen von drei Generationen*. Springer VS.

Ecarius, J. (2018). Vom Verhandlungs- zum Beratungshaushalt: Familie in der Spätmoderne und verantwortete Elternschaft. In O. Kapella, N. F. Schneider, & H. Rost (Eds.), *Familie—Bildung—Migration: Familienforschung im Spannungsfeld zwischen Wissenschaft, Politik und Praxis. Tagungsband zum 5. Europäischen Fachkongress Familienforschung* (pp. 139–153). Barbara Budrich.

Elias, N. (1991). *The society of individuals*. Continuum.

Elias, N. (1992). Figuration. In B. Schäfers (Ed.), *Grundbegriffe der Soziologie* (pp. 88–91). Springer VS.

Elias, N. (1984). *What is sociology?* (S. Mennell & G. Morrissey, Trans.), Columbia University Press.

Engel, N. (2019). Übersetzungskonflikte: Zu einer kritisch-kulturwissenschaftlichen Pädagogik. *Zeitschrift für Pädagogik, 65*(5), 730–747.

Faircloth, C. (2014). Intensive parenting and the expansion of parenting. In E. Lee, J. Bristow, C. Faircloth, & J. Macvarish (Eds.), *Parenting culture studies* (pp. 25–50). Springer VS.

Finch, J. (2007). Displaying families. *Sociology, 41*(1), 65–81.

Garfinkel, H. (1967). *Studies in ethnomethodology*. Prentice-Hall.

Gödde, G., & Zirfas, J. (Eds.). (2012). *Takt und Taktlosigkeit: Über Ordnungen und Unordnungen in Kunst, Kultur und Therapie*. transcript.

Göppel, R. (2010). *Pädagogik und Zeitgeist: Erziehungsmentalitäten und Erziehungsdiskurse im Wandel*. Kohlhammer.

Griesemer, J. R., & Star, S. L. (2017). Institutionelle Ökologie, "Übersetzungen" und Grenzobjekte: Amateure und Professionelle im Museum of Vertebrate Zoology in Berkeley, 1907–39. In S. Grießmann & N. Taha (Eds.), *Susan Leigh Star: Grenzobjekte und Medienforschung* (pp. 81–116). transcript.

Herbart, J. F. (1802/2022). Introductory lecture to students in pedagogy. In N. Friesen (Ed. Trans.), *Tact and the pedagogical relation: Introductory reading* (pp. 28–37). Peter Lang.

Jergus, K., Krüger, J. O., & Roch, A. (2018). Elternschaft zwischen Projekt und Projektion: Einleitung in den Band. In K. Jergus, J. O. Krüger, & A. Roch (Eds.), *Elternschaft zwischen Projekt und Projektion: Aktuelle Perspektiven der Elternforschung* (pp. 1–20). Springer VS.

Krinninger, D., & Müller, H.-R. (2012). Die Bildung der Familie: Zwischenergebnisse aus einem ethnographischen Forschungsprojekt. *Zeitschrift für Soziologie der Erziehung und Sozialisation, 32*(3), 233–249.

Krinninger, D., & Müller, H.-R. (2020). Familienerziehung als reflexive soziale Praxis. In A.-M. Nohl (Ed.), *Rekonstruktive Erziehungsforschung* (pp. 167–182). Springer.

Krinninger, D. (2015). Familiale Anerkennung diesseits und jenseits des Äquivalenzprinzips: Zur Pädagogizität der Familie aus einer Perspektive des Ökonomischen. In J. Bilstein & J. Zirfas (Eds.), *Geben und Nehmen: Sozialökonomische Zugänge der Pädagogischen Anthropologie* (pp. 68–81). Beltz Juventa.

Krinninger, D. (2020). Praktische Reflexivität und Übersetzungsarbeit: Zur Erziehung in der Familie. *Sozialer Sinn, 21*(2), 289–310.

Lange, A., & Thiessen, B. (2018). Eltern als Bildungscoaches? Kritische Anmerkungen aus intersektionalen Perspektiven. In K. Jergus, J. O. Krüger, & A. Roch (Eds.), *Elternschaft zwischen Projekt und Projektion: Aktuelle Perspektiven der Elternforschung* (pp. 273–293). Springer.

Macvarish, J., Lee, E., Bristow, J., & Faircloth, C. (Eds.). (2014). *Parenting culture studies*. Springer.

Mannheim, K. (1982). *Structures of thinking*. Routledge.

Merkens, H. (1997). Stichproben bei qualitativen Studien. In B. Friebertshäuser & A. Prengel (Eds.), *Handbuch qualitative Forschungsmethoden in der Erziehungswissenschaft* (pp. 97–106). Juventa.

Müller, H.-R., & Krinninger, D. (2015). Familie als Bildungskonfiguration: Theoretische und methodologische Aspekte eines erziehungswissenschaftlich begründeten Forschungszugangs. In D. Edelmann, A. König, & U. Stenger (Eds.), *Erziehungswissenschaftliche Perspektiven in frühpädagogischer Theoriebildung und Forschung* (pp. 203–220). Beltz Juventa.

Müller, H.-R., & Krinninger, D. (2014). Theorie gestalten: Auf dem Weg zu einer empirisch gestützten Bildungstheorie. In N. Engel, M. Göhlich, I. Miethe, S. Reh, & A. Tervooren (Eds.), *Ethnographie und Differenz in pädagogischen Feldern: Internationale Entwicklungen erziehungswissenschaftlicher Forschung* (pp. 63–78). transcript.

Müller, H.-R., & Krinninger, D. (2016). *Familienstile: Eine pädagogisch-ethnographische Studie zur Familienerziehung*. Beltz Juventa.

Müller, H.-R. (2007). Differenz und Differenzbearbeitung in familialen Erziehungsmilieus: Eine pädagogische Problemskizze. *ZSE: Zeitschrift für Soziologie der Erziehung und Sozialisation, 27*(2), 143–159.

Muth, J. (1962/2022). Pedagogical tact: Study of a contemporary form of educational and instructional engagement (selections). In N. Friesen (Ed. Trans.), *Tact and the pedagogical relation: Introductory readings* (pp. 85–117). Peter Lang.

Nohl, A. M. (2018). Zur intentionalen Struktur des Erziehens: Eine praxeologische Perspektive. *Zeitschrift für Pädagogik, 64*(1), 121–138.

Reckwitz, A. (2003). Grundelemente einer Theorie sozialer Praktiken: Eine sozialtheoretische Perspektive. *Zeitschrift für Soziologie, 32*(4), 282–301.

Reichenbach, R. (2015). Über Bildungsferne. *Deutsche Zeitschrift für europäisches Denken, 69*(1), 5–15.

Richter, M., & Andresen, S. (Eds.). (2012). *The politicization of parenthood: Shifting private and public responsibilities in education and child rearing*. Springer.

Schatzki, T. R. (1996). *Social practices: A Wittgensteinian approach to human activity and the social*. Cambridge University Press.

Schatzki, T. R. (2019). *Social change in a material world*. Routledge.

Statistisches Bundesamt Wiesbaden. (2020). Schutzmaßnahmen für Kinder und Jugendliche ab 1995 nach Art der Maßnahme. <https://www.destatis.de/DE/Themen/Gesellschaft-Umwelt/Soziales/Kinderschutz/Tabellen/schutzmassnahmen.html>

Steinberg, P., & Peters, K. (2015). Wet ontologies, fluid spaces: Giving depth to volume through oceanic thinking. *Environment and Planning D: Society and Space, 33*(2), 247–264. <https://doi.org/10.1177/0263775814560148>

Suzuki, S. (2010). *Takt in modern education*. Waxmann.

Waterstradt, D. (2015). *Prozess-Soziologie der Elternschaft: Nationsbildung, Figurationsideale und generative Machtarchitektur in Deutschland*. Monsenstein und Vannerdat.

Weinert Portmann, S. (2009). *Familie—ein Symbol der Kultur: Perspektiven sozialpädagogischer Arbeit mit Familien*. Springer VS.

Winkler, M. (2012). *Erziehung in der Familie: Innenansichten des pädagogischen Alltags*. Kohlhammer.

PART IV

Embodiment and Tact

Antinomies and Aporias: The Reciprocal Ambivalence of Tact and the Body

Norm Friesen

That education is a field constituted by oppositions, paradoxes, and tensions has its origin in Socrates' maieutic. It extends through the Scholastic *disputatio* and is still manifest in today's debate clubs and oral defenses. This chapter begins by describing ways of thinking of educational theory and practice in terms of opposites, paradoxes, and the tensions between them, looking at both traditional and contemporary sources. It then turns to a broadly aporetic understanding of the lived body as articulated in the phenomenological tradition, based largely on Merleau-Ponty's *The Visible and the Invisible* (1968). By highlighting the similarity of these two accounts, this chapter then defines and describes pedagogical tact specifically as the embodied negotiation of pedagogical antinomies. In this way, it highlights the indispensable role of the body as both an expressive and receptive presence in pedagogical engagement.

The Antinomies of Pedagogy

It may initially sound strange to think of possibilities for educational theory and practice as bound by antinomies, paradoxes, tensions, and double binds. To see education in this way is no longer to regard it as germane either to the gradual amelioration promised by progressive education or to claims of functional optimization offered by psychology.[1] It is instead to direct one's attention to certain challenges and choices that arise every day in being with children, for example: Balancing children's freedom with protective constraint; recognizing a child's individuality *and* their place in a family or classroom; helping with a task but not simply "taking it over" as one's own; or negotiating the subtle differences between being a teacher on the one hand and a friend on the other (see Friesen & Su, 2023). All of these situations involve a tactful balancing act between opposed possibilities, between freedom and constraint, individuality and collectivity, dependence and independence, a professional distance and the proximity of friendship. They all involve questions of *pedagogical tact*. This is the case whether this tact is defined as "a link intermediate between theory and practice" that "becomes the immediate director of our practice" (Herbart, 1802/2022, p. 34) or seen as a kind of "pedagogical professionalism… the subjective ability and willingness to tactfully balance pedagogical paradoxes" (Zirfas, 2012/2022, p. 192). The first definition locates tact within the opposition of theory and practice—suggesting it is a matter of a balance between these antinomies. The second applies the question of balance to any and all pedagogical tensions, suggesting that tact, so defined, is a general criterion of pedagogical professionalism.

Whether new or old, the notion that the practical pedagogical field is marked by antipodes, paradoxes, tensions, and aporia has long been important in the history of educational ideas. It can be traced as far back as Socrates' dialectic, his method of arriving at knowledge or at the "truth" through question and answer, dialogue and dispute. Referencing Socrates' early dialogues in particular, Meyer (2018) explains that

> in these aporetic dialogues, the double dimension of Socrates' questioning is most clearly revealed: on the one hand, questioning is used in order to reach the truth about the question debated, on the other hand, when Socrates questions, he puts the interlocutor himself in question by attacking his alleged knowledge. (p. 115)

These dialogues are aporetic, expressive of contradiction and paradox, in multiple senses: They not only show that truth and knowledge is reached through its opposite—doubt, skepticism, and ignorance—but they also expose the ignorance and impotence underlying individuals' presumed knowledge and mastery. Often, the only certainty and knowledge that Socrates arrives at in these dialogues is that he (or his interlocutor) *doesn't* know and *isn't* certain. Wisdom, paradoxically, arises through the realization of one's own ignorance.

Aristotle is second ancient Greek source relevant in this connection; of particular importance is his notion of the golden mean (*mesotēti*). In the *Nicomachean Ethics*, Aristotle explains how choosing a middle course between opposed extremes can provide a basis for defining "moral virtue" and thus for ethics more broadly:

> Virtue, then, is a state concerned with choice, being in the mean (*mesotēti*) relative to us, determined by reason (*logôi*), and as the man of practical wisdom (*ho phronimos*) would determine it. It is a mean-state between two vices, one of excess, and one of deficiency… virtue finds and chooses the intermediate [*to meson*]. (Aristotle, 1106b36–1107a6)[2]

What is good or excellent, what constitutes a moral state or disposition, in other words, is a mean, a middle point. This middle point, Aristotle continues, is not an absolute median—in the way that 3 is the median of 1 through 5, for example. It is instead determined from a *relative* position. This requires a kind of practical wisdom (*phronesis*) that is situational, reflecting sound judgment, rather than one that involves the application of universal rules and principles. In illustrating his notion of *mesotēti*, Aristotle refers to the example of an athlete who should be fed the right amount of food, rather than either too much or too little, in preparation for competition. Other examples provided by Aristotle include the virtue of courage, which represents a balance between cowardice on the one hand and recklessness on the other. In these and other contexts, virtue consists of navigating one's own way between two vices or between excess and deficiency. Although the pedagogical antinomies explored in this chapter also designate extremes, opposites like freedom versus constraint or distance versus proximity do not represent vices, deficiencies, or excesses on their own. These are instead possibilities for pedagogical action and reflection that are appropriate in varying degrees. But if this chapter were to describe "virtue" in teaching in Aristotelian terms, it would still largely conform to Aristotle's definition of moral virtue: Virtuous or excellent teaching consists in the practical ability, the state or disposition, to choose the middle path between opposing extremes—as they are relative to the individual and the situation.

A number of sources that implicitly link these ancient ideas and practices with more contemporary understandings of education are of German origin. Their authors include Immanuel Kant and also the theologian and hermeneutician Friedrich Schleiermacher. In framing a key question for education, Kant casts the matter as intrinsically oppositional or paradoxical: "How do I cultivate [the child's] freedom under [conditions of] constraint?" Kant's ambivalent response—"I shall accustom my pupil to tolerate a constraint of his freedom, and I shall at the same time lead him to make good use of his freedom" (1803/2007, p. 447)—reappears frequently in educational discourse in Northern Europe. The young toddler must be barred from stairways and other dangers to freely exercise their newly found ability to walk, just as the teenager must first study (e.g., for the driver's exam and other tests) before they can go enjoy the privileges of driving or can choose to go to university. As Helsper (2001) has remarked of the German context, Kant's "paradox" has come to represent a "foundational" opposition in pedagogical practice, one which can "repeatedly been seen as an object for reflection and reformulation" (p. 85).

Although the Kantian opposition of freedom and constraint is understood precisely as a *paradox*—with the two terms kept rigidly apart by their mutual exclusivity—both this paradox and the other pedagogical oppositions can be seen as rather more flexible and dialectical in nature. As the above examples of the toddler and the teenager suggest, freedoms of movement and choice, whether for children or young people, are meaningful only within certain constraints.[3] Understanding education in dialectical terms, as a dynamic movement between oppositions and antinomies receives perhaps its fullest and most sustained treatment only a few decades after the publication of Kant's *Lectures on Pedagogy* in F. D. E. Schleiermacher's *Lectures on Education* (newly translated, see 1826/2023).

The entirety of Schleiermacher's lectures can be seen as structured through a dialectic that works to define, heighten, and (in some cases) resolve the differences between the widest range of opposed terms (e.g., Friesen, 2023). These terms include the opposition or antinomy of individuality versus collectivity as well as of the present and the future in the life of the child. Of particular importance for the current discussion is Schleiermacher's opposition of "support" and "counteraction." Schleiermacher understands this opposition in ethical terms, specifically between what is *good* and to be *supported* and what is *not* and to be *counteracted*:

> From one perspective we act according to the maxim that education should and must be nothing but the awakening and the support of the Good in preparation for the [child's] entry to larger circles of life... From the other perspective we [should] act according to the maxim that education should and must be nothing but counteract[ion]... comprehensively counteracting that which is objectionable. (p. 74)

Both as parents and teachers, we go out of our way to encourage and assist with words and rewards behavior in children that we see as good; and we counteract—discourage, correct, redirect—those things we view less favorably. Do we necessarily know in advance precisely how and why such support or counteraction might occur? Schleiermacher—like Herbart before him—argues that theory cannot dictate precisely what should happen in these and other pedagogical moments. Schleiermacher concludes his initial discussion of support and counteraction by saying that "we... have to leave it to life itself to decide what should be done from moment to moment" (p. 76). It is only the realm of practice, in other words, in which the opposition between support and counteraction can be resolved.

Helsper and others have updated Kant's formulations and Schleiermacher's antinomies for today's education and for the contemporary professionalization of classroom teachers (see also the Postscript, "Pedagogical Tact and Teacher Professionalization"). In his 2017 book, *Antinomic Interpretations of Pedagogical Processes: Conceptual Sketches and Clarifications for Teaching and Learning*,[4] Jörg Schlömerkemper outlines how pedagogical antinomies in general can be understood in the context of today's teaching practice. In particular, he argues against a purely "binary understanding" of pedagogical oppositions, as if dealing with opposites was just "a question of... decision-making in the sense of 'either/or' 'good/bad' or 'true/false.'" Instead, he emphasizes that

> from a more sophisticated perspective, it becomes a matter of situations and structures in which two aspects, requirements or demands which are (almost) of the same weight... but nonetheless dialectically intermixed. Briefly put, one can at this point say: It should not be a matter of a polarizing "either/or" but of a consistent "also... but." (p. 28)

To understand freedom and constraint, support and counteraction, or distance and proximity not as an "either/or" but as an "also… but" can be seen as the aim of the responsive teacher or parent. It is to see these opposed possibilities as something that can be addressed through a certain *ambivalence* in pedagogical practice. An ambivalent awareness and practice is one which, for example, would present to the child choices or freedoms within a given set of constraints: "You can't have the chocolate bar, but do you want a sandwich with jam or honey?" It would be a kind of practice that sees a similar situation of correction or redirection ("counteraction") as always containing an element of affirmation and support. One possibility may be dominant and the other latent in any such moment of engagement (e.g., counteracting the request for a chocolate bar rather than supporting it). But as circumstances change or as insight increases, this dominance and latency might well be inverted (e.g., supporting the child's desire for a chocolate treat as a reward for good behavior). Schlömerkemper describes this type of "ambivalent" practice as a

> fluctuation between different perceptions and value judgments in which one assesses matters first one way and then another, without desiring or having to decide between them. Both can be seen as simultaneously valuable ("-valent"). Ambivalences can be seen as a more moderate form of antinomy, because the two poles actually are not mutually exclusive. (2018, p. 29)

For example: In the case of the freedom and constraint of the young child learning to walk, a parent might well prefer greater restraint in some settings (e.g., in public) as opposed to others (e.g., among the extended family). Similarly, a teacher might choose the "pole" represented by the individual versus the collective in order to give special praise to a challenged but hard-working student in class. In these cases, the adult's affirmation of one side or another of the antinomies in question is never final or absolutely definitive. It is instead ambivalent. It is an affirmation that is well aware that the opposite course of action could well have been the better choice. It is this oscillation between dominance and latency, or the simultaneous embrace of two opposed possibilities which then constitutes what can be called the dynamics or "dialectics" of pedagogical thought and action.

Indeed, in today's literature on educational practice and teacher professionalization (at least in the German language), such practical pedagogical antinomies and tensions are seen not only as a way (among others) for *understanding* educational practice, but as an essential, intrinsic part of this practice itself: "According to this understanding," as Helsper (2001) explains, "antinomies are *constitutive* for pedagogical teacher action. To try to suspend them would be to eliminate the pedagogical nature of the action itself" (p. 87; emphasis added;

see also the postscript to this collection). Or as Hainschink and Zahra-Ecker (2018) say, "pedagogical action is *comprised* of constitutive contradictions and/or antinomies which cannot be suspended, but only engaged with reflectively... [L]earning how to balance their opposed polarities is a *constitutive* element of [teacher] professionalization" (pp. 179, 182, emphases added; for an English-language discussion, see Didolet, Lundin, & Krüger, 2019). For the purposes of this chapter, however, these opposed possibilities and their dialectics are not seen as "objectively" pre-existing in practice, but as interpretations of the pedagogical field—ones that have been too often overlooked in English.

Prominent in contemporary discussions in the German language is an antinomy that is in some ways already implied in the tensions between freedom and constraint, support and counteraction discussed above. This is the opposition of *proximity* and *distance*. Again with an unmistakable emphasis on practice, Werner Helsper (2002) explains:

> A problem of professional pedagogical action is also evident in the repeated accusations that teachers neglect their educational duty through the distanced "transmission" of curriculum content. But if they were to orient themselves completely to the individual [student], then allegations would soon arise that they are improperly inserting themselves in the private realm of the child and their family. (p. 25)

To also invoke Schleiermacher's oppositions of support and counteraction *and* individuality and collectivity, one could say that the teacher must closely *support* and guide students and attend to them carefully—both as individuals and as a group. At the same time, though, the teacher must treat any one student like any other and retain sufficient distance to effectively remain a teacher rather than a friend—and be prepared to appropriately counteract, redirect, and correct the student.

The Mediating Potential of Pedagogical Tact

As the first to define tact as something specifically *pedagogical*, Friedrich Herbart (1776–1841) did *not* see pedagogical tact so much as a mediator of entirely practical tensions like those between proximity and distance, individuality and collectivity, present and future. Instead, as mentioned above, Herbart defined pedagogical tact as "a quick judgment and decision" able to link or apply *practice* as a whole to the universality and totality of *theory*. Pedagogical tact represents the conciliation, in other words, of the universal rules of theory to the vagaries and particularities of practice: "Tact inevitably occupies a place that theory leaves vacant, and so becomes the immediate director of our practice" (1802/2022, p. 32). In so doing, tact works as a medium (e.g., see Zirfas, 2012/2022): it mediates the gap between fixed theoretical prescriptions and the ever-changing demands of practice. And such tact, Herbart suggests, is a matter not of deliberate choice or volition, but a question of "attunement," of "a particular pedagogical disposition" (pp. 32, 35).

About 25 years later, in discussing pedagogical oppositions and antipodes as being specifically *dialectical*, Schleiermacher also emphasized tact's largely "unconscious" balancing and mediating function, describing tact very broadly as "the general medium of order and measure" (1826/2000, p. 255). After outlining two opposed possibilities for education similar to Kant's opposition of freedom and constraint ("personal freedom" versus "confin[ement]"), Schleiermacher explains his conception of tact:

> Only those who stand in the safest balance between the two extremes will have the right judgment about how to avoid them. An artful action, based on such insight and guided by the *right tact*, is also advantageously appropriate in relation to this difficult point, as one must always return to such an action in one's practice. (Schleiermacher, 1826/2000, p. 352; emphasis added)

Here Schleiermacher expands the potential role of tact beyond the mediation of the universality of theory and the particularity of practice, and places it firmly within the realm of *practice* (to which "one must always return"). He further grants pedagogical tact the role we are seeking to give it here: the function of Aristotle's *mesotêti*, of mediation, measure, and negotiation. Moreover, in doing so, Schleiermacher emphasizes that tact has the capacity not only to balance the extremes of confinement and freedom, but also to potentially overcome or "avoid" them altogether.

In his 1962 monograph *Pedagogical Tact*, Jacob Muth also locates tact squarely in the realm of practice. He defines pedagogical tact as a kind of *sensitivity* and *reserve* realized specifically in the face of that which is unpredictable and unplannable in pedagogical practice:

> *sensitivity* and *reserve* [are] its two essential defining moments... [both are] always realized in the concrete, unforeseeable situation in which one finds oneself suddenly confronted, needing to protect others, to help others—insofar as another is in need of help—in that one responds to the other, in no way hurting or imposing oneself on the other. (1962/2022, pp. 91, 92; emphasis in original)

The distance and reserve implied in pedagogical tact, Muth emphasizes, both work to preserve "the correct middle point between the educative help of the teacher and the possible self-help of the child" (pp. 107–108). Muth describes the second key characteristic of pedagogical tact—sensitivity—as "a feeling for the 'you' (or Thou[5]), for one's fellow human being, for the singularity and singular rights of the other; it is a respect for the ultimate inaccessibility of the other" (p. 91).

In 2015 (as well as in his later work on the subject) Jörg Zirfas focuses explicitly on pedagogical tact precisely "as the subjective ability ... to tactfully balance pedagogical paradoxes" in general (Zirfas, 2012/2022, p. 192; see also Burghardt & Zirfas, 2019, pp. 149–163). At the same time, Zirfas reinforces Muth's emphasis on the singularity and ultimate inaccessibility of the other, characterizing this aspect of pedagogical practice specifically as an *aporia*—a logical contradiction or impasse: "The experience of the singularity of the other," Zirfas explains, "exists only in the experience of an aporia" (2012/2022, p. 192). Zirfas concludes his discussion specifically by defining pedagogical tact in terms of one's relation to the aporia or "riddle" of the other:

> Pedagogical tact is resonance with the openness, dynamics, variability and unfathomability of the other; to put it more lyrically: tact is the response to the riddle of the other. However, pedagogical tact is not the solution to the riddle, but merely an educational response in which a specific responsibility for the protection and promotion of the other and of oneself is expressed. (p. 192)

To see the other as an insoluble riddle, as an aporia, is to introduce to the antinomic dynamics of pedagogical tact as something *more* than a question of balance, measure or mediation. It is to admit something that arguably can*not* be resolved or even addressed through dialectics or the simultaneous (ambivalent) incorporation of opposites. To deal with the question of aporia in pedagogy, this chapter now directs its focus first to illustrate how the body's capacity to incorporate polar opposites and antinomies give it a particular ability to engage tactfully— to mediate, balance, or at least ameliorate pedagogical tensions and oppositions. Second, and in concluding, this chapter illustrates that even with this ability, "the riddle of the other" necessarily takes one beyond any embodied performance, any mediation of which the body might be capable.

The Aporias of Embodiment

If the dialectical structures and dynamics of pedagogical thought and action can be seen as embedded in pedagogical situations, or as constitutive of pedagogical professionalism or the pedagogical "field" itself, then the dialectic of the lived body is manifest rather differently. As the study of lived experience, phenomenology shows the body to appear as a kind of dynamic meeting-point or "nexus," more a verb or a process than an object or thing. In its dynamism, the body appears both to integrate and manifest opposed phenomena simultaneously. Particularly important here is the profound predisposition to ambivalence that pedagogy and the body appear to have in common.

Phenomenology has conventionally understood the body in terms of the foundational notion of intentionality; the idea that our awareness is always an awareness of *something*, and that in everyday life, we regard this "something" in a particular way; we see this something-*as-something*: A tree is shade on a hot summer day just as a doorway might be a place for refuge on a windy or rainy one. The body is typically seen as having a mediating, enabling, sometimes even constitutive role in the subject's engagement in "intentional" action. It can not only take us to the cooling shade of a tree or to protection from the cold and rain, but it also stands literally as the source of experiences of heat, shade, cold and protection to begin with. Bernhard Waldenfels, one of Merleau-Ponty's students, invokes information theory in describing the body as functioning "simultaneously as sender, message, channel, and perhaps also as receiver" (2007, p. 468). "The lived body, as Edmund Husserl puts it, is a point of interchange between the physical and psychical worlds;" it is part of our everyday projects and (in this sense) also of our "project-ions" in the world (e.g., Heidegger, 1962). Writing in 1945 in the *Phenomenology of Perception*, Merleau-Ponty develops this further by saying that "consciousness is being toward the thing through the intermediary of the body"—with the body, in turn, presenting "our general means of having a world" (1945/2012, pp. 140, 147). The body, moreover, is expressive both of nature and culture, of biological necessity and human freedom:

> everything [bodily] is constructed and everything is natural, in the sense that there is no single word or behavior that does not owe something to mere biological being—and, at the same time, there is no word or behavior that does not break free from animal life that does not deflect vital behaviors ...through a sort of *escape* and a genius for ambiguity ... might well serve to define man. Behaviors create significations that are transcendent in relation to the anatomical structure and yet immanent to the behavior as such. (2012, p. 195)

We are simultaneously biological and cultural, with our every word and move expressing our anatomical and physiological limitations and possibilities. At the same time, these words and movements also express something about our individuality, our kinesthetic "style," our mood, and about the culture into which we are socialized. In initial congruence with the "dialectics" of pedagogical practice, Merleau-Ponty describes these opposites as being negotiated with an "ambiguity" (*équivoqu*; a close etymological cousin of ambivalence) that, he adds, may be nothing less than *definitive* of what it is to be *human*.

Later, however, Merleau-Ponty rejects the mentalist bias implicit in the primacy of "consciousness" in our relation to the world and in seeing the body (merely) as the "intermediary" or "space" for our conscious plans and devices. The body, as Merleau-Ponty later comes to see, can no longer be viewed just as a meeting-point for opposites like object and subject, mind and world. In *The Visible and the Invisible* (1968), he instead casts the body as *simultaneously* mind and world, object and subject, sensible and sentient. Body is flesh (*la chair*[6]). It is simultaneously constitutive of body, mind, *and* world, and is marked above all by its "visibility." "To properly designate it," Merleau-Ponty explains, "we should need the term 'element,' in the sense it was used to speak of water, air, earth, and fire, that is, in the sense of a *general thing*" (p. 139). The body, moreover, is emergent as the "intertwining" (*entrelacs*[7]) of self and world, characterized as "two phases" in a single process or as the "obverse and reverse" (p. 138) sides of a leaf or of two leaves:

> We say therefore that our body is a being of two leaves, from one side a thing among things and otherwise what sees them and touches them; we say, because it is evident, that it unites these two properties within itself, and its double belongingness to the order of the "object" and to the order of the "subject" reveals to us quite unexpected relations between the two. (p. 137)

The body is both subject and object, sensed and sensing, and it unites these oppositions doubly—arguably in both material and experiential terms. And the quite unexpected relations between the two orders, as Merleau-Ponty enumerates, include the oppositions of the "phenomenal body and objective body" (p. 136), "passivity" and "activity," "the visible" and "the seer," "material" and "spiritual" (p. 139), as well as the "In Itself" and the "For Itself" (p. 137). On its own, the body can realize these opposed possibilities simultaneously in multiple ways and through multiple senses; it shifts from one sense modality to another; it touches, hears, and sees itself and it combines activity and passivity in myriad habits, dispositions and ways of "being." However, shortly after describing these aspects as the "two sides" of the body, Merleau-Ponty (1968) puts this initial characterization into question:

> One should not even say, as we did a moment ago, that the body is made up of two leaves... it would be better to say that the body sensed and the body sentient are... two segments of one sole circular course which ...is but one sole movement in its two phases. And everything said about the sensed body pertains to the whole of the sensible of which it is a part, and to the world. (pp. 137, 138)

Here, Merleau-Ponty's emphasis is not exclusively on the lived body itself, but on this body's relation to the world. World and body are of the same visible substance, mirroring each other not only in sensory and material qualities, but also in the sense of the body as what Merleau-Ponty calls an *"exemplar sensible"* (p. 135)—as the basis or the measure for what we see and experience in the world. This can be seen to extend from the "foot" of a mountain through the "torso" of a work, to the "head" of a bed. The body, as Merleau-Ponty says, is "caught up in the tissue of the things," "draw[ing]" this tissue "entirely to itself, incorporate[ing] it, and, with the same movement, communicat[ing] to the things upon which it closes over that identity without superimposition…" (p. 138).

These oppositions of sensed and sentient, object and subject, touched and touching, visible and seeing—together with the myriad complexities and permutations to which they give rise—can be seen to form consistent antipodes in Merleau-Ponty's account of the lived body as "flesh." Insofar as the body is both nature and culture, both enabling and constraining of movements and habits, one might add to Merleau-Ponty's oppositions a version of the Kantian paradox of freedom and constraint: Our embodiment is the precondition for both our liberty as well as our own ultimate limitation. However, unlike Schlömerkemper's account of antinomic ambivalences, Merleau-Ponty here is suggesting that we do *not* fluctuate or switch emphasis at will from subject and object, nature and culture, sensing and sensed. These corporeal antipodes appear less as a "fluctuation… in which one assesses matters first one way and then another" (as Schlömerkemper characterizes the antipodes of pedagogical practice; 2018, p. 29) and more as *always-already interwoven* and *interlaced*. The "genius for ambiguity" that Merleau-Ponty earlier says might well be definitive for the human being appears decisively aporetic—much more a "both… and" rather an "either/or." In *The Visible and the Invisible* (1968), this aporetic ambiguity is arguably expanded to become not simply a characteristic of the body, but a comprehensive but fractured ontological *paradox* of material existence as a whole. Here, Merleau-Ponty describes the flesh as

> a being in latency, and a presentation of a certain absence …[a] prototype of Being, of which our body, the sensible sentient, is a very remarkable variant, but whose constitutive paradox already lies in every visible… it is indeed a paradox of Being, not a paradox of man, that we are dealing with here. To be sure, one can reply that, between the two "sides" of our body… there is an abyss that separates the In Itself from the For Itself. (p. 136)

Merleau-Ponty's ontology of the flesh, then, is one emphatically marked by paradox, and the abyss or gap he speaks of here strongly suggests in that any opposition that the body might integrate or manifest is never fully complete or symmetrical: As an "element," flesh is "decentered" (p. 138) and in the dynamism of this decentering it is never fully self-identical. Consequently, the interweaving, interleaving, and intertwining of Merleau-Ponty's *entrelacs* seems ultimately more a *process* or *event* than it is an intricate but fixed pattern.

Embodied Tact and the Pedagogical Paradox

As simultaneously structure and event, the body, it seems, may be particularly able to work with the fluctuation between pedagogical antipodes that are said to constitute both pedagogical professionalism and pedagogical tact. In other words: If the body incorporates both subject and object, nature and culture, sensing and sensed, would it not be particularly suited to the task of "balanc[ing]" or perhaps even overcoming "pedagogical paradoxes" that Zirfas (2012/2022, p. 177) and others see as constitutive of such tact?

To address this question, it is helpful to begin with the opposition of *proximity* and *distance*. Although an educator's balancing or mediating of these two antipodes can obviously be measured literally as the physical space separating them from the one being educated, this opposition can be expressed and "measured" in a wide range of ways—through classroom arrangements as well as words, gestures, and tone. Proximity and distance, moreover, can take on a range of different pedagogical valences. Helsper and Muth, above, have already framed proximity and distance in terms of impersonal instruction versus (overly) personal intimacy, or via the educator's temptation to intervene versus a careful deference to the capacity and singularity of the educand. Others see this opposition, for example, in terms of "mutual dependence" versus "self-assertion" in the student-teacher relation (Dörr, 2019). Distance versus proximity can also be understood in terms of "limitation" or "restriction" (*Begrenzung*) on the one hand versus "love" or "attention" (*Zuwendung*) on the other—as Kowalski (2020, p. 107) has framed it.

Nonetheless, in an exchange between an educator and educand, the body can express these different and opposed dimensions of proximity and distance simultaneously, perhaps even in a way that can be said to avoid the opposition to begin with. Praising a student or child using a positive tone from across a (class) room, for example, can have the effect of simultaneously identifying the student for support and positive attention while maintaining literal distance. The educator both does and does not single out or separate the student in this act—certainly, no one in the room is explicitly excluded from this moment of individual relation. One can perhaps say that it does not become *intimately* personal.

The mere presence of the teacher and the students in the room, on the one hand, only underscores the persistent relevance of Kant and Schleiermacher's opposition of freedom and constraint (or confinement): The classroom setting gives students a notable range of freedom for individual (or collective) action and expression. But at the same time, it constrains, or literally confines them. On the other hand, considering scenarios of teaching and learning *online* can illustrate how the body's inherent capacity for ambivalence selectively *removed* through different forms of technological mediation. In online video, for example, the presence of the body is often effectively abridged to become just a talking head; and in online text forums, flesh is even further reduced to inanimate text on a screen.[8] Certainly, words of praise alone (e.g., sent in a group email exchange, or even spoken in an online video meeting) cannot communicate this timing, openness, position and individualization with the same subtlety and nuance as is possible in classroom scenarios: If things like timing and individuation are not significantly impaired in these online settings, they are at least undermined through the vagaries of video compression and transmission.[9] As an early innovator in videoconference technologies observed, even the most advanced video communications appear "precisely configured to confound... non-verbal" communication (Lanier, 2001, p. 68)—thwarting mutual eye-contact, confusing conversational turn-taking, and distorting one's sense of position relative to others. In these and other ways, these mediating technologies seem to noticeably attenuate the body's aporetic or pedagogical tension and dynamism, its ability, in other words, to connect and perform two pedagogical possibilities at once.

Thinking further of Merleau-Ponty's account of the body-as-flesh, one might additionally—and with some imagination—come up with further scenarios, and show how they instantiate the delicate entwinement of nature and culture, sensing and sensed, seeing and seen, material and spiritual, all in myriad ways: For example, in a fleeting moment of eye-contact between teacher and student, not only are cultural expectations about the length and meaning(s) of such contact brought into play, but so are deeper dynamics and atavisms regarding glances and gazing, as well as visuality itself, as Merleau-Ponty suggests:

> I look at him. He sees that I look at him. I see that he sees it. He sees that I see that he sees it ... Well, even though in principle reflections upon reflections go on to infinity, vision is such that the obscure results of two glances adjust to each other, and there are no longer two consciousnesses with their own teleology but two mutually enfolding glances. (1964, p. 17)[10]

The manifold complexity of a moment of eye-contact is further evoked by thinking of Merleau-Ponty's account of self and world as "two segments of one sole circular course... one sole movement in its two phases" forming a kind of fleshly circuit, both semantic and material, consisting of gesture and of word, of sight and sound; activity and passivity—all "caught up in the tissue of the things" (1968,

p. 138). Activity and passivity, the semantic and the material, for example, can be said to be combined in these and other ways in a supportive or judging glance, in a strained or mellifluous tone of voice. Whatever the individual or collective student response to the moment of teacher praise across the classroom mentioned above might be, such response is invariably part of the "circular course" described by Merleau-Ponty.

Distance and proximity, support and counteraction, freedom and restraint, present and future, action and passivity, expression and reception: The way that these varied oppositions and antipodes can be balanced and bridged by the deep "ambivalence" of the body-as-flesh are a part of the body's unique power to communicate ambiguity and semantic multiplicity. It alone is arguably able to grant space and freedom while remaining immediately present; only it can be supportive while at the same time redirecting and counteracting. Only it—again thinking of a moment of eye-contact—both senses and expresses not only that one is looking, but also *how* one is looking and *that* one's look is directed to me. The body, moreover, accomplishes these and myriad other ambivalent communications and manifestations in a way that is singularly insistent and indubitable: While one can debate the precise meaning of any one of the multiple communications that are constantly radiating from the body, one certainly cannot question *that* the body is communicating and that its gestures and glances certainly mean *something*. At the same time, this precise "something" is rendered ambiguous not only by the body's ambivalent and aporetic nature, but also by what Merleau-Ponty referred to as an "abyss" or gap ("that separates the In Itself from the For Itself"; 1968, p. 146). Just as such a "fissure" (p. 235) separates what can be seen as objectively given from what is subjectively taken up, so too does a palpable non-coincidence and non-identity in these moments still separate educators not from the one being educated but from themselves.

Reference to the decentered and decentering nature of the body takes this chapter back to the riddle of otherness. In its otherness, the body of another, it should be noted, is neither transparent nor opaque. And this is the case not only for an outside observer, but also for one thus embodied. The "bodily self," as Bernhard Waldenfels explains, "is 'not a master in his own home'" meaning that "the Other arises as co-original with myself and to some extent as preceding myself" (2011, p. 56). We use mirrors to see what we look like (although they still don't show everything), and we wonder whether an unusual or tired feeling means we might be getting sick. This is also because the body's powerful ambivalence and ambiguity, its silent mimetic and empathic modalities, are always partly concealed to consciousness or reflection. And they can be seen to reach their limit in overcoming, mediating or balancing the kind of antipodes negotiated in everyday pedagogical contexts. For the other *as* other, even in the closest intimacy with the self, does not necessarily recapitulate the structure of proximity and distance, support and counteraction—or any of the other pedagogical antipodes discussed above. Instead, as both Muth and Zirfas have made clear, the openness, dynamics, variability and unfathomability of the other is *not* balanced by that of the self but instead represents a kind of aporia, a riddle, a cul-de-sac. It "is the label placed on a closed box for which everyone is looking for the key" as French educationist Muriel Briançon (2019) has put it—but it is one for which no key exists (p. 72). It represents an absolute surplus that cannot be offset through any one type of action, through any one moment of proximity or support. Instead, one of the few reactions adequate to it would be a kind of reserve, as both Muth and Zirfas note. "The experience of the singularity of the other exists only in the experience of an aporia. In pedagogical tact, one takes responsibility for or answers to the relationship with another …for something for which one cannot actually answer to or be responsible for" (Zirfas, 2012/2022, p. 192; Muth, 1962/2022, p. 72).

Notes

[1] Jerome Bruner's (1996) essay, "The Complexity of Educational Aims," represents an important exception in the psychological literature. Bruner explicitly identifies three "antinomies of early educational practice" (p. 81) as follows: 1) that education reproduces a collective culture while also optimizing individual ability and singularity; 2) that learning is ultimately intrapsychic, "in one's head," while effectively occurring only "interpersonally"; 3) that a perspective in school curricula is needed that is simultaneously particularistic and universal. Suggesting a deep affinity between antipodes and the dynamics of education, Bruner unwittingly echoes Schleiermacher (1862/2023) and the educational tradition discussed here in indicating that such antinomies are essential to (the goals of early) education, and that they "do not permit of logical but only of pragmatic resolution" (pp. 66–67). However, Bruner (perhaps as a reflection of his cognitivist commitments) ultimately departs from Schleiermacher and this dialectical tradition by coming down on the side of individuality and interpersonal development—at the expense of collectivity and intrapsychic development.

[2] This passage from Aristotle's *Nicomachean Ethics* is quoted as translated in Gill (2015, p. 94). Aristotle's text has its origin near the end of the third century B.C.

[3] To understand Kant's question, "How do I cultivate [the child's] freedom under [conditions of] constraint?" as outlining two paradoxical or mutually exclusive possibilities is arguably to see freedom specifically as "freedom *from*"—as what political theorist Isaiah Berlin refers to as "negative liberty" (1969, p. 120). Freedom in this sense can only be the *absence* of a constraint and interference, with any degree of heteronomy or intrusion from outside deemed to be a limitation. On the other hand, "freedom *to*"—what Berlin has called "positive liberty" (p. 121)—sees such heteronomy as being *integral* to freedom: One is free in this sense not simply to do something according to one's wishes; instead, one is free, for example, to have access to higher education, to be protected by the law, or to vote

in elections. To enjoy such freedoms not only presupposes a degree of heteronomy, external interference, or even constraint; it is also to see such heteronomy or constraint as positively *constitutive* of such freedom: To be free under the protection of the law is also to submit to it, to enjoy freedom of movement is also to respect restrictions regarding trespass, just as to cast one's vote is to constrain oneself to structured political systems.

4 *Pädagogische Prozesse in antinomischer Deutung: Begriffliche Klärungen und Entwürfe für Lernen und Lehren.*
5 "Thou" represents an antiquated form of informal address in English and is used in translation as a parallel to the German informal "you" to indicate immediacy and intimacy.
6 *La chair*, like the word "flesh," has both material and also antiquated (often Biblical) connotations regarding the body.
7 *Entrelacs* refers to fine tracery, also suggesting things like a latticework, maze, or tangle.
8 For a relevant investigation of the relationship of such written text to the body, see Edith Stein's discussion of *Wortleib* ("lived word-body") in: Stein, 1964, pp. 74–78.
9 In Friesen (2011), I discuss this in terms of a general attenuation of the significance of a phenomenon like shared silence (see pp. 134–135).
10 Bernard Waldenfels writes: "As gaze meets gaze, the simple attribution of seeing and of seeing-and-seen is broken in many pieces. The alternating gaze is characterized not only by a new object of vision, but by a more complex structure of vision. At first glance, this structure is as follows. When I look the other person 'in the eyes,' I not only see a seeing person, but I also see where the gaze of the other is going. I see what the other sees and to a certain extent, how he sees it. We encounter a 'look-gesture' like every gesture, this gesture has a certain direction and expressiveness. If there is no independent source of [the] color or form of [objects on] their own, there is a source of vision from which rays of sight emanate. This 'radiance' … which is also etymologically linked to the word 'glance,' has been part of the repertoire of all aesthesiology [study of the senses] since antiquity. It is connected with a materialization … that leads children to imagine our gazes crossing, colliding or intermingling in space" (2007, 497–498).

Bibliography

Berlin, I. (1969). Two concepts of liberty. In I. Berlin (Ed.), *Four essays on liberty* (pp. 118–172). Oxford University Press.

Briançon, M. (2019). *The meaning of otherness in education: Stakes, forms, process, thoughts and transfers.* Wiley.

Bruner, J. (1996). The complexity of educational aims. In J. Bruner (Ed.), *The culture of education* (pp. 66–85). Harvard University Press. <https://doi.org/10.4159/9780674251083>

Didolet, S., Lundin, S. & Krüger, J. O. (2019). Constructing professionalism in teacher education. Analytical tools from a comparative study. *Education Inquiry*, *10*(3), 208–225. <https://doi.org/10.1080/20004508.2018.1529527>

Dörr, M. (2019). *Nähe und Distanz: Ein Spannungsfeld pädagogischer Professionalität.* Beltz.

Friesen, N. (2011). The place of the classroom and the space of the screen: Relational pedagogy and internet technology. Peter Lang.

Friesen, N. (2023). Accentuate the negative: Schleiermacher's dialectic. In N. Friesen & K. Kenklies (Eds. Trans.), F.D.E. Schleiermacher's outlines of the art of education: A translation & discussion (pp. 177–213). Peter Lang.

Friesen, N. & Su, H. (2023). What is pedagogy? Discovering the hidden pedagogical dimension. *Educational Theory.* 73(1), 6–28 <https://doi.org/10.1111/edth.12569>

Gill, M. L. (2015). Virtue and reason in Aristotle's Nicomachean Ethics. In D. Henry & K. M. Nielsen (Eds.), *Bridging the gap between Aristotle's science and ethics* (pp. 94–110). Cambridge University Press.

Hainschink, V. & Zahra-Ecker, R. A. (2018). Leben in Antinomien – Bewältigungsdispositionen aus arbeitsbezogenen Verhaltens- und Erlebensmustern. *Pedagogical Horizons* 2(2), 179–194.

Heidegger, M. (1928/1962). *Being and time.* (J. Macquarrie & E. Robinson, Trans.). Harper.

Helsper, W. (2001). Antinomien des Lehrerhandelns – Anfragen an die Bildungsgangdidaktik. In Hericks, U. Keuffer, J., Kräft, H. C., Kunze, I. (Eds.), *Bildungsgangdidaktik. Perspektiven für Fachunterricht und Lehrerbildung.* Springer VS.

Helsper, W. (2002). Pädagogisches Handeln in den Antinomien der Moderne. In Krüger, H.-H. & Helsper, W. (Eds.), *Einführung in Grundbegriffe und Grundfragen der Erziehungswissenschaft.* Springer.

Herbart, J. F. (1802/2022). Introductory lecture to students in pedagogy. In N. Friesen (Ed. Trans.), *Tact and the pedagogical relation: Introductory readings* (pp. 28–37). Peter Lang.

Kant, I. (1803/2007). Lectures on pedagogy. In G. Zöller & R. B. Louden (Eds. Trans.), *Anthropology, history and education* (pp. 437–485). Cambridge University Press.

Kowalski, M. (2020). *Nähe, Distanz und Anerkennung in pädagogischen Beziehungen.* Springer VS.

Lanier, J. (2001). Virtually there: Three dimensional teleimmersion may eventually bring the world to your desk. *Scientific American* 284(4), 66–75.

Luhmann, N. & Schorr, K. E. (1988/2000). *Problems in the reflection in the system of education.* (R. A. Neuwirth, Trans.). Waxmann.

Merleau-Ponty, M. (1968). *The visible and invisible.* (A. Lingis, Trans.). Northwestern University Press.

Merleau-Ponty, M. (1945/2012). *Phenomenology of perception.* (D. A. Landes, Trans.). Routledge.

Meyer, M. (2018). Dialectic and questioning: Socrates and Plato. *Revue Internationale de Philosophie*, 2(284), 113–129.

Muth, H. (1962/2022). Pedagogical tact: Study of a contemporary form of educational and instructional engagement (selections). In N. Friesen, (Ed. Trans.), *Tact and the pedagogical relation: Introductory readings* (pp. 85–113). Peter Lang.

Schleiermacher, F. D. E. (1826/2000). *Texte zur Pädagogik. Kommentierte Studienausgabe*. (M. Winkler & J. Brachmann, Eds.). Suhrkamp.

Schleiermacher, F. D. E. (1826/2023). Outlines of the art of education. In N. Friesen & K. Kenklies (Eds. Trans.), *Outlines of the art of education: A translation & discussion*. (pp. 21–86). Peter Lang.

Schlömerkemper, J. (2018). *Pädagogische Prozesse in antinomischer Deutung: Begriffliche Klärung und Entwürfe für Lernen und Lehren*. Beltz/Juventa.

Stein, E. (1964). *On the problem of empathy*. (W. Stein, Trans.). Springer.

Waldenfels, B. (2007). *Antwortregister*. Suhrkamp.

Waldenfels, B. (2011). *Phenomenology of the alien: Basic concepts*. (A. Kozer & W. Stähler, Trans.). Northwestern University Press.

Zirfas, J. (2012/2022). Pedagogical tact: Ten theses. In N. Friesen (Ed. Trans.), *Tact and the pedagogical relation: Introductory readings* (pp. 175–196). Peter Lang.

Tactful Views: On Forms of Educational Measure and Precaution[1]

Jörg Zirfas and Daniel Burghardt

In this chapter, pedagogical tact is discussed in its aesthetic and ethical dimensions. Herbart has pointed out the specific, even necessary, connection between aesthetic-moral judgment and pedagogical action. *Aisthesis* (sensation or perception in contrast to conception or intellection) aims at that which occupies the senses, which connects people with sensations and feelings, and fills them with consciousness as a form of involvement. In this respect, pedagogical tact is always tied to aesthetic preconditions. For without sensory perception, the "other" would neither be visible, nor could he or she show himself or herself nor could anything be shown to him or her. Pedagogical glances are linked to the knowledge of how different looks and modes of representation can arise—and how they require different forms of educational precaution and indulgence.

Perception plays a generally inconspicuous and yet very central role in pedagogical events. This not only refers to the look of the pedagogical professional who is able to perceive and assess persons and facts, but also to that of the one being educated. And this, in turn, has an impact on this professional. Perception is first and foremost an intersubjective process that involves showing and being shown as well as visibility and invisibility, and it is part of practically every pedagogical interaction and pedagogical process.

In the following, the pedagogical gaze or look is understood as a perceptive-interpretive approach to the one educated on the part of the pedagogical professional, and from the perspective of education and development: "*Bildung*[2] is the overarching frame of every pedagogical gaze, which differs depending on the pedagogical field of action and thus shapes pedagogical perception differently" (Schmidt, 2012, p. 15). The pedagogical gaze can be motivated in very different ways: it can be a controlling, monitoring, or even punishing gaze, but it can also be a compassionate, help-signaling regard, a look of solidarity. The pedagogical look can be astonished and appreciative, hurtful or encouraging, censuring or praising. A pedagogical gaze can be roving and focused or contemplative and challenging. It can overlook everything, and it can (want to) overlook a great deal. It also triggers specific reactions in the recipient. Pedagogical gazes are institutionally anchored, they have a specific power and can create realities (see Schmidt et al., 2016).

Pedagogical perceptions thus always include (identity-related) attributions of meaning, and these concern not only the visible, but above all the invisible. For example: In a certain arm movement that the teacher notices,

> she not only perceives the movement of the arm. In this movement she may recognize an expression of anger and rage, joy, humiliation, or despair. Also, in this movement, aspects of social identity of the person being observed are recognized. In the arm movement, the child, the milieu, their movement or their gender is perceived. (Schmidt, 2012, p. 16)

This example illustrates that pedagogical perception does not simply depict the world, but that perception generates patterns, images, and symbols of the world; it behaves *poietically*.[3]

Perceptions, including pedagogical ones, can thus be traced back to a "systematic connection of seeing, insight, understanding, forming an opinion, being convinced, and knowing" (Schürmann, 2008, p. 20). Every perception happens within a specific horizon, which generally appears only implicitly and usually remains itself undetermined. Thus, perception is determined by the person's self-conception, by the knowledge (and skills) available to him or her, and by a perceptual focus, or rather: The implicit logic of perception is conditioned by mimetic, discursive, and habitual practice. In this sense, the professional pedagogical self-conception can be understood firstly as an expression of a mimetic practice gained in the biography and training of pedagogical professionals in their confrontation with others, secondly as "knowledge as an expression of a discursive perceptual practice, and finally the focus as an expression of a habitual practice of the gaze" (Schmidt, 2012, pp. 59–64, 98). Finally, it can be stated that the gaze is not only a form of empowerment, but also an act of representation, of showing oneself (Marx, 2017).

What follows concerns the pedagogical gaze, in which essential decisions of pedagogical tact have already taken place, because this gaze itself decides what it wants to perceive and *how it* wants to judge. It is about the fact that ethical and pedagogical judgments are already made with the pedagogical gaze as well as about the fact that these gazes can be themselves tactful, that is, appreciatively respectful and benevolently just. In other words, they should be cautious and lenient, and they should literally "keep an eye" on the educational and developmental possibilities of those being taught. We focus on the pedagogue's view of those they are working with and thus on the pedagogues' self-perception as well as on their views of the pedagogical environment and on questions of tactful supervision. In addition, we focus on the aesthetic-ethical aspects of a tactful gaze and "overlook" phenomenological, epistemological, and psychological aspects of the gaze, which go hand in hand with attention, mindfulness, encounter, experience, sensitivity, perspective-taking, and self-identification. Finally, we are not concerned with a critical view of the tactful gaze as a maneuver, ideology, deception, strategy, or theater, as characterized by Niklas Luhmann (2002):

> Education that wants to attain the free acceptance of its challenges and incitements—but at the same time strives for effects—operates under the imperative of protecting the pupil's self-respect. In normal engagement one would speak of "tact" … Tactful communication must not, of course, show that it is based on the assumption that the person thus treated needs such treatment; that there is something to hide. … The problem is that it is not always possible to conceal the furtive nature of the good intention. Students may suspect that the teacher's benevolence, kindness, and measure are strategic concepts. (p. 74–75)

The tactful look of prudence and measure is not a tactic, but a pedagogical attitude that intends what is good for the other and his *Bildung*. In this respect, we associate with the tactful gaze aspects of perception and judgment as well as those of attitude and behavior.

Pedagogical Tact

Johann Friedrich Herbart (1776–1841) occupies such a central position in the formation of general pedagogical theory and in related research in pedagogical tact that he can be considered, in a sense, the first researcher of pedagogical tact:

> But for every theorist… who does not proceed with pedantic slowness… who puts his theory into practice in particular cases … a link intermediate between theory and practice …a certain tact, a quick judgment and decision that is not habitual and eternally uniform… inserts itself. But this tact is unable to boast, as a fully developed theory *should*, that while remaining deliberately consistent with the rule, it can at the same time answer the true requirements of the individual case. (Herbart, 1802/2022, p. 32)

If we interpret Herbart's formula systematically, pedagogical tact requires, *first, a* quick decision and, *second*, a prudent and thus rational judgment or assessment. *Third*, these processes must be carried out flexibly, or not "uniform[ly]," and *fourth*, they must do justice to the individual in question. Finally, at this point Herbart refers for the first time to tact as a link, a mediating principle (*Mittelglied*). He casts the difference between theory and practice as an opportunity; in more modern terms, tact is born from an "in-between," it functions as a bridging principle between polarities and contradictions (see Zirfas, 2012/2022, pp. 181–182).

On the other hand, if we interpret pedagogical tact phenomenologically as dynamic, then the "quick judgment and decision" seems to us to be strongly dependent on the perception of the teacher. And this perception, in turn, is essentially co-determined by the personal development of this individual and their academic training:

> Only in *action* do we learn the art; only in this way do we acquire tact, aptitude, quickness, and dexterity. But even in action, one learns this art only if one has earlier thoughtfully learned the science, made it one's own, attuned oneself through it, and is able to make sense of future experiences through it. (1802/2022, p. 33)

According to Herbart, pedagogical tact also includes actions understood as conducive to moral development (*Moralentwicklung*). In this, he grasps the overarching function and general purpose of pedagogy. It is about the development of a moral disposition, reflected or condensed in maxims on moral action. The condition for this lies in the connection to one's own life practice and its integration into general scientific structures. In terms of educational theory and anthropology,[4] it is first necessary to develop a particular pedagogical disposition, one that is the result of certain beliefs about the nature of humans and their *educatability* (*Bildsamkeit*; Herbart, 1802/2022, p. 35).[5] Only this disposition can produce pedagogical tact. This specific type of disposition is in turn to be brought together with the genuinely aesthetic question of taste. According to Herbart, it is a matter of acquiring pedagogical taste, so to speak, for the development of a particular other and for moral generality (see Burghardt, 2015).

The ability to do what is morally and pedagogically tactful thus depends not only on a specific practical disposition enabling one to act, but above all on the aesthetic competence of a tactful "taste" that puts those acting into a comprehensive conception of a state of affairs and thus makes it possible to behave adequately, that is, tactfully (see Suzuki, 2008). According to Hans-Georg Gadamer,

> Taste is defined precisely by the fact that it is offended by what is tasteless and thus avoids it, like anything else that threatens injury. ... From this it ultimately follows that all moral decisions require taste... It is truly an achievement of undemonstrable tact to hit the target and to discipline the application of the universal, the moral law (Kant), in a way that reason itself cannot. (1960/2004, pp. 33, 35)

At the same time, however, it becomes clear how strongly tactful taste can also be directed against the aspirations and desires of those engaged in action. Taste thus demands a change in character traits, that is, in virtuous dispositions, in order to do justice to the valences of tact. Thus, the following relationship can be established: If the main business of pedagogy is to be grasped in aesthetic education for morality, and if pedagogy is always involved in mediating contexts—between theory and practice, educator and pupil, or perception and action—then tact as the "middle member," as both the facilitation and performance of appropriate taste, also acquires a genuinely aesthetic structure (see Suzuki, 2010). Pedagogical tact is centrally dependent on aesthetic perception and judgment as its precondition (see Burghardt, 2016).

Pedagogical Perception as Ethical Competence

That tact is dependent on aesthetic perception and judgment points to one's being determined by the other's ability to see. Jean-Paul Sartre describes a simple scene in a park (Sartre, 1956, p. 254): You are sitting on a bench, contemplating the lawn or the chairs placed at its edge. A person walks past these chairs and looks at you. A banal situation, you would think. Everything takes place normally, there is no catastrophe, a stranger walks past me, who perhaps, like me, was looking for respite or who just wants to enjoy the fresh air. And yet the fact that the other is looking at me strikes me with a terrible power. It is as if Jacques Derrida's remark, "the mere presence of the foreigner, the mere fact of his having his eyes open, cannot not provoke a violation" (Derrida, 1979, p. 113), seems to be true. But to what extent is the mere presence of an observer already an abuse of myself?

In the gaze, the Other enters into a fundamental connection with me. Sartre even goes so far as to claim that I only receive my being through the Other, so that the Other thus simultaneously deprives me of my being as they grant it (e.g., Sartre, 1956, p. 260). In the gaze of the Other, a certain perspective on me is expressed that I cannot get a hold of, and which nevertheless—or precisely because I can't hold it—radically affects my self-relation. It is to the Other that one owes this wonderful and terrible condition. This is a condition in which one finds oneself as the one who no longer knows who he is, because he knows that this understanding of himself also derives from the gaze of this Other—an Other whose understanding, in turn, he does not know. "The gaze of the Other reaches out to that in me which I cannot see except through the resonance of his gaze. My echo of his actions, which in turn respond to me, constitutes my field of subjectivity by taking up questions not asked by the self" (Meyer-Drawe, 2000, p. 117). What student would not know what this is all about?

By being seen, I am no longer the same: I am driven out of my natural disposition; I adapt myself, if necessary, to the expectations (and expectations of expectation) projected by me onto the other. I may feel ashamed of my worn-out clothes, check my memory to see if I have seen this face before, monitor my position on the bench, and so on. I become someone who is seen, observed, appraised, and thus I no longer belong (solely) to myself, but also to another who has involved me in his gaze and existence. He looks at me, and makes me an object, he "reduces" me to an "object" of his seeing. And because I "know" or intuitively experience this, I am no longer so sure of myself. The Other sees me with other eyes that do what they will with me and involve me in a double alienation: alienation by the Other and the alienation by myself. I have no power over these processes of dispossession, and therefore the gaze of the other is a form of violence exercised on me: It makes of me an Other, it changes me. That "hell is other people" as Sartre also writes (1989, p. 45) is related to the fact that we are at the mercy of others because we are assigned our identity by them.

However, this assignment also means that you may not be seen the way you would like. Again, students in particular can speak about this. All theories of recognition (e.g., Honneth, 1996) fail because of this fact—because the feeling of not being seen properly, of being misunderstood, can always arise. Non-recognition or lack of recognition is also a crisis of the consciousness of visibility, because "those in the dark are not seen."[6] A person's reputation depends on whether and how he is regarded. This refers to an anthropological difference: that people always want to be seen as others, that they desire to be seen differently. No theory of recognition can therefore do without a theory of knowing and without a theory of misrecognition. For recognition runs the risk of "never getting beyond misrecognition in the sense of a refusal of knowing and recognition" (Ricœur, 2005, p. 161). Or as Helmuth Plessner (1924/1999) formulates:

> The soul suffers from nothing more than from not being understood. This is, though, its fate elicited by its own nature. For such failure of understanding is not a simple mistake, an overlooking of reality. Rather, it is both failure *and* comprehension. An apt judgment applies to us but hurts just as much as a false one. As apt, we one-sidedly see ourselves from our own or a foreign perspective as determined. (p. 110)

Therefore, there is a certain tendency to make oneself inconspicuous in order to be able to cope with one's permanent visibility. The result of the gaze of the other is often embarrassment, a sizing up of oneself from the other's point of view which goes hand in hand with not knowing and not being able to go on. Literally as a reflex of being looked at, the person no longer knows where to look. But the reverse, embarrassment from *not* being observed by the other, is also pedagogically instructive. The unobserved and unheeded becomes inactive and an embarrassed silence prevails—if this is not intercepted by a tactful, polite silence that lets one's counterpart "save face" (see Rogge, 2020, pp. 133, 142). It is also necessary to be pedagogically careful and tactful toward those who are silent and embarrassed; and this behavior should not give the impression that those being taught are incompetent and lazy.

Thus, even a permanent inconspicuousness is risky, because only one who is visible can be held responsible and liable but is also considered competent, insofar as there is a visible continuum between them and their actions. And only one who is visible can attain identity, insofar as this is tied to an image mirrored by others. In short, "if the look is only a look, what might follow and make the gaze a particular kind of action lies in the imagination of the beholder. Tact consists in knowing how different looks can be interpreted" (Reemtsma, 2008, p. 128). The pedagogical gaze appears tactful when, on the one hand, it *recognizes* what it has to do with its counterpart—with "their needs and wants, their search and struggles, inability and abilities" (Volmer, 2019, p. 130). This look is both discerning—because it perceives what "is"—and at the same time reserved—cautious in judgment, not wanting to offend the other, to commit them to a position, to shame or stigmatize them.

> The tactful person knows about the vulnerability of the other, and therefore exercises a certain restraint: he would rather say too little than too much, because the "too much," in contrast to the "too little," cannot be corrected again. What he says hits the note and also the bull's eye. (Volmer, 2019, p. 134)

However, the tactful pedagogical gaze is also a *distinguishing* gaze because it records problematic facts and confronts its receiver with the possibilities of different behavior or a different attitude. But it does so only with possibilities which the other can also accept: "The tactful person avoids bringing up a truth that can only hurt but not alleviate or help; he is silent where words of truth may bring despair, he speaks softly, where a loud voice would bring shame" (Brenner, 2012, p. 155). In the tactful gaze, the sparing of the other goes hand in hand with the invitation for the other to develop further, to unfold his or her potential, and to change previous patterns of behavior and attitudes. The tactful gaze is a *"loving gaze,"* one that brings respect and trust to the other person (Volmer, 2019, pp. 129, 133). It is a gaze of benevolent proximity that nevertheless respects the dignity and self-determination of the other and therefore always requires distanced pedagogical reflection. And it is a *situational-creative* gaze that "finds and invents [*findet und erfindet*] connections for one another" (Rogge, 2020, p. 223). It does this in order not only to advance communication and interaction between the participants, but also and above all to foster the education and development of the pedagogical other.

On the Ethics of the Tactful Gaze

Pedagogical tact encourages the pedagogical gaze to be flexible, situational and individually appropriate. It demands a gaze of justice that, if necessary, also brackets the generally valid, applicable rules and norms in favor of the individual case. Not mercy before justice, but the individual case before universal justice. The pedagogical tact of the gaze (and the judgment derived through it) begins with the premise that a theory of universal justice fails in the concrete case and would not be appropriate. What is pedagogically appropriate is what the educatability and self-determination of the other person requires for development. And precisely because we do not (and *cannot*) know this with ultimate certainty, and because, moreover, we cannot be sure whether our measures will be perceived as tactless or even debilitating or degrading, pedagogues must proceed tactfully (see Puchegger, 2015). The tactful gaze is a gaze that on the one hand respects the intimate sphere of the other and does not illuminate the remotest "corners" of his or her individuality. On the other, it is the look of an individual, a precise perception of the other, which in turn is only a prerequisite for the recognition of his or her educatability and self-determination: "The art of tact lies in sufficiently perceiving and respecting the other's need for self-protection and inner balance, but without foregoing interventions that stimulate and promote development" (Gödde, 2012, p. 233). At this moment, with Dietmar Kamper (1996), aesthetics gains ethical weight as a "trace of the Other in the perception of the world" (p. 148). This is because only perception—now independent of perception as passion and perception as infallibility[7]—is in a situation to determine the difference with or to the Other. "Thinking has to be 'perceiving' for a long time, not taking what is true, but practicing 'awareness,' practicing sensing, paying attention, respecting, and holding in high esteem the Other" (Gödde, p. 152; see also pp. 146–152). Such an ethical aesthetics as knowledge of the other can no longer be justified in absolute terms, but "functions in the manner of a foundation" (p. 149), and can thus also be described as the basis for pedagogical thought and action. But it must, Dietmar Kamper further emphasizes, be formed and practiced.

The pedagogical tact of the gaze knows on the one hand that the rules and norms of (pedagogical) justice do not regulate the conditions of their own application, that it is therefore under a fundamental deficit in terms of its operationalization. On the other hand, this type of pedagogical tact knows that the individual case can never be completely grasped by a model of general justice. If such a view is aware that it operates situationally, contextually, and in a manner that is consequence-oriented—while also being singular and incomparable, as well as experimental, skeptical, and fallible—it can also be tactful: flexible, and hypothetical in a measured way.

Under the rubric of forbearance or moderation, we understand a hermeneutical-ethical stance (see Wils, 2006, pp. 21–44) that has to do with the complexity and contingency of situations, the epistemological processes of understanding associated with them, as well as the possibilities of action linked to them. Included under this rubric are considerations of the mutability (of conditions) of action, the uncertainties of judgment, and conflicts of interpretation. Those who practice such moderation know that situations do not "simply" unfold according to a presupposed logic—be it one of action, of understanding, or of judging and being judged—but that such situations should be reviewed with measure and appreciation. When the particularity of a situation does not conform to the generality of a (political, social, pedagogical, etc.) law, it is not because hindsight lacks precision or is sloppy and arbitrary, but because it is in search of an appropriate, singular and fair assessment. On the contrary, hindsight appears to be particularly accurate because it seeks to arrive not at a hasty judgment but at a meticulous assessment of the facts. In this respect, if individual cases are always assessed consistently or similarly, measure may well become a "practice of *creating* order and norms" (Wils, 2006, p. 23). In this respect, measure does not offer a better idea of justice but a different one, one which is not interested in the general, but in the individual; more precisely, it is an individual idea of justice, which claims validity against the background of general ideas of justice. In Aristotle's *Nicomachean Ethics* (2018) we read the following:

> Hence, while the equitable (*epikeia*) is just, and is superior to one sort of justice, it is not superior to absolute justice, but only to the error due to its absolute statement. This is the essential nature of the equitable: it is a rectification of law where law is defective because of its generality. In fact this is the reason why things are not all determined by law: it is because there are some cases for which it is impossible to lay down a law, so that a special ordinance becomes necessary. …he is [equitable] who by choice and habit does what is equitable, and who does not stand on his rights unduly, but is content to receive a smaller share although he has the law on his side. And the disposition described is equity; it is a special kind of Justice, not a different quality altogether. (1137b–1138a).

Because actions are always individual cases (as Aristotle goes on to explain) and because these individual cases cannot be anticipated, a special sense of measure, a sensitivity for the uniqueness of this situation and a benevolent interpretation of it is also required. In his *Rhetoric*, Aristotle offers a small phenomenology of those cases in which measure seems to be necessary, for instance in "what is proper," but also in "errors, wrong acts, and misfortunes." These considerations seem to be just as important for educators as the practical consequences that result from a measured attitude.

> And it is equitable to pardon human weaknesses, and to look, not to the law but to the legislator; not to the letter of the law but to the intention of the legislator; not to the action itself, but to the moral purpose; not to the part, but to the whole; not to what

a man is now, but to what he has been, always or generally; to remember good rather than ill treatment, and benefits received rather than those conferred; to bear injury with patience; to be willing to appeal to the judgment of reason rather than to violence; to prefer arbitration to the law court (2018, 1374b).

It is no coincidence that Aristotle then brings measure or forbearance into a close relationship with tact:

The quality termed Consideration [γνώμη, good judgment; translated in German as "tact"], in virtue of which men are said to be considerate [tactful], or to show consideration for others (forgiveness), is the faculty of judging correctly what is equitable. This is indicated by our saying that the equitable man is specially considerate for others (forgiving), and that it is equitable to show consideration for others (forgiveness) in certain cases; but consideration for others is that consideration which judges rightly what is equitable, judging *rightly* meaning judging what is *truly* equitable. (2018, 1143a)

According to Aristotle, the tactful person unites phronesis (practical prudence) with forbearance by combining the knowledge of the generally valid rules with the individual addition of case-by-case justness. He who acts with measured leniency knows about the complexity, contingency, and uniqueness of situations, perceptions, interpretations, and judgments (see Wils, 2006, p. 191). He is therefore not only particularly lenient, but also particularly cautious.

Late in his career, Derrida (1992) devoted himself to the idea of individual justice. Derrida understands justice as an unconditional openness toward the other, which far surpasses the traditional models of justice as justice. These are models, for example, of distributive, procedural, transactional, and participatory justice. His idea of a "deconstructive" justice is due to

its affirmative character; In its demand of gift without exchange, without circulation, without recognition or gratitude, without economic circularity, without calculation and without rules, without reason and without rationality. And so we can recognize in it, indeed accuse, identify a madness. (p. 25)

To behave justly toward the individual other is to think and practice an unconditional, impossible-possible justice. To put it differently: To be just toward the Other is to expose oneself to the experience of multiple aporias. Justice, as an experience of the impossible, is the experience of—at least—five aporias: 1) because it must appeal to a (principled) rule that does not (yet) exist, 2) because it must make a decision for the undecidable singular, 3) because it requires an immediate decision in the face of justice that is yet to come, 4) because responsibility *before the* Other disavows responsibility *for* him—and 5) because it must make a decision for *itself and for the Other* (see Zirfas, 2001). The decision to abstain from a decision is also a decision—one which may well be tactless. Self-righteousness cannot be had without justice *before* and *for the* other. Therefore, it amounts to an impossibility: an impossible justice, which, however, is the condition of the possibility of justice.

Summary

Against the background of our considerations elsewhere (see Burghardt & Zirfas, 2019, four forms of the tactful pedagogical gaze can be identified on the basis of the four systematic functions of pedagogical tact, namely 1) as a mediating principle, 2) as an antinomic concept, 3) as a boundary model, and 4) as a creative-responsive concept:

1. The tactful pedagogical gaze mediates between one's own thoughts, feelings, and attitudes and the behavior and actions of the other person. In this respect, it is to a large extent a mimetic gaze that seeks to comprehend the (physical and linguistic) representation of the other—in order to teach something or to learn something. The gaze also appears *pedagogically* tactful, however, when it simultaneously links a movement of attention and invitation with a movement of distance and reflexivity; one could call the first movement "focused attention," the second (using a term from psychoanalysis) a "free-floating attention." "He who is not perceived cannot be sympathized with. To have experienced empathy, however, only forms the prerequisite for being able to develop and show empathy oneself" (Volmer, 2019, p. 74). The characteristics of "free-floating attention," the counterpart to focused attention, include the ability to allow the other person to have an effect on one's senses and mind, the creation of an open atmosphere, the attitude of "not knowing," and a subtle perception of one's own feelings, fantasies, and bodily sensations (see Gödde & Zirfas, 2007). A focused perception is then linked to an individual problem-context, a specific situation, a particular task or object and requires a closer and more detailed look, a more intense and contextualized look—to do justice to the learner, the situation, the task, or the object.
2. In terms of perception and image theory, there is a fundamental antinomy of the pedagogical gaze in modern pedagogy. It is related to the fact that, on the one hand, one has to form an image of the learners in order to be able to initiate learning processes and, on the other hand, one should not form an image of the "pupils" because every image always-already blocks developmental and educational possibilities. In this respect, modern pedagogy is located between "intransparency" and "understanding" (Luhmann & Schorr, 1986).

This dilemma in educational theory can be fittingly described by the term "diagnostic sensitivity." This term draws attention to the fact that in pedagogical-diagnostic observations, a scientifically precarious conclusion is drawn from the direct observation of students to regarding their competencies that are not immediately apparent. Two errors can occur, for example, in the question of special educational needs:

> In the first case (error of the first kind), the diagnostic decision can falsely claim the existence of "special learning needs," whereas in fact there are no special learning needs. In the second case (error of the second kind), the diagnostic decision may falsely claim that there are *no* "special learning needs" when in fact there are such needs. (Arnold & Graumann, 2005, p. 361)

And of course, this perspective of special education can also be formulated more generally: One can falsely assume individual competencies in one's diagnosis where there are none; and one can claim that students do not have any, although they certainly do.

Even if one has developed a systematic diagnostic view that has been professionalized through behavioral observations, interviews, performance assessments, parent and colleague interviews, self-diagnoses and supervision, the transition from the visible to the invisible remains precarious. And the required diagnostic sensitivity does not prevent the "inverse coupling of decision errors" (Arnold & Graumann, 2005, p. 362). To put it differently: A teacher who is so tactful and follows the principles of heterogeneous learning processes and individual justice, for example, will hardly make mistakes of the second kind (falsely claiming that individual students do not possess specific competencies). Such a teacher may consequently give more difficult tasks to many students without promising grades or evaluations—which in turn may become problematic for these teachers. Conversely, if you are tactful enough to follow the principles of a general performance ethic, you will hardly make mistakes of the first kind (falsely assuming individual competencies where there may be none). However, you may not pay attention to some students who have special talents that are worthy of support.

3. A tactful pedagogical view is also aware of the limits of its own perception—limits that can be biographical, institutional, training-related, subject-related, or focus-specific. Of course, these limits are not fully present in teachers' ongoing perceptions and actions, and yet teachers should be aware of these limits in (important) decisions and actions, and also make

them clear to students in certain situations. For example, teachers are often overwhelmed by the many mental diagnoses among their students. Even the increased sensitivity of one's pedagogical view due to personal interest or further training hardly leads to adequate assessments of the students. Psychological professionalism is often lacking here, which leads, among other things, to the fact that pedagogical views often attest to the presence of psychological disorders, although these are not present (a false-negative diagnosis: error of the second kind); and conversely, in the case of aggressive behavior (disruptions in the classroom, significantly impaired attention), errors of the first kind (false-positive diagnosis) are often committed: It is assumed that there is no "predisposition" to aggressiveness (Arnold & Graumann, 2005, p. 369).

4. Finally, a tactful pedagogical gaze will also perceive the unusual, the special, the extraordinary, and assess it as such. It is an attentive gaze that also knows how to register the "new" and "unfamiliar" without immediately adapting it to the common patterns of knowledge and ability: "Noticing does not yet constitute intentional or even propositional knowledge; at most, it is a preliminary form of knowledge, which as subliminal attention can certainly remain ephemeral and selective so that it eludes awareness and memory" (Waldenfels, 2004, p. 96).

In terms of tactful attention, some important differences can be noted: In terms of temporalities, current attention can be distinguished from remembering and anticipatory attention. The degree of accuracy and precision of attention can also vary greatly. Occasionally it can be useful—not only pedagogically—*not* to know facts too precisely. And finally, one should also realize that actual perception always represents only a fraction of what is sensually apprehended. In this respect, the pedagogical gaze can see new possibilities for development through attention: "In attention, we do not see other things, but we see what we see differently than before" (Waldenfels, 2004, p. 26). The tactful pedagogical gaze is also able to see facts and people differently, to assess them anew—in order to be able to offer learners different and better educational opportunities. It also serves to change attitudes and actions toward the other—or to put it briefly: It educates not only those who are to be educated, but also the educators.

Aspects of perception and judgment, as well as those of attitude and behavior, are connected with the (tactful) gaze. In this respect, questions of the gaze touch not only aesthetic principles—because the way I look at a state of affairs determines that state of affairs, but also ethical ones—because the way I look at a state of affairs determines the (un)just, (non)empathic, (non)benevolent, (non)supportive, etc., way I deal with it. Therefore, pedagogical looks should be tactful, that is, appreciatively respectful, benevolently just, and individually nurturing. They should see, for example, when it is fair to treat everyone equally and when it is fair to educate everyone individually. Tactful looks are cautious and indulgent, and they promote the educational and developmental possibilities of those who are being educated—especially because they themselves are open to other pedagogical forms of perception.

Notes

[1] *Blick* in German is translated as gaze, look, or view as well as glance; *Nachsicht* is translated as "measure," but could just as well have been rendered as "forbearance," which refers to abstinence (especially regarding enforcement), to endurance, and to leniency.
[2] *Bildung* refers to the holistic development of the individual in dialectical relation to the world, including their self-development.
[3] In the sense of *poiesis*, of being generative or creative.
[4] Anthropology is used here in the sense of the philosophical study of what it is to be human.
[5] "Herbart defined *Bildsamkeit* as a key pedagogical concept, as a latent arsenal of 'powers' [in the young] that is to be educationally awakened and released" (Böhm & Seichter, 2018, p. 73).
[6] Attributed to the film version of Bertold Brecht's *Threepenny Opera*.
[7] In German, perception is *Wahrnehmung*, literally "taking (nehmen) as true (wahr)." In speaking of perception as possibly independent of passion and of infallibility, Zirfas and Burkhardt first emphasize Wahr*nehmen* as passion and *Wahr*nehmen as infallibility.

Bibliography

Aristotle. (2018). *Nicomachean Ethics*. (H. Rackham, Ed. Trans.) Perseus. <https://perseus.uchicago.edu/>

Aristotle. (1999). *Rhetoric*. (H. Rackham, Ed. Trans.) Persius. <http://www.perseus.tufts.edu/hopper/text?doc=Perseus:text:1999.01.0060>

Arnold, K.-H. & Graumann, O. (2005). Schüler mit besonderen Lernvoraussetzungen. In H.-J. Apel & W. Sacher (Eds.), *Studienbuch Pädagogik* (2nd ed.) (pp. 359–380). Klinkhardt.

Böhm, W. & Seichter, S. (2018). *Wörterbuch der Pädagogik*. Ferdinand Schöningh.

Brenner, A. (2012). Der richtige Abstand: Takt trumpft Ethik. In G. Gödde & J. Zirfas (Eds.), *Takt und Taktlosigkeit. Über Ordnungen und Unordnungen in Kunst, Kultur und Therapie* (pp. 147–164). transcript.

Burghardt, D. (2015). Zwischen der Differenz: Zum Pädagogischen Takt in der Ethnographie am Beispiel Japan. In D. Burghardt, D. Krinninger, &

S. Seichter (Eds.), *Pädagogischer Takt: Theorie – Empirie – Kultur* (pp. 131–143). Ferdinand Schöningh.

Burghardt, D. (2016). Ästhetische Notwendigkeit. Johann Friedrich Herbarts ästhetische Ethik als Grundlage der Pädagogik. In D. Lohwasser, J. Zirfas, L. Klepacki, T. Höhne, & D. Burghardt (Eds.), *Geschichte der Ästhetischen Bildung* (vol. 3.2). *Klassik und Romantik* (pp. 145–156). Ferdinand Schöningh.

Burghardt, D. & Zirfas, J. (2019). *Der pädagogische Takt. Eine erziehungswissenschaftliche Problemformel*. Beltz Juventa.

Derrida, J. (1979). *Of Grammatology*. (G. C. Spivak, Trans.). Johns Hopkins University Press.

Derrida, J. (1992). Force of law: The "mystical foundation of authority." In M. Rosenfeld, D. Gray & D. Cornell (Eds.), *Deconstruction and the possibility of justice*. Routledge.

Gadamer, H.-G. (1960/2006). *Truth and method* (2nd ed. rev.) (J. Weisenheimer & D. G. Marshall, Trans.). Continuum.

Gödde, G. (2012). Takt als emotionaler Beziehungsregulator in der Psychotherapie. In G. Gödde & J. Zirfas (Eds.), *Takt und Taktlosigkeit. Über Ordnungen und Unordnungen in Kunst, Kultur und Therapie* (pp. 213–246). Transcript.

Gödde, G. & Zirfas, J. (2007). Von der Muße zur "gleichschwebenden Aufmerksamkeit": Therapeutische Erfahrungen zwischen Gelassenheit und Engagement. *psycho-logik. Jahrbuch für Psychotherapie, Philosophie und Kultur*, 2, 135–153.

Herbart, J. F. (1802/2022). Introductory lecture to students in pedagogy. In N. Friesen (Ed. Trans.), *Tact and the pedagogical relation: Introductory reading* (pp. 28–37). Peter Lang.

Honneth, A. (1996). *The struggle for recognition: The moral grammar of social conflicts*. (J. Anderson, Trans.). MIT Press.

Kamper, D. (1996). *Abgang vom Kreuz*. Fink.

Luhmann, N. (2002). *Das Erziehungssystem der Gesellschaft*. Suhrkamp.

Luhmann, N. & Schorr, K. E. (1986). *Zwischen Intransparenz und Verstehen. Fragen an die Pädagogik*. Suhrkamp.

Marx, B. (2017). *Der doppelte Blick. Zum Phänomen der Sichtbarkeit*. Königshausen & Neumann.

Meyer-Drawe, K. (2000). *Illusionen von Autonomie: Diesseits von Ohnmacht und Allmacht des Ich*. (2nd ed). P. Kirchheim.

Plessner, H. (1924/1999). *The limits of community: A critique of social radicalism*. (A. Wallace, Trans.). Prometheus.

Puchegger, R. (2015). *Der pädagogische Takt im Unterrichtsalltag.* Akademiker Verlag.

Reemtsma, J. P. (2008). *Vertrauen und Gewalt: Versuch über eine besondere Konstellation der Moderne.* Hamburger Edition.

Ricœur, R. (2005). *The course of recognition.* (D. Pellauer, Trans.). Harvard University Press.

Rogge, P. (2020). *Der aufeinander einspielende Takt: Hüter leiblicher Würde.* [Doctoral dissertation, Sport University Cologne]. <https://fis.dshs-koeln.de/files/5935343/978_3_534_40531_2_Rogge_aufeinander_spielender_Takt_gesamt1.pdf>

Sartre, J.-P. (1956). *Being and nothingness: An essay on phenomenological ontology.* (H. E. Barnes, Ed.) (H. E. Barnes, Trans.), Simon & Schuster.

Sartre, J.-P. (1944/1989). *No exit, and three other plays.* Vintage.

Schmidt, F. (2012). *Implizite Logiken des pädagogischen Blicks. Eine rekonstruktive Studie über Wahrnehmung im Kontext der Wohnungslosenhilfe.* VS Verlag.

Schmidt, F., Schulz, M., & Graßhoff, G. (Eds.) (2016). *Pädagogische Blicke.* Beltz Juventa.

Schürmann, E. (2008). *Sehen als Praxis. Ethisch-ästhetische Studien zum Verhältnis von Sicht und Einsicht.* Suhrkamp.

Suzuki, S. (2008). Takt als Medium. Überlegungen zum Takt-Begriff von J. F. Herbart. *Paragrana. Internationale Zeitschrift für Historische Anthropologie, 17*(1), 145–167.

Suzuki, S. (2010). *Tact in modern education.* Waxmann.

Volmer, J. (2019). *Taktvolle Nähe. Vom Finden des angemessenen Abstands in pädagogischen Beziehungen.* Psychosozial-Verlag.

Waldenfels, B. (2004). *Phänomenologie der Aufmerksamkeit.* Suhrkamp.

Wils, J.-P. (2006). *Nachsicht. Studien zu einer ethisch-hermeneutischen Basiskategorie.* Schöningh.

Zirfas, J. (2001). Dem Anderen gerecht werden. Das Performative und die Dekonstruktion bei Jacques Derrida. In C. Wulf, M. Göhlich, & J. Zirfas (Eds.), *Grundlagen des Performativen. Eine Einführung in die Zusammenhänge von Sprache, Macht und Handeln* (pp. 75–100). Juventa.

Zirfas, J. (2012/2022). Pedagogical tact. Ten theses. In N. Friesen (Ed. Trans.), *Tact and the pedagogical relation* (pp. 175–196). Peter Lang.

Creating Contact, Making Things Sound: Resonance and the Expression of Tact in the Classroom—Respect and Timing as Mediators of Self-World Relations

Jens Beljan

Introduction: Tactfulness and the Pedagogy of Resonance

For a general understanding of pedagogy, the aim of educational efforts lies either in the utilitarian acquisition of skills, knowledge, and competences, or in the realization of the student's inner self and their ability to create and construct their own reality and learning processes. Between the acquisition of objective facts and abilities and the realization of one's own potential lies another pedagogical dimension that focuses on the development of meaningful relations between the self and the world. If one takes the self-world-relation as the core concept of educational activities and processes, the question arises: Which qualities must these relations have in order to be educationally meaningful? Instead of measuring skill acquisition and performance, and rather than evaluating whether a person can construct, assess, and manage her own learning process, it is the form or quality of connectedness itself that is the analytical and normative criteria of what has been termed a "pedagogy of resonance" (cp. Rosa, 2019, pp. 238–248; Rosa & Endres, 2016; Beljan, 2019; Beljan & Winkler, 2019).[1] This account of pedagogy locates pedagogical meaning in resonating relations, in which students and teachers experience their relatedness to themselves and to each other, but also to topics, spaces or temporal structures as touching, moving, and reaching—also, finally, as touchable, reachable, and movable.

A similar account that focuses on the relational qualities in pedagogy can be found in the works of Max van Manen. Van Manen (2012) defined the pedagogical relation as a state in which an adult is open to the call of contact of a child (pp. 8–34). To react, to respond to and to answer this call, van Manen argues, parents, teachers, and pedagogues must possess a practical sensitivity and thoughtfulness that he defines as pedagogical tact. Focusing on relational qualities, van Manen (2015, p. 103) refers to the Latin meaning of the word *tactus*, which means to touch. Shōko Suzuki (2010) points out in her study on tact in modern societies, creating contact can be understood as a fundamental issue for the concept of pedagogical tact in intellectual history as well as in recent debates. For this reason, Suzuki defines "Takt as a contact point" (p. 153).

But while van Manen focuses on the social relation between a pedagogue and a child or a teacher and a student, the pedagogy of resonance has a wider perspective: The call of contact is not only one of the child, but of the world. We can experience ourselves in contact with the world in its social dimension (as van Manen argues), but we can also be in contact with other aspects of the world, like a piece of art, a scientific theory, a landscape, a political procedure, a material feature or an activity, but also with our own body and with the world within: our thoughts and feelings. The criterion that we experience certain qualities of contact when we learn and teach applies to everything human beings can come into contact with. Pedagogical tact is obliged to integrate these aspects of the world and their forms of contact, too. Moreover, van Manen's account is child-oriented, while, as I will show, resonance is relation-centered. While tact describes primarily a mode of action that influences and modulates the relation to the child, in the pedagogy of resonance it is the relational quality that is conceived as the primary locus of self-world-experiences and of a corresponding mode of action.

The pedagogy of resonance assumes that there are three different modes or qualities of self-world-relations. In the mode of resonance we experience ourselves as moved, reached, and touched by the world or by aspects of it, but we also have the experience that we are able to reach, move, and touch these aspects. The "world" is everything human beings can relate to; it can be other persons, but also books, materials, challenges, or thoughts, for example. To teach, as van Manen (2015) says, is indeed "to touch and to be touched" (p. 103). Resonance describes a quality, tension, or interplay that occurs in the self-world-relation. A resonant world relation may be experienced as answering, listening, and responding—frequently in ways that are benevolent or accommodating. In our daily communication we sometimes speak of resonance as the magical moment when sparks arise between students, the teacher, and a topic. In those moments the interchange between students, teacher, and the educational material intensifies and appears as meaningful and resonating.

In some respect the concept of resonance is already implicit in the original ideas about pedagogical tact that Herbart presented in his first lecture on pedagogy. Herbart defines tact as "a mode of action that gives vent to feeling and expresses how one has been affected from the outside" (Herbart, 1802/2022, p. 32). Consequently, for Herbart, pedagogical tact is neither an objective theory, nor merely a subjective state. Rather, tact follows from a specific relation between both, the self and the world, especially between objective theoretical and empirical knowledge on the one hand, and subjectively lived practice on the other. Tact, for Herbart, is the result of a connection, so that theoretical concepts and knowledge resonate with the educators' practice. For Herbart the result of such a resonance between practical experiences and formal educational theory is, as we know, tactful pedagogical action.[2]

As a quality in the interrelationships of students, teachers, and educational materials (or: the world), resonance can be distinguished categorically from two other modes of self-world-relation. When resonance appears in relations in which the self and the world are open to be affected by each other, *repulsion* describes a quality in which the self and the world are still in contact, but in a negative way. Repulsion is a relational mode in which the self and the world repel, deny, or reject each other so that their connection is characterized by hostility, defense, distance, reserve, exclusion, and tactlessness. Repulsion is manifest in experiences in which the school world, for example, is perceived as a fearful space filled with situations in which one can be blamed, ashamed, hurt, assaulted, rejected, excluded, or discriminated against. In such atmospheres, the probability increases that students as well as teachers take an attitude of rejection, defense, and control toward the world for the tactical sake of strictly regulating that with which they are confronted.

A third mode of self-world-relation can be described as indifference. In this relational quality, contact to the world, with others, and with one's own self is neither open nor closed, it simply breaks off. In her book on *Alienation*, the German philosopher Rahel Jaeggi defines indifference as a "relation of relationlessness" (Jaeggi, 2014, pp. 3–50). We experience ourselves as cut off from the world around us and within us. The world becomes "lifeless and insignificant" as Jaeggi puts it (p. 145). In the mode of indifference, students and teachers can have the experience that the world out there is not reacting or responding, that nothing resonates. They may have the feeling of not being seen and heard by others. Indifference is a relational quality in which the subject is not touched, moved, reached, or affected by what is encountered outside of or within it. Such a quality can therefore be described as a relation of "muteness" or "rigidity"—our connection to the world is "silenced," our relations remain devoid of resonance (Rosa, 2019, p. 9).

The analytical and normative basis of the pedagogy of resonance lies in the assumption that repulsion and indifference are deficient modes of the self-world-relation when repulsion or indifference become the dominant relational quality. The connection between students and teachers, as well as with educational materials and the corresponding aspects of the world fails. Admittedly, in our daily life we all experience resonance, repulsion, and indifference from time to time, and there is nothing wrong with that. But if students and teachers, either in some or in all aspects of their school life, suffer permanently from repulsion or indifference, they develop feelings of alienation, a sense of not being in touch with the world around them and—as world relations correspond to self-relations—also of not being in contact with themselves. In this case the school becomes a zone of alienation, in which classmates, teachers, and subject matter fail to generate a sense of meaning, and in which the (un)affected person develops the feeling that he or she is not heard, seen, or addressed. Students and teachers can come to the conclusion that they are not able to reach, move, or touch what they discover in this world. Obviously, alienation will reduce or block our ability to participate and reduce our capacity to be involved in learning processes.

Whether we experience our connection to the world as open and responsive (resonance), as closed and defensive (repulsion), or as a-pathic and mute or silenced (indifference) is not exclusively the product of the school environment. The experiences that children already have in their family and with their peers have an influence on their ability to or disposition for being open or closed in face of new learning experiences involving the an encounter of with unknown subject matter, unusual topics, or unconventional thoughts and practices. Also, the structure of society, and of the administrative system—as well as cultural self-understandings—will influence how children relate to the world in the medium of school life. Yet, schools by themselves undoubtedly also modulate in significant ways the quality of young people's and teachers' relationships to their own self, to others, and to the world. Schools are indeed a key institutional setting that relates and connects young people to the world (e.g., see Biesta, 2021).

I want to suggest that it is here that tact plays the most crucial role in educational processes, insofar as tact is a practical sensitivity for the modulation of relational possibilities: Tact modulates the quality of the self-world-relation. Obviously, in the history of pedagogy, the concept of tact was promoted by the conviction that a modern and supportive education is not driven by repulsion and educator aggression. Hence, Jörg Zirfas (2012/2022) sees as one precondition of pedagogical tact the recognition of human vulnerability that calls for a negation of violent relationships: This anti-repulsive attitude is expressed through the avoidance of "humiliations, insults, intimidation, and disrespect" (p. 186). Similarly, Volker Schubert (2015) speaks of pedagogical tact as a measure to prevent educational aggression, while for Jakob Muth (1962/2022), tact expresses itself in the avoidance of injury to the child. But tactfulness, as Max van Manen argues, is also an effective interdiction against educational indifference. He describes tactfulness as a form of awareness of and responsiveness to the lived experiences of the child. For the same reason Micha Brumlik (2015) defines "tactlessness" as a form of disinterest in and detachment from the child.

Traditionally, the concept of tact emphasizes that meaningful learning experiences and productive pedagogical situations cannot be produced, constructed, or controlled willingly. The corresponding German notion of *Unverfügbarkeit* that Jakob Muth takes as a key feature of pedagogical tact—and that Hartmut Rosa identifies as a central component of resonance—has no direct translation in English. The meaning is perhaps best expressed as "unavailability" or "undisponibility." It emphasizes that pedagogy cannot be reduced to instrumentalism or, as Biesta (2015) puts it, to a mechanical orientation. These approaches are manifest precisely in concerns about educational outcomes, evidence, control, and accountability that dominate public debates and educational policies. From the perspective of the pedagogy of resonance, the spread of instrumental reasoning (for example in the form of standardized testing) in educational systems globally tends to produce mute, cold, ossified, or lifeless and alienated self-world-relations (e.g., see Senkbeil, 2021). Indeed, the crucial difference between pedagogical tactfulness and instrumental tactics—a form of tact that is superficial, manipulative, egocentric, or just "naked external power" (Adorno, 1951/1974, p. 2)—may be found in the relational qualities in which it is embedded. While tact is based on mutual sympathy, responsiveness, and resonance, a tactic aims at one-sided instrumental control and at a neutralized world that is predominantly mute, incapable of speaking or answering. A school environment that is predominantly shaped by repulsion and indifference is likely to encourage young people to develop a tactical orientation, instead of connecting them to a world that is marked by diverse possibilities to resonate with environments, materials, and others.

The Vibrating Wire to the World: Experiences of Resonance

Before I explore some forms of resonance in the classroom that are mediated by pedagogical tact—and as I suggest, also by pedagogical tone—I will examine further what is involved in an experience of resonance. There is general agreement that resonance, as understood here, contains four main components: the openness to be affected, the conviction of self-efficacy, a moment of undisposability, and a structural transformation.

Without the openness to be affected by students, materials, colleagues, or even by one's own thoughts, one is literally not open to be touched, moved, or "affected" from "the outside" (as Herbart put it; 1802/2022, p. 32)—or from the world within (as the pedagogy of resonance would add). An openness to be affected and a willingness to be reached, touched, and moved by something, as the first component of resonance, corresponds with intrinsic interest in the world, in other persons, in challenges, in learning experiences, and in the growth of others. Being affected is primarily a bodily experience (Beljan, 2019). As the phenomenologist Thomas Fuchs (2013) specifies: "The body is a 'resonance body,' a most sensitive sounding board in which interpersonal and other 'vibrations' constantly reverberate" (p. 221). Understanding the body as a "sounding box" is different from conceiving it as a mere object or tool whose use is to be optimized. While the body can be treated as a mute object that can be used and formed instrumentally, tactful comportment toward students as embodied beings requires sensitivity for intercorporeal responsivity—not intrusive and controlled interventions. Similar to the concept of resonance, pedagogical tact is not oriented to an external outcome, but to the intrinsic features of the pedagogical relation itself.[3]

Though resonance can be said to be a form of inter-affectivity (affect shared bodily and otherwise between individuals), it is not a specific affective state or emotion, for example a feeling of happiness or enthusiasm. Resonance describes a specific way of being interconnected (Rosa, 2019), an intensity in pedagogical relations that can occur in shared happiness (instead of mocking laughter), as well as in shared sadness (in contrast to the isolation of depression), and even in feelings of anger (as opposed to toxic hate speech[4]). Instead of asking which emotions are instrumentally useful to increase the outcomes of learning processes, the pedagogy of resonance describes emotions as a primary form of self-world-relation, a bodily voice that tells us something about the meaning of our connection to the world.

But human beings don't just have the need to be touched, moved, and reached passively by the world, they also want to experience their capacity to actively reach, move, touch, and affect the world. This leads to self-efficacy as the second component of resonance. Taking the notion from Bandura's psychology, Rosa (2019) argues that we must trust or believe in our ability to touch and affect the world both out there and within us. In the context of a pedagogy of resonance, self-efficacy doesn't mean to believe in one's ability to control a complex or challenging situation, as Bandura (1993) suggested; it means that we can participate actively in or creatively be part of what we relate to. Obviously, such beliefs in one's self-efficacy cannot be accessed or produced instrumentally. They depend on the resonating features of the surrounding world—whether they are social, natural, political, or aesthetic in nature—which respond or answer to the subject's attempts to influence and affect them. While resonance describes a relational quality, tact captures a practical capability that results from this quality, in which experiences of affection (first component) and of self-efficacy (second component) are possible: "Tactful means full of touch, and it also means to be able to have an effect" (van Manen, 2015, p. 103).

The undisposability or unavailability of resonance is the third component. Resonance cannot be produced instrumentally or created willingly; it needs a free-floating medium. A teacher who tries to force his students to resonate with him or with school tasks would immediately produce alienation. Similar to tact, resonance should not be seen as a one-sided or one-way reflection of one's own self, but as a relation in which the poles or partners respond to each other. Rosa consequently differentiates resonance from "echo":

> Resonance is not to be confused either literally or figuratively with the concept of *echoing* for precisely this reason. An echo lacks its own voice; it occurs in a way mechanically and without any variance. What resounds in an echo is never a response, but only ever oneself. (Rosa, 2019, p. 167; emphases in original)

Resonant relations occur in the encounter of two or more voices, tones, or frequencies that reach, move or touch each other mutually. Therefore, the pedagogy of resonance aims at the development of the student's own voice and tone through which they address and respond to the world. In contrast, schools can tend to organize educational processes effectively as echoes, defining beforehand what they want to see or hear from their students—giving students no option to develop their own voice, connecting them only to predefined aims and procedures that cannot be individually or creatively appropriated.

When resonance means something other than the resounding of one's own voice, the phenomenon is best defined as an experience of difference: in resonating relations one is touched by a voice or frequency that is not one's own. Similarly, tact is often described as a practical attitude toward differences. Adorno (1951/1974) for example characterized tact as "the discrimination of differences" (p. 37). Similarly, Herman Nohl was convinced that teachers realize pedagogical tact not through the mechanical invariance that for Rosa corresponds to the echo—but through "a singular *distance* to his subject as well as to his student" (Nohl, 1933/2022, pp. 80–81; emphasis in original). Following Nohl, Schubert (2015) writes that "tact secures the obligatory space of freedom … that children and educators need to be able to shape educational relations productively" (p. 9). To develop one's own voice or to hear the "voice" of a subject or topic at hand, students, teacher, and the subject itself need an autonomous space in which their own connection to the world can be unfolded, explored, created, and expressed.

Because neither tact nor resonance can be produced instrumentally, both phenomena can never be understood fully as mere techniques of control, as methods of accountability, or as recipes for managing educational resources and assessments. Both tact and resonance capture the compassionate involvement and the responsive engagement of our primary self-world-relations. In its most elemental meaning, tact is a mode of contact (so that the partners and poles can reach, touch, move each other) and a sensitivity to preserve a distance toward the other so that the genuine voice or frequency of the other is hearable and sensible. To act tactfully, Muth (1962/2022) writes, one has to be encompassed by and involved in "the individual situation," not be entangled with one's own self, not isolated or coldly distanced (p. 103). One has to be touched by the existence of the other. In the same text, Muth emphasizes that tact relies on a certain kind of distance and reservation to mind the relational difference. To put it simply, resonance can occur when we come in contact and in touch with the voice and frequencies of others or of the other.

In this discussion of affectedness, self-efficacy, and undisposability, I have examined the intertwinement of the concepts of tact and resonance. The concept of pedagogical tact corresponds with resonance, as tact stresses the practical requirement to accept the elusive, intangible, unpredictable, surprising, and situational character of pedagogical relations (e.g., see Burghardt & Zirfas, 2019). In this sense tact can be understood as a practical comportment and sensitivity that results from resonant relationships, as well as being the precondition for the appearance of resonance in relations. I will now go on to show how both concepts are implicated in "transformation."

Through mutual reverberation and co-vibration, new qualities can arise which would otherwise be unavailable to student, teacher, or subject matter on their own. Being touched by something can and often does transform persons and how they see the world (Buchleitner, 2017), corresponding to the fourth component of resonant relation: transformation. As theories of transformative learning from Jack Mezirow (1978) and Andrea English (2013) to Hans-Christoph Koller (2018) imply, the reconfiguration of the self-world-relation is not a one-sided but a multi-sided transformation. When teachers and students reach each other, it is not only the student who learns to see the educational material and the aspect(s) of the world it represents in a new way, but also the teacher is touched by the student's perspective and may also see or experience the subject matter anew. In a similar way Alex Aßmann defines tact (with reference to Jacob Muth and Herman Nohl) not as a possession or property of the isolated subject, but as a relational quality between subjects and the world (Aßmann, 2008, p. 63).

Moreover, without transformation, there might be a greater risk in producing only "simulations of resonance" (Rosa, 2019, p. 186) or what Rosa calls "resonance bubbles." In the famous novel *The Wave* by Todd Strasser from 1981—a story based on true events—teacher Ben Ross establishes a rigid, disciplinary high school-regime (called "the wave") to explore how it was possible that so many Germans became Nazis. At first it seems that the fascistic developments that follow create intense experiences of resonance: A very strong feeling of community, bonding, enthusiasm, and inspiration arises between its members. Even those students who formerly were victims of mobbing and exclusion became recognized members and were able to experience self-efficacy. However, the atmosphere soon came to be hostile and repulsive: students were forced into line, while critics of the project, like a student-journalist, were excluded, isolated, and threatened. When a Jewish student was attacked, the teacher had to end the experiment.[5]

What comes to light here is that some forms of apparent "resonance" are not based on affective openness, individual self-efficacy, undisposability, and transformation, but on the contrary, are formed by the instrumentalization of affects, the establishment of rigid disciplinary regimes, controls, and manipulations. The atmosphere of resonance being considered is in fact a "resonance simulation," a "filter bubble," and a "realm of the echo," in which the voice of the other is suppressed. As a bubble and simulation, resonance is instrumentally created and controlled from the inside, by actively producing alienation outside, so that no external disruption or critique can be articulated and reach the bubble, encouraging only hostile repulsion and solidifying indifference. For this reason, resonant relations can never flourish and be sustained without the acceptance of alienation, as I argued above. Transformation does not mean bringing everything into resonance, for this would represent coercion to resonate, which would lead directly to alienation. A teacher who forces his students to be enthusiastic about his topic would very soon produce its contrary: repulsive seclusion and indifferent coldness. Bildung here does not aim at amelioration by simply forcing everything to resonate. Rather, Bildung is a vivid, dynamic, dialectical process between experiences of alienation and an attempt to bring aspects of the world to resonate through transformative acquisition. Through this process both poles, the subject and the world, can change together. Jacob Muth (1962/2022) and Micha Brumlik (2015) are right in their intuition that tactfulness requires a moment of ascetism, the ability to hold back: When profuse affect, like overwhelming enthusiasm, mutes the other—without an openness to alienation—it can do harm to the resonance axis of the students.

Pedagogical Tact: Creating Contact in the Social Axis

Nearly every theoretical account of pedagogical tact locates the concept primarily in the social relation of an educator and those educated or, between a teacher and their students. As I suggested, in the pedagogy of resonance, tact is the practical sensitivity and attunement by which a person is able to establish and maintain contact by participating in what the other is experiencing. In moments of tact-mediated resonance, certain kinds of self-world-experiences can be enacted which I have described as ones of familial, jovial, and collegial contact, and also as experiences of dignity, recognition, deference, and devotion (Beljan, 2019). Here I want to explore tactfulness more closely in its potential to create strong moments of resonance via its ability to deal respectfully with boundaries and limits.

A facet of pedagogical tact is its manifestation as respect. Respect can be described as a tactful sensitivity in dealing with boundaries of the Other and of others. In fact, pedagogy can be understood as continuous work on the edge. Boundaries and limits can be of every sort; they can be personal (e.g., limits of a subject's knowledge, abilities, ideas, experiences or control), social (the limits of trustworthiness, encounters, mutual understanding, cultural backgrounds, languages etc.), or material (the access to resources, tools, and techniques). The sensitive treatment and acceptance of boundaries and limits can, in turn, be called *respect*.

Respect and tact are related concepts, but they are not the same. A relation to a subject or to a task can appear respectful because one fears authority and the consequence of repulsive rejection (e.g., see Reichenbach, 2011, pp. 160–161). Respect can also be the result of a loss of contact and indifference. To "respect" each other could mean to simply privilege one's own autonomy and not intervene or even care when another may appear to be endangered.[6] Both forms of respect imply some kind of tactlessness. To be tactful, respect has to manifest in an atmosphere of resonance. When teachers treat the boundaries of their students tactfully—with sensitivity and openness—children can experience being respected. Experiencing oneself as being respected in this way can be a very strong moment of contact, an experience of resonance and of touching and being touched.

If tactful action aims to encourage resonance, it does not demand solely that the other be able to open up (something that can be undermined by repulsive or indifferent forms of respect), it requires also that the person affected remain autonomous; that her borders and limits are respected so that she can speak or address the world with her own voice, interest, or questions. If the subject's boundaries are violated by bodily or psychological aggression or other forms of tactlessness, the self closes itself and loses its openness. It becomes fossilized, defensive, protective, and control-oriented. If, on the other hand, the boundaries of the child are indifferently ignored—either by pushing the child beyond their limits or by being artificially contained in an overprotecting environment (so they can never sense their limits)—the self can become diffuse, empty or "cold" to affect around it. The self can lose its ability to speak with its own voice and to resonate with the world in an individual, personally transformative frequency.

> In the pedagogy of resonance, tact means neither to break nor to ignore personal, social, and material boundaries. It means to "liquefy" them. Resonance appears whenever and wherever subjects, in the course of a given interaction, are touched or affected by an Other or by others, and, moreover, are themselves capable of touching or affecting

others; wherever one's relationship to the world and thus also to oneself appears to be at least potentially fluid or liquefiable. (Rosa, 2019, p. 179)

Boundaries are needed not only to structure teaching and learning processes, but also to make some frequencies sound and to mute others. Without boundaries on the institutional and organizational level, the classroom would decay into an area in which multiple voices, affections, and frequencies are chaotically confused. Students would not be able to pick up a sound which they can become attuned to—mentally, emotionally or socially. They would simply not be able to hear a highlighted frequency with which they could resonate.

On the personal level, creating contact by respectfully dealing with limits, boundaries, and conditions depends on the tactful behavior of the teacher. Sometimes students are confronted with situations in which they are in danger of losing their personal boundaries. Young people might need help from a teacher to maintain their self-defined personal boundaries which secure the autonomous space from of which they can speak with their own voice and address the world with their own "frequencies" (e.g., interests, thoughts, ideas, feelings, or values). The blackout phenomenon is a paradigm case in which the student loses contact with herself and the world. A blackout can be described as the total breakdown of boundaries, which makes it impossible to find one's voice. Imagine a student standing in front of a class and freezing up while she is giving a presentation. Her wire to the world literally becomes "frozen." Not only her mind, but also her body suddenly stops. Not only has she lost contact with her own thoughts, but she has also lost contact with her classmates, who may feel her silenced self-world-relation and sense the disconnected discomfort of her muteness. One may well imagine how much she wants to cancel her relation to the situation and the world of the school in total. In such a case it may be a good idea to help the student to recover her own boundaries. This would happen neither by pushing nor by ignoring her limits, but by being as fully present to her as possible. The teacher can become a compensating border guard, directing attention away from the student thus buying her some time, allowing her to get in contact with herself and with her task (e.g., see van Manen, 1991, pp. 162–164). Respecting boundaries in this case means allowing the other to secure or recover her personal space, a space out of which she can speak and address the world from her own position and with her own voice.

Muth (1962/2022) explains that tactful reserve, is neither an indifferent state of not-wanting-to-be-involved, nor an attitude of pressure and rejection—but instead a way of being in contact with the Other and with others (p. 89). In so doing, Muth allows us to see how tact is a special sensitivity to other's personal boundaries. But while Muth argues that this reserve is for the sake of the other, the concept of resonance focuses on the relation itself. While Muth perhaps overemphasizes the passivity of the teacher, in the pedagogy of resonance, the teacher is ascribed a more active role. He or she is cast as a constitutive part of the world, one that affects students with ideas, questions, challenges, new experiences, and alternative perspectives, and who intensifies, reverberates and transforms students' affections.

But tact is also conceptualized as a practical consciousness of the limits of educational intentions, expectations, and possibilities. Pedagogical tact can be described as the ability of the teacher to distance herself from the claim, having direct and linear effects on the students learning. This seems to be important for avoiding cold and indifferent relations that arise as a result of frustration, anger, or ignorance, particularly if one does not reach one's predefined goals or prescribed learning outcomes.

While in the pedagogical literature, tact is often associated with respectful sensitivity to personal limitations, I want to suggest that tact is also manifest as support for the overcoming of fixed boundaries and limits. Sometimes students reach boundaries that affect their capacity to grow, limits which they cannot overcome by themselves. In such cases it may be necessary to help them to rid themselves of personal doubts, inner conflicts, or external barriers. Education has always to deal with the questioning of established self-understandings and worldviews. In the famous movie *Dead Poets Society* (1989) the unconventional teacher John Keating pushes an excessively shy student to express his poetic gift and sensitivity in front of the class. In an intense scene, Keating provokes the student by yelling at him, so that he comes in touch with his expressive energy. The teacher talks insistently to him, so that the student forgets the gaze of his classmates, something that has always limited him. By insistently encouraging and pushing him, Keating leads the student to raise his own voice and to find his own personal style. But at the same time, the teacher stands in close contact with his student, remaining at the student's side until the young man comes into contact with his poetic potential. In this way, the student overcomes his boundaries and expresses himself, touching the teacher and the students deeply. Of course, this is a fictional and dramatic representation, but what it highlights is a daily experience, at least in the realm of pedagogy: In order to break through the boundaries limiting of our self-world-relation, we sometimes need the tactful yet provocative intervention of a teacher.

In this scene, tact turns out to be the crucial element for an educational process in which the experience of alienation leads to a newly established axis of resonance in the aesthetic dimension. Tact allows the teacher to retain contact with young people when they suffer from experiences of repulsion and indifference, from moments of crises. In this way, tact allows old orientations and self-understandings to dissolve and new relations to the self and to the world emerge.

In other cases, it might be a significant moment of resonating contact or of the experience of being "seen" and respected, which allows a child to escape their limitations. Listening to a child actively might give them the space to have an experience of self-efficacy as this term is understood by Rosa (2019). A child who talks about a project, an idea, a worry, or a hope might not long for an answer from an adult that would solve a problem, but for someone who really is able to understand them for who they are. In some moments, not presenting a solution, not doing something directly for them, can be an expression of trust in the child. The aim of solving every problem of a child immediately can cultivate a muted self-and-world relation in which children become little more than an echo of the adult. A pedagogy of resonance is more concerned with responsive incitement than instrumental instructions.

Last but not least, tactfulness that aims to facilitate resonances will initiate and provoke interactions and exchanges across borders. Community life can provide resonating inspiration for learning processes, as the concept of service learning or as place-based pedagogy affirms. Teachers sensitive to resonance may also provoke exchanges and encounters within the student body: Whether one can ride horses, play role games, speak Japanese, or practice boxing, different interests can be used to create spaces in which students enter different segments of their world and further fields of resonance. The school can be a space in which the openness to resonate with another or others is cultivated.[7]

Pedagogical Tone: Making Things Sound in the Material Axis

Educational relations are always interpersonal, but they are also always connected to the part of the world that is represented in educational material or the subject being taught—whether it is an historic episode, a mathematical formula, a poem, the use of a toothbrush, or one's own thoughts, feelings, and judgments. In this respect, we not only establish a relation to others, but also to the Other: For example, to things, materials, challenges, pieces of art, nature, or idealistic principles that have aspects of the unknown or unexpected. Therefore, the teaching process in the classroom (as everywhere else) is constituted of two dimensions, the social and the material axis—the relation to another and the relation to the world and the alterity encountered in the world. These two axes define what one can call with Norm Friesen the relational "pedagogical triangle" (Friesen & Osguthorpe, 2019).

While pedagogical tact describes a certain way of contacting others—of interacting—pedagogical tone defines a way of connecting students (and also teachers) to the educational material. "Hitting the right tone" makes things sound, it makes our wire to the educational material vibrate. Unfortunately, van Manen's (2002) book *The Tone of Teaching* does not differentiate consistently between tact and tone, and the word "tone" is referenced only ten times. Nevertheless, in his thoughts about the acquisition of knowledge, van Manen refers precisely to a notion of tone that is quite compatible with the understanding I suggest in my interpretation of a pedagogy of resonance. Acquiring knowledge, van Manen argues, is not only a matter of cognitive processes, a collection of objective facts, or something completed through the curriculum. Knowing is instead described as a relation to the world, a way of connecting and responding to the things we discover out there:

> Obviously, to know a particular subject means that I know something in that domain of human knowledge. But to know something does not mean to know just anything about something. To know something is to know what that something is in the way it speaks to us, in the way it relates to us and we to it. (van Manen, 2002, p. 61)

Obviously, the material is not literally speaking. "Speaking" here refers to the phenomenological fact that artifacts, objects and materials express a meaning in the way they address and relate to us. This relation expresses its meaning in the educational material and in the significance that this part of the world around us has in our life. Advocates of a pedagogy of resonance are convinced that the moment of realizing a relation is essential for every pedagogical process. But such moments are also fragile and cannot be taken for granted. Probably every one of us has had the experience in school that curriculum (and the aspect of the world that it highlights) does not "speak" to us, that we cannot relate to what is presented—or even that the teacher has lost their connection to the subject. In this case the relation and the meaning of the object stays "mute" and "silent." In short: The pedagogy of resonance focuses on the relational quality itself.

If we regularly experience topics and educational materials as dangerous impositions, as threats to our integrity, as a one more chance to feel ashamed in front of the class—and if we feel ourselves helplessly overwhelmed or exposed to the frustration of the teacher—the relation to the lesson content will certainly appear as one of hostility and repulsion. To refer to van Manen's metaphor: The material would not speak to us, but reject us. If we have the experience that the subject being covered has nothing to do with our lives, that it is just an arbitrary requirement to complete the lesson, if we are not able to experience it reaching, moving, or touching another (a person or thing), we will probably develop a relationship of indifference in the material axis.

But every topic "makes relationships possible," offering an opportunity for relation, van Manen writes. And he adds: "Our responsiveness, our 'listening' to the subject, constitutes the very essence of the relationship between student and subject matter" (van Manen, 2002, p. 133). Now the central questions of the pedagogy of resonance are: What happens in the classroom, what are teachers doing, what attitudes and sensitivities do they have, what organizational and didactical preconditions are given—so that students and teachers can relate to the material, that it can speak and resonate? It is this moment of resonance, the moment of speaking and responding, the moment in which an objective becomes an educational subject that is important. The ability and sensitivity needed for fostering such relational moments of contact with educational materials can be called "tonal behavior."

Writing elsewhere, I have identified at least seven forms of pedagogical tone (Beljan, 2019). The first of these is motivational tone, the ability to express interest and enthusiasm about the subject, and the sensitivity to respond to students' motivational and inspirational responses. The second is personal tone, the intuition needed to give abstract concepts and content a personal touch, animating them through the people involved, for example, experts, explorers, scientists, emperors, or reformers. The next is biographical tone, a way of making sense of the curriculum by connecting it to the lifeworld and life-stories of the students. The fourth is curricular tone, the ability to explore connections and relations within different parts of the curriculum. Next is practical tone, based on Dewey's insight that learning experiences are the result of practical interactions with the world. Spatial or place-based tone involve facilitating experience of places, architecture, and locations enacting meanings and telling stories. The last is aesthetic tone, the ability to make things "sound" through dramaturgy, artistic forms of expression, and compelling reenactment. This list does not claim to be final. One might want to add more forms of tonal behavior. Next, I use an example to sketch out pedagogical tone in its temporal dimension.

Because self-world-relations are realized in time, they are always also time-relations. In the temporal dimension pedagogical tone manifests as a sense of timing (Zirfas, 2015, p. 28). Timing has several facets. One aspect is the practical awareness that some topics, developmental steps, or learning experiences are more likely to be taken or happen in certain windows of opportunities or "fruitful moments," as Copei (1962) has put it. Being sensitive when the time may be ripe for a child to be confronted with a given aspect of the world can be understood as an essential component of tonal behavior.

Another facet of timing is its connection to what Aristotle called *kairos*. In contrast to its counterpart *chronos* (the objective and measurable timeline that flows continuously), kairos is a temporal experience in which a relation to the world is suddenly transformed into something meaningful and opportune. Love at first sight, grasping a once in a lifetime chance, experiencing the one moment that changes everything, are kairotic moments. But those moments in which our relation to time changes and resonates must not only be grasped as rare, improbable, and extraordinary events. They can also be found in the daily routine of school life. In the kairotic moment, "time becomes more intense, more filled with significance, more memorable for the students," as Rowntree and Gambino (2018, p. 73) argue. In time-intensifying situations of kairos, we can experience the world, God, or society as if they had formed an alliance with us, as if they had heard or seen us and are answering affirmatively to what we are doing and waiting for. Here temporal tone can be manifest as an awareness and sensitivity regarding moments that become alive and biographically significant for students.

Kairos expresses itself in the classroom, for example, in epistemic Aha-Moments or affective Wow-moments, where a curricular topic, mediated by the teacher, starts to speak and resonate within one or more students. Such moments are in themselves uncontrollable or nondisponsble: They cannot be produced willingly by the teacher, by the students, or by institutional arrangements. But at the same time, they are not just a matter of sheer luck. These fruitful epistemic, affective, motivational, or evaluational moments can be provoked, invited, opened up, cultivated, or welcomed. School arrangements can either enable or block these moments of resonance that are tantamount to the transformative appropriation of educational materials.

Another facet of temporal tone that makes things "sound" in the classroom can be described as the art of waiting. Every teacher knows situations in which a more or less complex question is met by a blank and mute reaction from students. This could be an expression of repulsive defensiveness or an atmosphere of enmity, but it can also be a symptom of indifference, a loss of contact or inner disconnection. Of course, it may be the manner of questioning that makes students become merely an echo of the teacher. When the teacher knows exactly what he wants to hear (for example by only asking for facts), it is difficult for students to speak with their own voice. But there may be something else that closes spaces of resonance, that is not so much bound to the art of questioning, but to the rhythm of waiting for an answer. Resonance is a time-consuming and time-intensive process. Concerning this issue, Mary Budd Rowe (1986) provides a simple explanation:

> To put it briefly, when teachers ask questions of students, they typically wait 1 second or less for the students to start a reply; after the student stops speaking, they begin their reaction or proffer the next question in less than 1 second. If teachers can increase the average length of the pauses at both points, namely, after a question and, even more important, after a student response, to 3 seconds or more, there are pronounced changes (usually regarded as improvements) in student use of language and logic as well as in student and teacher attitudes and expectations (p. 43).

Rowe (1986) is saying here that the lengthening of wait time is not just a technical modulation of chronos (the objective time), but an intensification of kairos. When waiting corresponds with a change in the teacher's and students' attitudes and expectations, lived time has the power to transform. Rowe clearly argues that a modulation of wait-times intensifies the responsiveness and interchange among students, and between the students, teacher, and the educational material: Students give longer and more complex answers, support their conclusions with stronger evidence or logical arguments. They also speculate more, ask more questions and propose more experiments, and the exchange between students increases while muteness decreases. Even the most "invisible people become visible," Rowe writes (p. 45). But the teacher also encounters her educational material and her students in new ways: Responses become more flexible, discourse increases, more kinds of questions related to understanding are asked, and expectations for the performance of certain students seems to grow. Tonal sensitivity for Rowe means a kind of temporal calmness and a sense for how much time students need to formulate and articulate their own answers in their own voice.

There can be no doubt that teaching and learning occur "in time," within temporal parameters. One can therefore say it is, among other things, a temporal practice. The temporal structure therefore modulates how we can come into contact with the world and how we can engage within it. Time can therefore be experienced as our friend, who is on our side, supporting and regulating what we are doing. But it can also be experienced as our enemy, something that only means the acceleration of our life and that drives us to exhaustion.

In a technical understanding of education, time comes into sight almost exclusively as a resource, one that must be used, banked, and controlled to manage learning and teaching processes, a resource that can be used effectively, saved efficiently, spent lavishly or be killed through meaningless activities. Since Kounin's (1970) groundbreaking studies on "learning-time," this kind of time is seen as the core variable for the outcome-effect of learning and teaching. What is easily missed here is that we as teachers and parents not only manage time like we do a scarce resource like money, but we are also participating in the practice of "rooting" or "embedding" young people (as well as ourselves) in time. Educators not only work with time, but they also connect human beings to time. As a resource, we control and manage time instrumentally and we make it into an echo of our aims, goals, and purposes. What this amounts to is that time "speaks" with its own voice, that we encounter as the other.

It is here where rituals acquire an essential meaning for personal, social, and organizational development, growth, and transition. Rituals can be embodiments of transformative transitions; they can bring temporally induced transformations to the awareness of those who are involved. Familiar rituals are not, as Hans-Ulrich Grunder puts it, "stiff and empty ceremonies" (Grunder, 2001, p. 226). They can instead relate us to time. They do this by enacting a practical and bodily dimension of change, instead of its merely being observed cognitively (e.g., "You are fourth grade now!") Tone can be understood as the ability and sensitivity required to make rituals "sound" in time. Jan Assmann (2011) spoke of the "connective structure" that human societies create by enacting rituals, by establishing a shared narrative within their symbolic world (pp. 2–4).

Scheduling, from daily routines up to annual plans, can be organized as dramaturgical tension. Those arcs create phases of intense strain and softened relaxation. Resonance is a bodily experience, and the body is not able to resonate continuously in high frequencies of inter-affection. In my research on a German summer-program for gifted students (Beljan, 2019), these tension arcs turned out to be the central ingredients for the experience of resonance. The tone of teaching can also work on the level of physiology. As the debate about biorhythms has shown, some students (and teachers) are just not open to be affected and touched by educational topics and materials, simply because they are tired in the morning or exhausted in the afternoon. The school as a space of resonance therefore has to be realized with sensitivity to various temporal dynamics that allow students and teachers to fall into (and out of) sync.

Classes are scheduled often only in reference to the objective or administrative time, wherein the event or subjective time is ignored or pressed into objective limitations. Temporal time regimes are not only quantitatively given, measured in minutes, days, or years, indifferent to subjective experience. Moreover, time is a medium through which we experience our connection to others, to the world, and to ourselves. In this last sense, time can be something we work with synergistically, giving our life structure, meaning, and depth. (The meaning of being, as Heidegger [1927/2005] showed, is deeply bound up with our temporal dwelling in the world.) But time can also be repulsive and indifferent, something in danger of running out, something that relentlessly drives us forward, something that destroys possibilities to intensify our relation to the world, to others, or to ourselves. In this sense, acceleration and shortage of time is, according to Rosa, a cardinal enemy of resonance (Rosa, 2010).

Human beings develop an understanding of who they are and what gives their life meaning by placing themselves in time, which includes not only one's personal lifetime, but also the historical or higher spiritual timelines. Our relation to all of these aspects define who we are, answering the question where we come from and where we are going. Maybe tonal behavior that makes things sound is characterized also by a sensitivity for the attachments to these different dimensions of time. There can be no doubt that referring to these timelines and the positions of the students in them can become a strong moment of temporal resonance.

In this last section of my chapter, tact and tone have been reinterpreted from the perspective of a pedagogy of resonance. While pedagogical tact describes primarily one-sided or mutual action to realize contact with the other, resonance defines a special relational quality. There are several advantages or shifts that occur when this relational quality is taken as the core concept of learning and teaching processes. First, pedagogical tact must no longer be understood substantially as "correct" or "right" behavior. Whether a behavior is tactful or not depends on its contribution to open interactions and spaces for resonance. The primacy of resonance and the relational quality it suggests enables us to conceptualize tact as historically and culturally variable. Second, the pedagogy of resonance is not so much concerned with the subjective experience of resonance, but with the intersubjective and objective preconditions for its appearance. The question would be, then, whether personal, social, institutional, temporal, architectural, and didactical components of the school-world-relation can be reconstructed either as spheres of resonance or as areas of alienation. Tactful behavior could be conceived as an indicator of a resonant school environment. Conversely, the promotion of tactful behavior might require a reduction in spaces of alienation and the cultivation of spaces of resonance in school.

Notes

[1] See Rosa, H. (2019). *Resonance. A sociology of our relationship to the world.* Polity, especially pp. 238–248; see also a number of German-language books from Belz Juventa: Rosa, H., & Endres, W. (2016). *Resonanzpädagogik. Wenn es im Klassenraum knistert*; Beljan, J. (2019). *Schule als Resonanzraum und Entfremdungszone. Eine neue Perspektive auf Bildung*; Beljan, J. & Winkler, M. (2019). *Resonanzpädagogik auf dem Prüfstand. Über Hoffnungen und Zweifel an einem neuen Ansatz.*

[2] Before Herbart, it was Herder who spoke of a teacher ability (and a quality in the classroom) to touch and reach students. Herder called this quality *Grazie* (grace). For example, Herder, J. G. (1765). Schulreden. Von der Grazie in der Schule. In: *Herders Werke in fünf Bänden* (vol. 5) (pp. 241–254). Aufbau. Helmut Plessner (1924/1999) argued that grace in this

same sense is the "adequate foundation for the healing effect of tactful conduct" (p. 165). For a reinterpretation of Grazie in the context of resonance, see Beljan, J. (2019). *Schule als Resonanzraum und Entfremdungszone*, pp. 67–76

3   The description and analysis of pedagogical relations that Max van Manen introduced to English scholarship, has a long tradition in the German account of the *geisteswissenschaftliche Pädagogik*. See: Friesen, N. (2017). The pedagogical relation past and present: Experience, subjectivity and failure. *Journal of Curriculum Studies, 49*(6), 743–756. Van Manen consistently privileges internal, intrinsic features of pedagogical relations over external, extrinsic ones: "Situational pedagogy focuses on the intrinsic rightness and goodness of what is required in the concrete situation itself—it is not concerned with some abstract principle or the eventual consequence of action" (van Manen, 2015, p. 200). Earlier in the same book, van Manen writes: "Pedagogical action that is motivated by the external setting of learning outcomes and achievement goals inevitably turns into instrumental action—action in the service of calculative ends... However, pedagogy does have internal goals that determine the appropriateness of how to act with children and young people" (p. 43).

4   Concerning feelings of anger, one can differentiate a sensation of anger in which a person responds with repulsion or indifference to the perspective of the other and in which she wants to silence or "destroy" the opposing voice. In contrast to such a destructive attitude, constructive anger (and opposition) is distinguished by an orientation in which the opponents are still open to each other's perspective. This, in turn, is the precondition for a transformation to a mutual shared understanding of the situation, one in which mutual resonance becomes possible again.

5   See Beljan (2017, pp. 142–145) for a more extensive discussion

6   Regarding conceptions of respect based on the autonomy of the individual, see Giesinger, J. (2014). Wirksamkeit und Respekt. Zur Philosophie des Unterrichts. *Zeitschrift für Pädagogik 60*(6), 817–831.

7   I describe an actual classroom in this sense as an "oasis of resonance-learning" in Beljan (2019, pp. 350–374).

Bibliography

Adorno, T. W. (1951/1974). *Minima moralia: Reflections on a damaged life*. (E. Jephcott, Trans.). Verso.

Assmann, J. (2011). *Cultural memory and early civilization: Writing, remembrance, and political imagination*. Cambridge University Press.

Aßmann, A. (2008). *Pädagogik und Ironie*. Springer VS.

Bandura, A. (1993). Perceived self-efficacy in cognitive development and functioning. *Educational Psychologist, 28*(2), 117–148.

Beljan, J. (2017). *Schule als Resonanzraum und Entfremdungszone: Eine neue Perspektive auf Bildung*. Beltz Juventa.

Beljan, J. (2019). *Schule als Resonanzraum und Entfremdungszone: Eine neue Perspektive auf Bildung* (2nd ed.). Beltz Juventa.

Beljan, J., & Winkler, M. (2019). *Resonanzpädagogik auf dem Prüfstand: Über Hoffnungen und Zweifel an einem neuen Ansatz*. Beltz Juventa.

Biesta, G. (2021). *World-centered education. A view from the present*. Routledge.

Biesta, G. (2015). On the two cultures of education research, and how we might move ahead: Reconsidering the ontology, axiology and praxeology of education. *European Educational Research Journal 14*(1), 11–22.

Brumlik, M. (2015). Pädagogische Taktlosigkeit. In D. Burghardt, D. Krinninger, & S. Seichter (Eds.), *Pädagogischer Takt: Theorie – Empirie – Kultur* (pp. 53–57). Ferdinand Schöningh.

Buchleitner, A. (2017). Wie Resonanz emergiert. In T. Breyer, M. B., Buchholz, A., Hamburger, S. Pfänder, & E. Schumann (Eds.), *Resonanz – Rhythmus – Synchronisation: Interaktion in Alltag, Therapie und Kunst* (pp. 105–116). transcript.

Burghardt, D., & Zirfas, J. (2019). *Der pädagogische Takt: Eine erzieherische Problemformel*. Beltz Juventa.

Copei, F. (1930/1962). *Der fruchtbare Moment im Bildungsprozess*. Quelle & Meyer.

English, A. (2013). *Discontinuity in learning: Dewey and Herbart as transformation*. Cambridge University Press.

Friesen, N., & Osguthorpe, R. (2019). Tact and the pedagogical triangle: The authenticity of teachers in relation. *Teaching and Teacher Education, 70*, 255–264.

Fuchs, T. (2013). Depression, intercorporeality, and interaffectivity. *Journal of Consciousness Studies, 20*(7–8), 219–238.

Giesinger, J. (2014). Wirksamkeit und Respekt: Zur Philosophie des Unterrichts. *Zeitschrift für Pädagogik, 60*(6), 817–831.

Gödde, G., & Zirfas, J. (2012). Die Kreativität des Takts: Einblicke in eine informelle Ordnungsform. In G. Gödde & J. Zirfas (Eds.), *Takt und Taktlosigkeit: Über Ordnungen und Unordnungen in Kunst, Kultur und Therapie* (pp. 9–29). transcript.

Grunder, H.-U. (2001). *Schule und Lebenswelt: Ein Studienbuch*. Waxmann.

Heidegger, M. (2005). *Being and time*. Oxford University Press.

Herbart, J. F. (1802/2022). Introductory lecture to students in pedagogy. In N. Friesen (Ed.), *Tact and the pedagogical relation. Introductory readings* (pp. 28–37). Peter Lang.

Herder, J. G. (1765/1978). Schulreden. Von der Grazie in der Schule. *Herders Werke in fünf Bänden* (vol. 5). (pp. 241–254). Aufbau.

Jaeggi, R. (2014). *Alienation*. Columbia University Press.

Koller, H.-C. (2018). *Bildung anders denken: Einführung in die Theorie transformatorischer Bildungsprozesse*. Kohlhammer.

Kounin, J. (1970). *Discipline and group management in the classroom.* Holt Rinehart and Winston.

Mezirow, J. (1978). Perspective transformation. *Adult Education Quarterly, 28*(2), 100–110.

Muth, J. (1962/2022). Pedagogical tact: Study of a contemporary form of educational and instructional engagement (selection). In N. Friesen (Ed.), *Tact and the pedagogical relation. Introductory reading* (pp. 85–113). Peter Lang.

Nohl, H. (1957). *Die pädagogische Bewegung in Deutschland und ihre Theorie.* Vittorio Klostermann.

Plessner, H. (1924/1999). *The limits of community: A critique of social radicalism.* (A. Wallace, Trans.). Prometheus.

Reichenbach, R. (2011). *Pädagogische Autorität: Macht und Vertrauen in der Erziehung.* Kohlhammer.

Rosa, H. (2010). *Alienation and acceleration: Towards a critical theory of late-modern temporality.* Nordic Academic Press.

Rosa, H., & Endres, W. (2016). *Resonanzpädagogik: Wenn es im Klassenzimmer knistert* (2nd ed.). Beltz Juventa.

Rosa, H. (2019). *Resonance: A sociology of our relationship to the world.* (J. C. Wagner, Trans.), Cambridge University Press.

Rowe, M. (1986). Wait time: Slowing down may be a way of speeding up! *Journal of Teacher Education, 37*(1), 43–50.

Rowntree, N., & Gambino, A. (2018). Pedagogy as slow time in the extra ordinary bush. In P. Renshaw & R. Tooth (Eds.), *Diverse pedagogies of place* (pp. 70–90). Springer.

Schubert, V. (2015). Maßnahmen gegen erzieherische Aggressivität: Vergleichende Perspektiven zum pädagogischen Takt am Beispiel Japan. In D. Burghardt, D. Krinninger, D. Burghardt & S. Seichter (Eds.), *Pädagogischer Takt: Theorie – Empirie – Kultur* (pp. 145–159). Ferdinand Schöningh.

Senkbeil, T. (2021). Takt, Resonanz, Widerstand, oder "Was braucht es zur Revolution?" In T. Senkbeil, O. Bilgi, D. Mersch, & C. Wulf (Eds.), *Der Mensch als Faktizität: Pädagogisch-anthropologische Zugänge* (pp. 189–212). transcript.

Strasser, T. (1981). *The wave.* Delacorte Press.

Suzuki, S. (2010). *Takt in modern education.* Waxmann.

Van Manen, M. (2002). *The tone of teaching: The language of pedagogy.* Althouse Press.

van Manen, M. (2012). The call of pedagogy as a call of contact. *Phenomenology & Practice*, 6(2), 8–34.

van Manen, M. (2015). *Pedagogical tact: Knowing what to do when you don't know what to do*. Routledge.

Weir, P. (Director). (1989). Dead poets society [Film]. Touchstone Pictures.

Zirfas, J. (2012/2022). Pedagogical tact. Ten theses. In N. Friesen (Ed.), *Tact and the pedagogical relation* (pp. 175–196). Peter Lang.

Zirfas, J. (2015). Zur Ethnographie des pädagogischen Takts. In D. Burghardt, D. Krinninger, & S. Seichter (Eds.), *Pädagogischer Takt: Theorie – Empirie – Kultur* (pp. 25–42). Ferdinand Schöningh.

Postscript

Pedagogical Tact and Teacher Professionalization: A Conceptualization

Thomas Senkbeil and Norm Friesen

This document offers a conceptualization of pedagogical tact formulated for course development at the Institute of Kindergarten and Primary school (IKU) of the University of Applied Sciences Northwestern Switzerland (PH FHNW). This overview emphasizes the field of practical teacher training and explains the significance of pedagogical tact for the professionalization process.

In German-speaking Europe, teacher professionalization aims above all to develop the pedagogical ability to "relate directly and immediately" to an autonomous other; "to another who has their own sense of what is meaningful, and their own interpretive authority" (Helsper, 2020, 1:50; Helsper, 2021, pp. 20, 94). Significantly, such an ability relies on the teacher's capacity for tactful words, actions, and decisions—ones that are appropriate for the student(s) and the circumstances of a given pedagogical situation. Pedagogical tact is conceptualized here as having four areas of practical application: 1) it starts from and protects the vulnerability of the child; 2) it offers a concept of difference operative in normative and reflexive terms; 3) it serves as a heuristic, an analytic in the professionalization process, and 4) in this context, it stands as a principle of mediation between theory and practice and other pedagogical tensions and oppositions. These aspects of pedagogical tact are relevant not only for teacher practice, but also for the development of programs or courses of study which prepare teachers for practical action. Pedagogical tact in this and other senses incorporates characteristics of Aristotelian entelechy or goal-orientation. In this conception, the final goal and the way it is achieved are the same—both involve the exercise of tact. Similarly, professionalization has awareness and reflection as its precondition, yet it is also the means by which such awareness and reflection—as well as the action they enable—are practiced and cultivated.

There are several concepts and assumptions to be explicitly highlighted and defined. The first is reflection, or more specifically, *reflectivity* (*Reflexivität*). Particularly in discourses of professionalization, this term encompasses but also goes beyond metacognition (thinking about thinking), self-reference, or learning from experience (reflective practice). Reflectivity is ultimately less a technique and more a disposition or way of being. It describes a decentered self or subjectivity, rather than one that is egocentric or centered in itself. It designates the ability to take up another's perspective and to see oneself as another does—indeed, to welcome such scrutiny. In his 2021 book, *Professionalism and Professionalization in Pedagogical Action*, Werner Helsper speaks of *"critical reflective knowledge"* (*kritisches Reflexionswissen*) which subjects "framework conditions, prerequisites, and the integration of one's own professional actions and practice… to reflection" (p. 136). The concept of *meta*-reflectivity (Cramer et al., 2019) goes even further, subjecting research findings and literature to critical reflection based on experience and observation. Reflectivity can characterize more than just an individual's relationship to themselves and their own thinking. It is also applicable to a given professional context, a theoretical system or a historical epoch. Reflexivity in these different senses—again, going well beyond reflection on practice—is an essential part of pedagogical professionalism.

Boundary reflection, a heightened awareness of and sensitivity to boundaries and limitations—whether corporeal, affective, or pedagogical—represents a sub-type of reflection, and is directed to the definition of boundaries through otherwise unreflected habit. Pedagogical action, perhaps especially in elementary and early childhood settings, is based on a sensitivity to and negotiation of boundaries. On the most basic terms, education and pedagogy designate the exercise of influence on others, on children and youth (see Friesen & Kenklies, 2023). This influence cannot be coercive or overbearing, nor can it completely refuse its educational function—for to refuse to exercise influence on the child is to nonetheless influence, indeed, often to amplify the influence of others (e.g., see Mollenhauer, 2014, pp. 6–8). Boundaries determined by cultural and organizational rules and norms, and by ever-changing situational parameters, are a constant concern. Another way of putting this is to say that pedagogical tact is a matter of distinguishing differences and engaging in deviations, both in thought and action. Tact according to Theodor Adorno (1951/1974) is "the determination of difference. It consists of knowing deviations" (p. 36).

Besides reflection, *habitus* and *role theory* also deserve clarification: Sociologist Pierre Bourdieu's notion of habitus refers to deeply ingrained habits, skills, perceptions, and dispositions that individuals acquire through extended periods of participation in a social group or context. These contexts include professional memberships and ones found in institutional settings, with a shared habitus being manifest in "intuition" or "gut feelings" that can guide both thinking and action in these contexts. Role theory, on the other hand, focuses on how such thinking, feeling, and acting can also be understood in "dramaturgical" terms—as the performance of a professional role. As sociologist Erving Goffman (1956) pointed out, one's professional role or identity stands in dynamic and sometimes contested relationship with one's "authentic" or biographical personhood. Goffman also posited that the maintenance of others' and one's own roles requires tact—often in the form of "tactful withdrawal" (p. 149). In this context, tact can be again said to work as a sensitivity to difference, acknowledging existing deviations in regulating the situation between role requirements and actual performance. A tact of difference and deviation is important for professionals, given that the two moments, role requirements and actual performance, almost never coincide (see Burghardt & Zirfas, 2019).

Conditions and Challenges Facing All Teachers

Because pedagogical tact is a way of dealing with difficulties and challenges that arise in teaching, it is first important to briefly consider some of the general and the more specific conditions that teachers face today. The first of these can be identified in a manner canonical to German educational studies: Through sociologist Niklas Luhmann's insight that everyday pedagogical life and practice is inevitably characterized by a "technology deficit" (see Töpper, 2023). This is not about a lack of new technology in the classroom, but instead brings attention to the absence of a clear cause-and-effect relationship between pedagogical measures and student learning. It refers to the inevitable abrogation of the intention and influence of the pedagogue by the emergent autonomy of those to whom their intention and influence is addressed. Teachers cannot plan or act in a primarily instrumental way, they cannot simply "cause" students to learn. Like teaching, learning is a process entered into freely. There is, in other words, a fundamental unpredictability and contingency that marks all pedagogical processes.

The lack of control and certainty in pedagogy is exacerbated by the increasing heterogeneity of student backgrounds and needs. As a result, flexibility and improvisation are required now more than ever in lesson planning and in instruction itself. The teacher is also called upon to invest ever greater effort to offer students shared time or space for favorable experiences. Often, this kind of time and space must be carefully patterned and regulated to provide a foundation of safety and trust—elements indispensable for the risks and uncertainties inherent in learning and teaching. These patterns and sequences have been studied anthropologically, and can be seen specifically as *rituals*, as preplanned collective events that are repeated regularly and have a symbolic meaning.[1] Particularly in the early grades, these ritual performances exist in many forms. Show and tell, choral reading, carpet time, a morning greeting: These enactments structure the time and space of the school and classroom, orienting children within a social order and facilitating constructive interaction. The morning ritual in class consciously creates an expected start to the day and promotes group cohesion. Other rituals can assist with transitions between different fields of socialization (e.g., playground vs. assembly) and institutions (e.g., school vs. home and family), enabling social learning that is vital for growing children. Such performances give interaction an overarching meaning and can be used to mitigate or resolve difficult situations and potential crises. Rituals are also useful when standard methods and techniques do not suffice, for example, in situations of evaluation, criticism, or of completion of a work phase.

Conditions and Challenges Facing Primary Teachers

Children in the primary grades are existentially dependent on spaces of opportunity in which they can develop and release their curiosity as well as have their energies directed constructively. Many things are happening in their lives for the very first time. From the perspective of developmental psychology, these children are in a permanent process of experimentation and transformation. In these processes, personality development and the promotion of social skills and self-regulation must all be initiated, facilitated, and expanded.

When designing and constructing learning opportunities and methods of support, the primary school teacher is always guided by the child's developmental level and individual perspective as well as by the curriculum. Lessons in primary school are different from those in the higher grades in that they are organized and designed to incorporate multiple disciplines and subjects. Various kinds of subject-specific knowledge must be acquired while learning different "modes of accessing the world" (Dressler, 2013)—such as reading, writing, and mathematics. The teacher not only cares for children but must also be a specialist in early childhood education and curriculum, as well as a generalist in those aspects of the larger world that are relevant. According to Bachmann et al. (2021), "this raises the question of the development of a professional self-image with regard to the relationship or interplay between subject-specific expertise and generalist teaching design and, associated with this, the specific professional habitus of generalists" (p. 19).

Processes that are particular to certain stages of personal development and maturation—such as student-teacher attachment—introduce still further difficulty and unpredictability. Needless to say, primary education deals with a sensitive phase of development in which secure emotional bonds between teachers and children can contribute significantly to maturation. These and other factors mean that teaching in primary school is often improvisational, involving rapid decisions—with classroom challenges frequently forcing the teacher to deviate from advanced planning. Finally, under contemporary conditions, teachers in primary school are given an increasingly comprehensive educational mandate:

They must address the holistic development of each child in addition to imparting curricular knowledge and skills.

Pedagogical Tact

We have shown how teaching is a profession that combines multiple areas of ability and knowledge, and that is marked by intersecting and also diverging moral, interpersonal, and epistemic demands. In this context, tact refers to the ability of a teacher, in the midst of this manifold complexity, to engage with and respond to the needs, both of the class as a whole and also of the individual student. The locus of pedagogical tact is the context where at least two singularities—the teacher and the student(s)—engage and overlap. In a broader sense and in line with its etymological relation to touch or tactility, tact implies a concrete physical-psychological experience, a sensory cognition. In its canonical definition, it is a "quick judgment and decision" that is capable of doing justice to the requirements "of the individual case" (Herbart, 1802/2022, p. 32). Pedagogical tact also serves as "a link intermediate between theory and practice" (p. 32), one that enables this rapid judgment and action. This tact is about the teacher's attention to and involvement with the child *and* also with the world. It is these two essential pedagogical elements—child and world, or more narrowly, student and curriculum—that the teacher wishes to open up to each other. The pedagogue's primary task, in other words, is to influence the relation of child and world, so that it becomes deeper, more open, and more productive (see Friesen & Kenklies, 2023).

As understood in the tradition of continental pedagogy,[2] the aims of education—for learners of any age—are manifold and interrelated. While imparting knowledge and facilitating children's "learning to learn" are indispensable, these processes are only a part of the general pedagogical aim to awaken and foster the children's individual *self-activity*. This term refers to activity that appears either spontaneously or through prompting, but always arises "from the child's own initiative, and according to their own goals" (Böhm & Seichter, 2018, p. 430). This activity is realized by allowing children to pursue their own interests and to develop their own abilities—allowing them to engage actively, creatively, and independently with each other and with their environment. The accomplishment of the child's eventual autonomy—the ultimate goal of all education, according to continental pedagogy—is in this way nurtured for the future and prefigured in the present. In supporting the child's current self-activity and eventual autonomy, pedagogical tact is realized in the space between what is already real for the child and what is possible for them in their potentiality. In an influential German monograph on pedagogical tact, Jakob Muth (1962/2022) says that this tact works to find "the correct middle point between the educative help of the teacher and the possible self-help of the child" (p. 36). Tact is not an explicit set of rules, nor a response calibrated to the sum total of moral, interpersonal, and epistemic demands. Instead, while not contravening or invalidating any of these rules and demands, tact relies crucially on the professional *habitus*, on the disposition, sense, and temperament of the individual teacher. And it is through knowledge of rules and requirements—for example, as gained through professional preparation—that this habitus, this disposition, can be cultivated.

Counterintuitively, one of the most important exercises of tact—and thus also of teacher professionality—is knowing what *not* to say and what *not* to do. As Jakob Muth (1962/2022) explains, this reserve or "holding back" is appropriate in encountering and engaging with alterity and vulnerability in ways that are expressive of "a feeling for the 'you' (or Thou)... a respect for the ultimate inaccessibility of the Other" (p. 92). This respect is registered through acts of omission, via the intentional suspension or attenuation of the influence on the other that is central to pedagogy as a whole. This inaction or reserve is an expression of the teacher's recognition of the limits of their own knowledge and authority, an acknowledgment of the ultimate recalcitrance and ungovernability of the learning process. It is also an affirmation of the intrinsic value of the self-active child's own interests and initiative. As Müller (2015) puts it, tact represents the self-limitation of pedagogy, the deliberate restraint of "pedagogical rationality" in recognition of the child's individual character and their vulnerability. This susceptibility of the child is further underscored through the German developmental concept of *Bildsamkeit*—or what Dewey referred to as "plasticity." While for Dewey, this concept is about "the adaptability of an immature creature for growth" (1916, p. 52), in the continental tradition, *Bildsamkeit* (and also *Perfectabilité*) refers to the combination of latent "'forces' that are to be awakened and unleashed educationally" (Böhm & Seichter, 2018, p. 74). This is to occur through a kind of interactive shaping that (ideally, at least) can lead to perfection. To reference Müller (2015) again, *Bildsamkeit* means that the young person's individuality should unfold in relative independence, and never "be subsumed without remainder into their role in the educational context" (p. 21). One is never just a student or a learner, but always an individual person. Together, *Bildsamkeit* and self-activity describe a dialectic[3] between the child's impressionable character, their *receptivity*, and their equally important incipient personality and expressivity, their *spontaneity*. This establishes the first area of tact's practical application in teacher professionalization: *Its capacity to protect the vulnerability of the child—and which arises their susceptibility to injury, particularly in terms of their development, plasticity, and openness, and their emergent and labile individuality.*

A tactful pedagogy frames the professional treatment of the vulnerability of the child by taking the child's boundaries as its measure: Neither curricular nor relational engagement should overtax or violate the integrity of the child. This represents a principal moment in the *ethos* of tact. In this context, *ethos* refers to deeply held and guiding beliefs and responsibilities possessed not only individually but shared by a (professional) group. Helsper explains that like other professionals—such as medical doctors—the pedagogical professional is subject to a special, universal claim or expectation:

> [Despite what] they may be called to address, [they] cannot refuse to address [a child in] crisis, but must provide ... services regardless of the person, in the sense of strict universalist equal treatment. This makes it clear that professional action is subject to a special ethos and cannot be regulated by money, the market, or bureaucracy. (Helsper, 2021, p. 20)

And this applies at least as long as the child is on school grounds—if not also well beyond them. The pedagogical ethos involves the teacher not just as a professional, but as a responsible adult, a whole person, shaped by their own biography, and upbringing. It is ingrained via practice and expertise, and it is realized through an embodied mindset that Rödel, for example, describes in Chapter 2 in this collection: "A pedagogical ethos… only becomes manifest in certain actions or practices of positioning oneself in front of others, of positioning oneself in a pedagogical situation" (p. 70). A pedagogical ethos, Rödel continues, "has to be acquired and refined in the field of practice itself, and by actually doing something, creating something, or interacting with someone" (p. 66).

Pedagogical tact also enables the mediation of theory and practice; in this sense it designates the exercise of the practitioner's power of judgment. Pedagogical theory cannot be seen as separate from practice; rather, the two are co-emergent. Nonetheless, practice is sometimes characterized by assumptions that are untested through formal investigation; these are often supported by mutually reinforcing routines, rituals, habits, convictions, and beliefs. At the same time, sound professional practice requires a variety of theoretical heuristics and practical alternatives for action. One of the most important of these heuristics is an understanding of a kind of dialectical set of oppositions and tensions, a number of which can be said to be identifiable in reflection on any given pedagogical situation (comprised of teacher, child[ren], and pedagogical purpose). These oppositions begin with the opposition of theory and practice but extend much further. As Friesen shows in his chapter in this collection, continental pedagogy views the field of pedagogical action and decision as being marked by "antinomic structures," by opposed possibilities for teacher action. These include, for example, the opposition of distance and proximity (literal and figurative, between student and teacher), student individuality and classroom community, support for or counteraction of student behavior, teacher authenticity (i.e., biographical personhood) and performance or dramaturgy (i.e., professional role), and the opposition of skill acquisition and holistic development. Underlying these oppositions is a foundational aporia or paradox that becomes clear with the focus of pedagogy on the eventual realization of the child's or student's autonomy. This paradox was first pointed out by Immanuel Kant at the beginning of the nineteenth century (1803/2007):

> One of the biggest problems of education is how one can unite submission under lawful constraint with the capacity to use one's freedom. For constraint is necessary. How do I cultivate freedom under constraint? I shall accustom my pupil to tolerate a constraint of his freedom, and I shall at the same time lead him to make good use of his freedom. (p. 453)

To cultivate student autonomy, in short, it is paradoxically necessary to balance it with its opposite, the constraint of certain student freedoms. Another way of putting this would be to say that educational action is embedded in an ambivalent structure in which children are trusted to do something they are not yet able to do. The task of the professional educator, in this context, is to be bold in the face of ambiguity and complexity; it is to balance, reconcile, and resolve the tensions between the contradictory possibilities for pedagogical practice. Again, this happens through finely tuned adaptability, discrimination, and differentiation. But where is the "golden mean" between any two pedagogical extremes? For example: How can counteraction be provided supportively, or space be offered through a presence that remains close enough to help? How can a teacher be fair to all students while compensating for the challenges experienced only by a few?

Professionalism, then, is characterized by self- and boundary-reflections, marked as distancing from and rediscovery of pedagogical boundaries, which are framed and reframed depending on the situation and context, and at the same time determined by the field-specific rules within cultures and organizations. Failure to navigate these borders and the opposites these often delimit may lead to a variety of pitfalls. These include various forms of tactlessness, for example, as can be manifest through coercion, micromanagement, favoritism, a loss of face, or a loss of patience. In avoiding these hazards through the careful navigation of opposed possibilities for action, the teacher must attempt to do justice to every unique student and pedagogical situation, each with its manifold and often contradictory requirements. "Tact," to again reiterate Adorno's (1951/1974) point, "is the determination of difference. It consists of knowing deviations" (p. 36). *Pedagogical* tact, meanwhile, can be said to operate precisely in terms of determination or discrimination, as well as difference and deviation—specifically to *offer a form of differentiation that operates both in normative and reflexive terms.*

Pedagogical Tact and Professional Teacher Competencies

So far, we have outlined a specialized vocabulary (e.g., reflectivity, habitus, *Bildsamkeit*, self-activity) related to today's teaching and teacher-student engagements. We have also highlighted the pedagogical skills, abilities, and forms of knowledge that constitute a teacher's professionalism, as well as the fact that many of these qualities involve the teacher's whole person, their biography, as an indispensable constituent. We have defined tact, meanwhile, as a way of navigating the tensions that exist between opposed demands and expectations, and the responses, capacities, and sensitivities that they entail. By establishing the interrelationship of these components, it is possible to develop a framework for general pedagogical activity, competence, and professionalism. It is, in other words, now possible to sketch out the conceptual and performative space within which tact operates as an indispensable mediating element.

As suggested above, pedagogical competencies include knowledge (importantly, knowledge of a disciplinary, specialized, theoretical, *and* experiential nature), skills (manifest in the performance of expertise), professional self-concept or role (developed and revised via reflectivity or self-reflection), dispositions (as the propensity to act in a certain way), and finally, motives (beliefs about self and world; Vazirani, 2010, p. 122). Each of these components is indispensable in the professionalization process, and as mentioned, together they allow tact to be understood as the process of moving from theory to practice, from competencies *in potentia* to readiness for action in situated practice. These interrelationships are represented in Figure 1. This diagram also offers the context for discussion of the remaining two of the four applications of pedagogical tact enumerated at the outset of this document—*namely, that it serves as an analytic in the professionalization process,* and that *it stands as a principle of mediation for teacher education.*

The left side of the figurative lists the components that together constitute professional pedagogical competence. Formal knowledge, both in relevant subject areas, and in general pedagogical and instructional principles and theories, is needed to be able to act professionally. "This theoretical knowledge," Wadepohl (2015) explains, "is supplemented by implicit experiential knowledge, which, in professional contexts, is to be transformed into reflected experiential knowledge" (p. 11). Professionals and practitioners are also expected to possess experiential

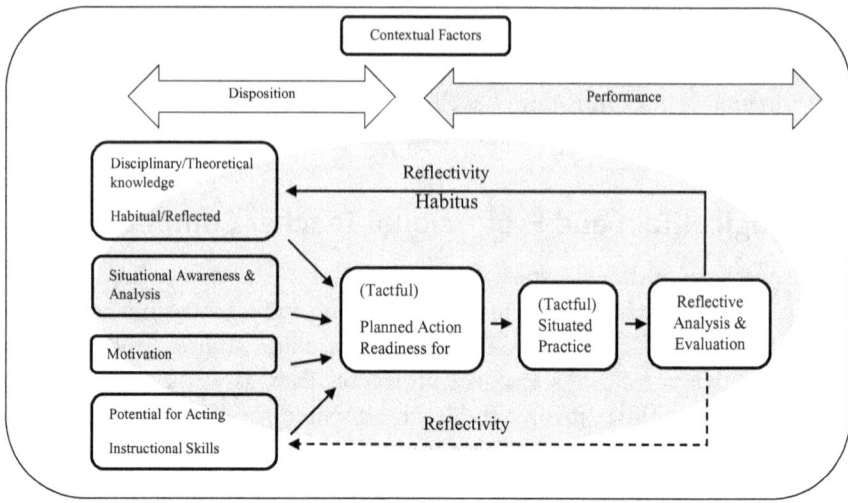

Figure 1: General Competence Model (adapted from Wadepohl, 2015, p. 11).[4]

knowledge that is simultaneously habitual and reflected: "This includes knowledge gained not only in teacher programs but what has been learned biographically" (Wadepohl, p. 11). Disposition, for example, is shaped not only by experiences in one's professional role but by one's personal experience as well. Both quotidian and specialized knowledge are subject to reflection as experiences relevant to pedagogy are sedimented over time. Reflectivity circulates from practical action and evaluation primarily to theoretical and experiential knowledge and secondarily to instructional skills and social abilities. These skills and abilities, together with motivation and situational awareness, draw on a broad base of individual experience and education, underscoring the extent to which practica and other opportunities to engage in and reflect on practice are central to teacher professionalization. Other concepts and terms introduced above can motivate and inform reflection and action. Significantly, these include habitus (center in the diagram), a concept relevant to nearly all elements in this model, and one that is interpenetrated by knowledge, action, and reflection. Ethos, meanwhile, can be seen to combine motivation with various forms of explicit and implicit knowledge, and to give embodied expression to the values, convictions, and principles that, in part, comprise the teacher's professionality and are performed via the teacher's attitude.

Finally, the intermediate stage between competency and performance (left, bottom of the diagram), readiness and action planning, can unfold very quickly, even unconsciously:

> In the phase of action planning and readiness, the professional will also draw on their existing repertoire of methodological skills (forms of observation, instructional principles) as well as their (dispositional) social skills such as perspective-taking or empathy in addition to the components already mentioned, and develop an action plan for the specific situation on the basis of their existing dispositions. (p. 12)

The often implicit feedback on action also mapped out in diagram 1 also has an effect on the disposition and leads to an enrichment of experiential knowledge. Furthermore, this reflective evaluation could also have an influence on other dispositional factors (e.g., on one's self-efficacy or on theoretical knowledge that can be expanded through study either in pedagogy itself or on the topics being taught).

Despite the absence of a controllable or technical structure, tact is not "unruly" or "arbitrary"; it is instead enabled by moral developments through which people are sensitized, stimulated, and strengthened in relation to their professional, pedagogical goals. Through professionally meaningful action and individual reflection, insights are gained that are assessed as significant and valuable and are subsequently internalized as guiding principles for action both in and across individual situations. These principles must be critically questioned, contextualized, and evaluated so that they are able to prove themselves in practice.

Tact as a Heuristic and a Principle of Mediation in the Professionalization Process

How can a program of study be designed to cultivate and develop teachers' pedagogical tact? This can be achieved: 1) through academic preparation using established methods, subject-specific and instructional guidelines, illustrative examples, and practical demonstrations; 2) through experience and practice in the context of practicum placements; and, 3) through reflection on examples as provided in classroom materials and through practica in "reflection seminars." While the first of these methods for cultivating tact—academic preparation—has been referenced above, the second and third—experience and reflection on it—is the focus here.

Utilizing experience and practice from students' practicum placements generally involves working with documentation of what was encountered in the classroom. These records include video or audio recordings, observational notes, academic records, and exercises in thick description. To make responsible use of these records, student-teachers must first be trained in ways of ensuring their own students' (and others') confidentiality and anonymity. This constitutes an important but preliminary step in the reflection seminar. In the next stage, these documented experiences are shared. Participants may be made comfortable to describe their difficulties in their practicum by first offering examples of their favorite moments or experiences: Their students' parting gift, moments of relational connection, a favorite lesson, or teachable moment. Of greater educative value, however, are challenges, problems, even failures. It is when things go wrong rather than when they "go" right that the mundane familiarity of routine pedagogical action and judgment breaks down and gives rise to reflection. Some of these moments can result in one being thrown back on oneself, enabling deeper reflection on and diversification of one's ways of acting and judgment. It is in these more difficult moments of reconstruction and reflection that implicit, situation-specific knowledge can be made explicit, and then expanded or corrected. Because *generalizations* about difficulties with student behavior (e.g., a child with an IEP,[5] an oppositional defiant child) so often foreclose on rather than invite further reflection and interpretation, it is important to be as concrete and specific as possible in descriptions and discussions. The focus should be on particularities of very specific incidents and situations in their uniqueness rather than on labels or explanations.

Teacher practicum experiences are diverse and provide many examples of how the demands of practical action and decision so often present exceptions to theoretical preconceptions and categories—consistently challenging even the best made plans. Moreover, examples or cases are so valuable in this context because they raise questions, recollections, and engage the imagination regarding past, present, and possible future experience (reasoning from the specific and concrete to the abstract and universal). Examples do this specifically by offering moments and situations in their specificity, facilitating a collective dialectical process of induction. This is a process that can lead to conclusions of some generality but that still do not betray the particularity of their origin and potential application. As those who are discovering and experimenting in the physical and social worlds, school students' actions by definition disturb convention and reflect individual idiosyncrasy: One student might blurt something out, another might start jostling with a neighbor, yet another might not be able put away a toy or device. Utilizing a ritual or routine (such as clapping out a pattern with the class or starting a countdown) may work in dealing with some disruptions. And some of these routines or rituals may even be realized with tact. But the exercise of a developed and sensitized tact would consist in knowing when these routines might not, do not, or will not work, when the class might, for example, benefit from a brief discussion on the disruption itself, or whether it can for the moment be ignored.

In the context of these myriad difficulties and possibilities, tact is only very rarely manifest in a solution, something that in a single stroke provides a quick fix and does away with the problem. The educative value of dealing with problems and challenges can be leveraged not by coming up with a quick solution or pointing out a distinct error or oversight—or simply wishing it were not so. The educational value of examples and dilemmas is realized instead by asking student-teachers to imagine how the situation, the incident, might have been otherwise—worse, better, or simply different—in a concrete and practical way. This is to practice reflectivity in the sense that it was described above: Learning how to decenter the self or subjectivity, to take up another's perspective in understanding events that are unavoidably multifaceted, ambivalent, and equivocal. This can only be undertaken collectively in an atmosphere of mutual support and trust; and this atmosphere is to be cultivated in parallel with student-teacher reflectivity itself.

Another type of reflection is constituted by stepping further outside of the situation and considering aspects of theory, specifically the dialectical theoretical framework described above within which tact can be located. *It is here, then, that tact as a principle of mediation—for theory and practice, and for many other pedagogical oppositions—comes to fruition.* In this case, these opposed extremes or possibilities—such as proximity and distance, freedom and constraint, individuality and community—delimit a space, a continuum of possibilities for the developing pedagogical imagination. This dialectical framework allows students to analyze and construct options and alternatives for pedagogical engagement that can be applied to the widest range of situations and questions: Do I consider a disruption to be a teachable moment for student development, or do I press on with my lesson plan? How much freedom of choice is too much when helping this child select a book for silent reading? Do I support, laugh along, at joke made at my expense, or should I stop and deliberately counteract it?

Reflection later expands still further to include the "framework conditions, prerequisites and the integration of one's own professional actions and practice" (Helsper, 2021, p. 136). This involves an attempt to examine the unique combination of circumstances that both constrain and enable teacher and student action and response. These factors include what the teacher may know about the life of the child outside of the classroom, the teacher's own experience as a student, and/or the circumstances of the classroom itself (e.g., number of students, seating layout, schedule of classes, or activities for the day). This reflection can be developed further to include not only school and classroom policy and circumstances but also the frameworks of the curriculum or the constraints of a given instructional method. None of this is undertaken to assign blame or to find fault—either with one's circumstances or others' actions. As the term reflection itself suggests, this epistemic activity is undertaken with a spirit of openness and curiosity.

Openness becomes especially important in what can be seen as the final phase of reflection—one that is likely not for all student-teachers. This type of reflection is what Cramer et al. (2019) refer to as meta-reflectivity. This is reflection on reflection, which focuses on how different reflections on various topics arise from different circumstances (Cramer et al., 2023). This would even include perspectives provided by established theories and frameworks:

> Knowledge of different theoretical approaches and empirical findings related to the teaching profession, the ability to locate them with regard to their respective foundations and claims of validity, to relate them to each other, to engage critically with them, and to make consistent, generalizing interpretations of the complex field of action that is school. (p. 410)

Developmental categories (like those of Piaget or Kohlberg) or theories of learning (from Vygotsky to Holzkamp or Gardner) offer valuable guidelines and frames for practice. So too do theoretical readings in educational equality and equity, and individual identity and collective diversity. However, these theories should neither be regarded as final nor applied unquestioningly; and teachers' own reflected experiences and observations can themselves be seen as evidence that may confirm or counter theories and findings. The same can be said for demographic research, and even for widely-promoted pedagogical "best practices": The idea that some practices are "best" is inevitably undermined by a teacher's (and by students') fundamental freedom in the pedagogical situation. In this context, the uniqueness intrinsic to all developing persons and to all pedagogical situations renders the superlative "best" nothing less than delusional.

In its different forms, reflection offers a way to enrich and validate one's skills and knowledge—including implicit or tacit knowledge—and to (re)form them as professional skills and dispositions. Clearly, the development of practical skills requires concrete pedagogical practice and experience in the context of professional performance, rather than simply academic or theoretical exercises alone. All these forms of reflection lead to the fact that on the one hand the situation can be shaped responsively and on the other that the knowledge about this situation is extended. We can say that tactful moments relate to ethical ideals, instructional norms, social frameworks, theories of psychological development, and other pedagogical abstractions but nonetheless realize practical results in concrete situations. Pedagogical tact can in this sense be defined as an art of pedagogical action that cultivates a practice of questioning and instills a desire to understand (see Müller, 2015).

The idea of tact as providing an analytic, a heuristic for professionalization now becomes clear. Tact allows reflection to be exercised at multiple levels, from the most concrete circumstances of a specific child in a specific situation, to the most general and least individualized aspects of teaching: curriculum, school policy, or basic human learning processes. Tact also allows for the representation of the components in the professionalization process, and for the delineation of their interrelationship, showing how they are united in a cyclical flow that courses more deeply and swiftly—and with less resistance—over time. Integrating specific moments of trial and error, failure and accomplishment requires careful judgment. As no two cases and decisions are the same, each one entails an intelligent personal contribution. Still, teachers also learn with every act of judgment, whether it is simulated or lived directly. Through each incident and each reflective cycle, the teacher's ability to discriminate and differentiate, to engage in "knowing deviations" (Adorno, 1951/1974, p. 36) becomes more developed. In this context, pedagogical tact gains the potential to be activated as "the immediate director of our practice"—as Herbart put it in first introducing the notion over 200 years ago (1802/2022, p. 32).

Notes

1. Rituals "are characterized on the one hand by their constantly repetitive and always recurring regular nature, as well as by the possibility of (historically and culturally determined) change. ... The performative dimension of rituals is of particular importance for educational research and theory in the fields of socialization, education, and learning" (Böhm & Seichter, 2018, p. 408).
2. Continental pedagogy "refers to a way of thinking about educational practice that coalesced in Europe some 250 years ago and that continues to be elaborated today" (Friesen & Kenklies, 2023, p. 245).
3. Dialectic is used here neither in a Hegelian nor Marxist sense. It is understood only in the broadest meaning of the term, as "any systematic reasoning… that juxtaposes opposed or contradictory ideas and usually seeks to resolve their conflict" (Merriam Webster).
4. In turn, this model was adapted by Wadepohl from: Fröhlich-Gildhoff, K., Nentwig-Gesemann, I. & Pietsch, S. (2011). Kompetenzorientierung in der Qualifizierung frühpädagogischer Fachkräfte. *WiFF Expertisen Nr. 19*. München: DJI.
5. An Individual Educational Plan, utilized for students with special educational needs.

Bibliography

Adorno, T. W. (1951/1974). *Minima moralia: Reflections on a damaged life*. (E. Jephcott, Trans.). Verso.

Bachmann, S., Bertschy, F., Künzli David, C., Leonhard T. & Peyer, R. (2021). Die Bildung der Generalistinnen und Generalisten. Einleitung, Problemaufriss und Fragehorizont. In S. Bachmann, F. Bertschy, C. Künzli David, T. Leonhard & R. Peyer (Eds.), *Die Bildung der Generalistinnen und Generalisten. Perspektiven auf Fachlichkeit im Studium zur Lehrperson für Kindergarten und Primarschule* (pp. 17–40). Klinkhardt.

Böhm, W. & Seichter, S. (2018). *Wörterbuch der Pädagogik*. Ferdinand Schöningh.

Burghardt, D. & Zirfas, J. (2019). *Der pädagogische Takt. Eine erziehungswissenschaftliche Problemformel*. Beltz Juventa.

Cramer, C., Harant, M., Merk, S. Drahmann, M. & Emmerich, M. (2019). Meta-Reflexivität und Professionalität im Lehrerinnen – und Lehrerberuf. *Zeitschrift für Pädagogik, 65*(3), 401–423.

Cramer, C., Brown, C., & Aldridge, D. (2023). Meta-Reflexivity and teacher professionalism: Facilitating multiparadigmatic teacher education to achieve a future-proof profession. *Journal of Teacher Education, 74*(5), 467–480. <https://doi.org/10.1177/00224871231162295>

Dewey, J. (1916). *Democracy and education*. Macmillan.

Dressler, B. (2013). Fachdidaktik und die Lesbarkeit der Welt. Ein Vorschlag für ein bildungstheoretisches Rahmenkonzept der Fachdidaktiken. In K. Müller-Roselius (Ed.), *Bildung – empirischer Zugang und theoretischer Widerstreit* (pp. 183–202). Barbara Budrich.

Friesen, N. (Ed. Trans.) (2022). *Tact and the pedagogical relation: Introductory readings*. Peter Lang.

Friesen, N. & Kenklies, K. (2023). "Continental Pedagogy & Curriculum." In R. Tierney, F. Rizvi, & K. Ercikan (Eds.), *The international encyclopedia of education* (4th ed.) (pp. 245–255). Elsevier.

Goffman, E. (1956). *The presentation of self in everyday life*. University of Edinburgh.

Herbart, J. F. (1802/2022). Introductory lecture to students in pedagogy. In N. Friesen (Ed. Trans.), *Tact and the pedagogical relation: Introductory readings* (pp. 28–37). Peter Lang.

Helsper, W. (2020, December 14). Prof. Dr. Werner Helsper: Pädagogische Professionalität [Video]. *YouTube*. <https://www.youtube.com/watch?v=_E--4ZHigko&t=132s&ab>

Helsper, W. (2021). *Professionalität und Professionalisierung pädagogischen Handelns. Eine Einführung*. Barbara Budrich.

Mollenhauer, K. (2014). *Forgotten connections: On culture and upbringing*. (N. Friesen, Trans.). Routledge.

Muth, J. (1962/2022). Pedagogical tact: Study of a contemporary form of educational and instructional engagement (selections). In N. Friesen (Ed. Trans.), *Tact and the pedagogical relation: Introductory readings* (pp. 85–117). Peter Lang.

Müller, H.-R. (2015). Zur Theorie des Pädagogischen Takts. In. D. Burghardt, D. Krinninger, & S. Seichter (Eds.). *Pädagogischer Takt: Theorie – Empirie – Kultur* (pp. 13–24). Ferdinand Schöningh.

Töpper, D. (2023). Technology deficit or technologies of schooling – seeing curricular planning and teachers' knowledge within a systems-theoretical understanding of technology. *Paedagogica Historica: International Journal of the History of Education*, 60(6), 1105–1124. <https://doi.org/10.1080/00309230.2023.2266708>

Vazirani, N. (2010). Review paper competencies and competency model-a brief overview of its development and application. *SIES Journal of Management*, 7(1), 121–131.

Wadepohl, H. (June, 2015). Professionelles Handeln von frühpädagogischen Fachkräften. *KiTaFachtexte*. <https://www.kita-fachtexte.de/fileadmin/Redaktion/Publikationen/KiTaFT_Wadepohl_2015.pdf>

Zirfas, J. (2015). Zur Ethnographie des pädagogischen Takts. In D. Burghardt, D. Krinninger & S. Seichter, (Eds.), *Pädagogischer Takt: Theorie – Empirie – Kultur* (pp. 25–42). Ferdinand Schöningh.

Notes on Contributors

JENS BELJAN works in the fields of educational science and philosophy of education. He has held various positions at Friedrich Schiller University, including at the Chair of Education and Culture and the Chair of School Development Research. He was involved in the program for Democratic School Development at the Free University of Berlin and currently trains special education teachers at Martin Luther University Halle-Wittenberg. His doctoral thesis explores the phenomenon of resonance in the classroom, an inquiry that he developed further in his Habilitation or postdoctoral thesis as a research program with a focus on expressivity as central to human learning. He is also the editor of the "Pedagogy" volume and contributed to the "Psychology" volume in the Critical Complete Edition of the writings of Friedrich Schleiermacher.

DANIEL BURGHARDT is Professor of Educational Science with a focus on social inequality and political education at the University of Innsbruck. His research areas are critical theory, educational philosophy, psychoanalytical pedagogy, and educational work critical of anti-Semitism and racism.

NORM FRIESEN, Professor at the College of Education, Boise State University, specializes in pedagogy, educational technology, and qualitative research. He has worked as a visiting researcher at the Humboldt University (Berlin), the University of Vienna, the University of Göttingen, the University of British Columbia (Canada), and held a Canada Research Chair position at Thompson Rivers University. Friesen studied German and philosophy at the Johns Hopkins University and is the translator of two German monographs and a collection of pedagogical "classics." He has published 9 books and over 100 peer-reviewed articles and book chapters. His work has been translated into German, Chinese and Spanish.

NOTES ON CONTRIBUTORS

KAJA KESSELHUT is Postdoctoral Researcher at the Institute of Educational Science at the Osnabrück University. Her work focuses on childhood studies, family research, pedagogy of early childhood, theories of social practices, as well as qualitative methods. She is the author of the 2021 book *"Deine Mama kommt ja wieder" (Your mommy will be back): An ethnography of "acclimation" in daycare*, published by Beltz/Juventa.

MORTEN KORSGAARD is Adjunct at VIA University College, Denmark and an Associate Professor of education at the Department of Childhood, Education and Society at Malmö University, Sweden. His research is focused on the philosophy of education, educational theory and history, as well as the work of Hannah Arendt.

DOMINIK KRINNINGER is Professor for Educational Childhood and Family Studies at Osnabrück University. His main research topics are Family Studies, Childhood Studies and Transitions, and Theory of Education.

HANS-RÜDIGER MÜLLER studied education, sociology, and child and adolescent psychiatry at the University of Göttingen. Until his retirement in 2020, he worked as Professor of General Education at the University of Osnabrück. His work focuses on the theory and cultural history of education and upbringing, pedagogical anthropology and pedagogical family- and generational-research. He has recently completed the edition of the 10-volume Klaus Mollenhauer Complete Edition (KMG; https://mollenhauer-edition.de) as co-editor. His most recent publications on the topic of pedagogical tact include an article co-authored with Dominik Krinninger entitled "Why and how should we talk about pedagogical tact?" (2024) and the book publication *Familienstile* (2016, with Dominik Krinninger).

EIRICK PRAIRAT is Professor of Education at the University of Lorraine (France) and Associate Researcher at l'Université du Québec in Montreal (UQAM). He was a member of the Institut Universitaire de France (First laureate of the Chair of Science and Philosophy of Education, 2011–2016). He published the book-length study, *Eduquer avec Tact* in 2017; his most recent monograph, *L'école des Lumières brille toujours*, mobilizes the Enlightenment origins of the modern school to address challenges in our post-truth era.

SEVERIN SALES RÖDEL has spent more than ten years researching and teaching educational theory and philosophy at various German universities. He wrote his doctoral thesis at Humboldt University in Berlin on a phenomenological topic related to learning theory ("Failure and negative experience in school learning"). In addition to pedagogical learning theory and phenomenological pedagogy, his research areas include: pedagogical professionalization and pedagogical ethos, democracy and education, right-wing extremism and pedagogy, as well as theories of situated knowledge and their connection to educational theory (Bildungstheorie). Severin Sales Rödel is currently refining his exercise of pedagogical tact: He switched to practical work and now teaches Math and Science at a primary school in Southern Germany.

THOMAS SENKBEIL, Ph.D., is an educator, researcher, and practitioner specializing in the relational dimensions of education. He is co-editor of *The Human Being as Facticity: Educational Anthropological Approaches* and of a special issue of *Ethics and Education* titled "Pedagogical Tact: Connections Old & New." His dissertation at the University of Innsbruck, *Border Relations*, explores educational, social, and cultural categories through an ethnographic lens on pedagogical tact. With extensive experience as a social pedagogue and Dialectical behavior therapy co-therapist, his research focuses on professionalization in Swiss education, school development, pedagogical tact, educational psychology, and scientific theory. He is a senior lecturer at the Institute for Special Learning Needs (ILEB) at the University of Teacher Education in Special Needs (HfH) in Zürich.

JÖRG ZIRFAS is Professor of Educational Science with a focus on Educational Anthropology at the University of Cologne. Chairman of the Society for Historical Anthropology (FU Berlin), he is also a member of the working groups Psychoanalysis and the Art of Living (Berlin) and Pedagogy and Vulnerability (Cologne). Main areas of work: Pedagogical and historical anthropology, philosophy of education and psychoanalysis, pedagogical ethnography, and cultural pedagogy. His publications include a co-edited multi-volume history of aesthetic formation, *Geschichte der Ästhetischen Bildung* Paderborn 2009–2021, and two co-edited handbooks, one on philosophy of education (*Handbuch Bildungs- und Erziehungsphilosophie*, Wiesbaden 2019) and one offering interdisciplinary perspectives on optimization (*Optimierung. Ein interdisziplinäres Handbuch*, Berlin 2024).

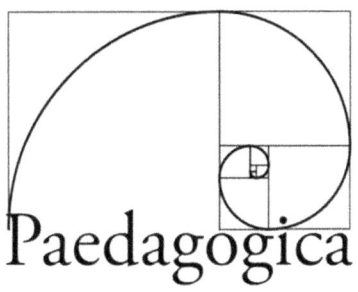

Sebastian Engelmann, Norm Friesen, and Karsten Kenklies
General Editors

Paedagogica publishes original monographs, translations, and collections reflecting the thought and practice long known, for example, as *le pédagogie* in French, *pedagogía* in Spanish, and *Pädagogik* in German. Pedagogy in this sense starts with the influence of one person or group on another—often an older generation on a younger. Pedagogy is not just about school or college, but interpenetrates many spheres of human activity, forming a domain of practice and study in its own right—one that is ethical in its implications and relational in its substance. This pedagogical tradition has been developed over hundreds of years, for example, by John Amos Comenius (Komenský), Jean-Jacques Rousseau, Johann Friedrich Herbart, Maria Montessori, and Janusz Korczak.

For additional information about this series or for the submission of manuscripts, please contact:

> sebastian.engelmann@ph-karlsruhe.de
> normfriesen@boisestate.edu
> karsten.kenklies@strath.ac.uk

To order books, please contact our Customer Service Department:

> peterlang@presswarehouse.com (within the U.S.)
> orders@peterlang.com (outside the U.S.)

Or browse online by series:

> www.peterlang.com

www.ingramcontent.com/pod-product-compliance
Lightning Source LLC
Chambersburg PA
CBHW052019290426
44112CB00014B/2307